Changing Lives!

Changing Lives!

DAILY READINGS for women who want more than a makeover

EDITED BY CATHERINE BUTCHER

Published by
The Bible Reading Fellowship
First Floor, Elsfield Hall
15–17 Elsfield Way, Oxford OX2 8FG

ISBN 1 84101 419 2
First published 2005
1 3 5 7 9 10 8 6 4 2 0

Acknowledgments

Scripture quotations taken from the Holy Bible, New International Version, copyright ©1973, 1978, 1984 by International Bible Society, are used by permission of Hodder & Stoughton Limited. All rights reserved. 'NIV' is a registered trademark of International Bible Society. UK trademark number 1448790.

Scripture quotations taken from The New Revised Standard Version of the Bible, Anglicized Edition, copyright © 1989, 1995 by the Division of Christian Education of the National Council of the Churches of Christ in the USA, are used by permission. All rights reserved.

Scriptures quoted from the Good News Bible published by The Bible Societies/HarperCollins Publishers Ltd, UK © American Bible Society 1966, 1971, 1976, 1992, used with permission.

Scripture quotations taken from The Revised Standard Version of the Bible, copyright © 1946, 1952, 1971 by the Division of Christian Education of the National Council of the Churches of Christ in the United States of America, are used by permission. All rights reserved.

Extracts from the Authorized Version of the Bible (The King James Bible), the rights in which are vested in the Crown, are reproduced by permission of the Crown's patentee, Cambridge University Press.

Scriptures taken from The Amplified New Testament copyright © 1958, 1987 by The Lockman Foundation. Used by permission.

Scripture quotations taken from the New Jerusalem Bible, published and copyright © 1985 by Darton, Longman and Todd Ltd and les Editions du Cerf, and by Doubleday, a division of Bantam Doubleday Dell Publishing Group, Inc. Used by permission of Darton, Longman and Todd Ltd, and Doubleday, a division of Random House, Inc.

The Living Bible copyright © 1971 by Tyndale House Publishers.

Scripture quotations marked (NLT) are taken from the Holy Bible, New Living Translation, copyright © 1996. Used by permission of Tyndale House Publishers, Inc., Wheaton, Illinois 60189. All rights reserved.

Scripture quotations from *The Message*. Copyright © by Eugene H. Peterson 1993, 1994, 1995. Used by permission of NavPress Publishing Group.

A catalogue record for this book is available from the British Library

Printed and bound in Great Britain by
Bookmarque, Croydon

Contents

Learning from others

Transformed!

Introduction

Changing Places, *Changing Rooms*... life-changing transformation seems as easy as changing TV channels. For a few hundred pounds I can renovate my garden, refurbish my home or even change the shape of my body. But most of us come to realize that changes on the outside don't make much difference in the long run.

People who change partners often discover themselves arguing over the same old issues after only a couple of years in a new relationship. *Life Laundry* victims find that they are just as untidy in their new environment. And the garden transformed by the *Ground Force* team soon reverts to its overgrown state once the weeds start growing through the decking.

If you are looking for permanent change, it has to start on the inside. Transformed lives need transformed hearts. Even starting the year deciding to develop a deeper relationship with God needs more than an act of will. Something needs to happen in my heart if dogma and discipline are to be truly life-changing.

The Bible points to the future when 'we will all be changed, in a moment, in the twinkling of an eye' (1 Corinthians:15:51, NRSV). But here and now, images of change sound more of a lengthy process: we will be refined like silver and tested like gold, or we will shine like jewels—which have to undergo the painful process of cutting and polishing to make them fit for a crown.

Fortunately, the process of change is not left to our own efforts. History changed for ever when Jesus died in our place. Up to that point, God had been screened off from mortal view. A curtain separated worshippers from the holiest place in the temple. But at the moment Jesus died, that curtain was ripped apart, torn from top to bottom by an invisible hand. Now ordinary people like us have instant and unlimited access to God's presence—all because of what Jesus has done.

That results in transformed lives, as Paul wrote: 'We, who with unveiled faces all reflect the Lord's glory, are being transformed into his likeness with ever-increasing glory, which comes from the Lord, who is the Spirit' (2 Corinthians 3:18, NIV).

I don't know about you, but I've already reached that age when no amount of exercise, careful dieting or special creams will stop the inevitable wrinkles and other signs of ageing. But Paul's letter talks about 'our lives gradually becoming brighter and more beautiful as God enters our lives and we become like him' (3:18, *THE MESSAGE*).

I see people around me losing heart as the efforts they make to change their lives fail to have the desired effect. But Paul writes, 'We're not giving up. How could we! Even though on the outside it often looks like things are falling apart on us, on the inside, where God is making new life, not a day goes by without his unfolding grace' (4:16, *THE MESSAGE*).

If I live long enough, I want to be one of those old people who radiate the beauty of God. So what's Paul's secret for that lasting inward beauty? 'Fix our eyes not on what is seen, but on what is unseen. For what is seen is temporary, but what is unseen is eternal' (2 Corinthians 4:18, NIV).

So that's the secret. As you take time out with God each day, using your Bible with this book, fix your eyes 'on Jesus, the author and perfecter of our faith, who for the joy set before him endured the cross, scorning its shame, and sat down at the right hand of the throne of God' (Hebrews 12:2, NIV).

Jesus has gone ahead of us. He has finished life's race. He is our example, and the gift of his Holy Spirit is like the adrenalin we need to start the race, the stamina we need to keep going and our personal trainer to whisper words of encouragement. These daily reading notes drawn from the first five years of *Day by Day with God* start by focusing on Jesus. As we look to him, he will be reflected in our daily lives and we will be changed. That's God's promise!

So how will we know that our lives have changed if the changes are on the inside? Changed hearts lead to changed actions. If we are looking to Jesus, we will treat others as he treated them, with love, justice, mercy and humility. Jesus came to serve others, giving up his life so that others could live. But we don't need to work out our own programme for change. As we keep our eyes focused on Jesus, concentrating on loving him, listening to him and inviting him into every aspect of our lives, he will make the changes in his own way at a pace that is perfect and uniquely planned for each one of us.

Contributors to Changing Lives!

Beryl Adamsbaum is a language teacher living in France, just across the border from Geneva, Switzerland, where she and her husband have been engaged in Christian ministry for 30 years. She is involved in teaching, preaching and counselling. She is the editor of her church magazine and writes short devotional articles.

Diana Archer is a writer and editor, working with the Damaris Trust in Southampton to produce *Connect* Bible studies. Starting a church in her lounge with her husband Graham, an Anglican vicar, led to her writing *Who'd Plant a Church?* (Christina Press), a warts-and-all account of church and vicarage life.

Fiona Barnard lives in Scotland. As a staff member of Friends International, her principal work is among international students and researchers, and encouraging local Christians to reach out in friendship to those temporarily far from home.

Celia Bowring compiles the CARE Prayer Guide, which highlights family and community issues as well as political and ethical concerns. Her book *The Special Years* is for parents of children under five. She works closely with her husband Lyndon in CARE and is a contributor to several periodicals.

Wendy Bray is a freelance writer, journalist and speaker with a special interest in family and relationship issues. She lives in Plymouth, Devon.

Shelagh Brown was BRF's commissioning editor when *Day by Day with God* was first conceived. She responded enthusiastically to the vision for Bible reading notes written by women for women and was to have edited the notes. Sadly she died after a fall down the stairs of her Oxford home.

Anne Coomes and the Revd Taffy Davies, a well-known vicar/artist, own and run www.Parishpump.co.uk, a resource website for church magazine editors. Anne has written five books on various Christians involved in mission. She holds a degree in theology and is working on her Masters Degree in Mission Studies.

Molly Dow is the Spirituality Adviser for Carlisle Diocese. She is married to Graham, the Bishop of Carlisle, and they have four adult children. She has produced and taught courses on prayer and other aspects of spiritual life and growth, and has written *Mountains and Molehills*.

Rosemary Green left the staff of Wycliffe Hall, Oxford, in order to have more time for grandchildren and for her local parish. She continues to be involved with Women in Mission, and she loves writing for BRF, trying to make the Bible alive and relevant in a world that is increasingly ignorant of this book.

Pat Harris is past president of the Mothers' Union and is now a member of the BRF Board of Trustees. A vicar's wife, she has a special concern for the poor and under-privileged.

Margaret Killingray is a tutor at the London Institute for Contemporary Christianity. She has assisted Dr John Stott and others in running *Christian Impact* conferences in the UK and overseas. Margaret and her husband David have three grown-up daughters.

Jennifer Rees Larcombe is one of Britain's best-loved Christian authors and speakers. She contributes regularly to Christian magazines and has written many books for adults and children. Her most recent book for BRF is *Beauty from Ashes*.

Chris Leonard has a degree in English and theology and her twelve books range from biography and devotional to children's stories. She enjoys leading creative writing workshops. Her most recent BRF publications include *The Heart of Christmas* and *The Road to Easter* (co-written with Jacqui Gardner).

Janet Lumb lives and works in North Yorkshire, where people come for a holiday or time out in a Christian setting. She spends her time writing, meeting visitors and counselling.

Hilary McDowell is a deaconess in Belfast with a ministry of reconciliation and outreach through poetry, art, drama and music. Her book *Some Day I'm Going to Fly*, with a foreword by Adrian Plass, has made her name known internationally.

Kristina Petersen works for BRF and as a freelance writer for a number of Christian newspapers and magazines. She started writing when she lived as part of the Lee Abbey Community in Devon, where she was the editor of their quarterly magazine *Rapport*. Kristina lives in Oxford.

Bridget Plass has a gift of seeing Jesus in the ordinary messiness of real life. She has recently written a Lent book, *Challenges of the Narrow Way* and speaks at occasional Quiet Days for BRF. As well as writing and speaking herself, she arranges her husband Adrian's diary and, when family commitments allow, she accompanies him on tour.

Christine Platt worked for ten years with The Navigators, living in Ivory Coast and travelling widely throughout Africa. She has written booklets, articles, and the SU Lifebuilder Bible study book on 'Forgiveness'. She now lives in New Zealand.

Elaine Pountney and her husband Michael, an Anglican priest, work with the International Fellowship of Evangelical Students Eurasia senior leadership team as consultants and co-ordinators of the work among Christian students in Ukraine and Moldova. They have two married daughters, one in England and one in Canada.

Wendy Pritchard is the wife of John, Bishop of Jarrow. She is a learning support assistant at a church secondary school, and mother of two daughters. Wendy has enjoyed each different phase of her life, from vicar's wife and maths teacher to mass caterer.

Christina Rees was born in America and came to live in England more than 20 years ago when she met and married Chris Rees. She is a freelance writer and broadcaster, speaker, preacher and member of the General Synod of the Church of England.

Mary Reid is the former editor of *Day by Day with God*. A trained teacher, and former magazine and book editor, she is married to Gavin and they have two sons, a daughter and several grandchildren.

Elizabeth Rundle is a Methodist minister living in London. She has written books of daily readings, Bible studies and articles and has contributed to religious programmes for both radio and television. She has led church weekends, women's conferences and pilgrimages to the Holy Land.

Alie Stibbe has a degree in natural sciences and spent five years in medical research before beginning to write for *Renewal* and other Christian magazines. Alie has recently completed post-graduate studies in the Department of Scandinavian Studies at University College, London. She is married to Mark, an Anglican minister, and they have four children.

Ann Warren started her career in the BBC as scriptwriter and producer and has written a number of Christian books. She is a trained counsellor. Ann and her late husband Peter spent many years working overseas. She has three married daughters.

Sandra Wheatley's life changed abruptly in 1987 when she was diagnosed with MS. No longer able to continue her nursing career, her life is nonetheless lived to the full as she seeks to know God and make him known through the struggles and 'delights' of living with a progressive disability. She is single and lives in County Durham.

PART ONE

Jesus—the one worth following

What's God like? How can we know the invisible God? When Philip, one of the disciples, asked Jesus, 'Lord, show us the Father', Jesus answered, 'Don't you know me, Philip, even after I have been among you such a long time? Anyone who has seen me has seen the Father. How can you say, "Show us the Father"? Don't you believe that I am in the Father, and that the Father is in me?' (John 14:8–10, NIV).

If the disciples who spent three years with Jesus were still asking to see God, what hope is there for us after two thousand years? Jesus answered the disciples' question and ours by promising to send the Holy Spirit: 'When he, the Spirit of truth, comes, he will guide you into all truth. He will not speak on his own; he will speak only what he hears, and he will tell you what is yet to come' (John 16:13, NIV).

Then Jesus prayed for us, the ones who would believe in him after he had returned to heaven. Talking to his Father, he said, 'I have made you known to them, and will continue to make you known' (John 17:26, NIV).

The Gospels show us what God is like through Jesus' words and actions. The Holy Spirit goes on making God known to us through the Bible and in many other ways—all of creation reveals what God is like (Romans 1:20).

In this first set of readings, we will be focusing on Jesus, the one worth following. If you are reading through the year, the first nine notes (pp. 15–25) have a Christmas and New Year theme and the last eight notes in this section (pp. 107–116) focus on Easter, but you can use them at any time of year.

As you use the readings, invite God to change you as you look at

Jesus. Ask for his help to get to know Jesus as well as getting to know about him. There is a difference. I know a lot about famous people in the news, but I don't know them in the way I know my best friend. When I get to know someone intimately, I'm changed by that relationship. I want to do things to please them. I change my daily schedule to adapt to theirs. I want to spend time with them. It's the same when we get to know Jesus, and it's amazing to discover that he longs to spend time with us and loves to give us good gifts to enjoy.

THE LIGHT OF THE WORLD

GENESIS 1:1–4a (NIV)

Light!

In the beginning God created the heavens and the earth. Now the earth was formless and empty, darkness was over the surface of the deep, and the Spirit of God was hovering over the waters. And God said, 'Let there be light,' and there was light. God saw that the light was good.

It's that time again. Christmas! How go your festive preparations? Do you find yourself remembering six essential presents you must buy, on the way to picking up supermarket mince pies because your home-made attempts collapsed? (Experience speaks.) Does Christmas anticipation fill you with joy or dread? Perhaps there is pain to be faced, loved ones to be unbearably missed. Do you look forward to some fun, or are you exhausted by it all?

Christmas seems to be inescapably momentous, no matter what. Of course we in the West have made the pre-Christmas shopping pressure into a somewhat hysterical art form, totally embarrassing when we think of our developing world cousins for whom just clean water would be an ecstatic Christmas treat. But no, I am not diving off into a Christian battering Christmas-commercialism rant. Because it was extravagant Christmas lights that pulled me back to Genesis.

Christmas lights can be fantastic. In a street near us, every house outdoes its neighbour in innovative external Christmas lighting. Visitors come to view the sleighs on roofs, the gardens ablaze, the electric snowmen. Extra effort with light is an integral part of our northern winter-darkened Christmases. With apologies to our beach-barbecuing friends in the southern hemisphere, I appreciate all this creativity with light. For who created it in the first place? Who saw that it was good? Who gave us light, invented electricity?

The same creator who sent a tiny baby to be the light of the world. This is what Christmas is about. Do not let Christmas busyness take that away from you. At least let the next Christmas lights you see remind you of your creator.

Is Jesus the light in your world?

✣

LUKE 1:27b–31 (NIV)

Surprised by light

The virgin's name was Mary. The angel went to her and said, 'Greetings, you who are highly favoured! The Lord is with you.' Mary was greatly troubled at his words... But the angel said to her, 'Do not be afraid, Mary... You will... give birth to a son, and you are to give him the name Jesus.'

I have heard these words so many times. They are spoken at carol concerts, narrated at pre-school nativity plays, and recited in church as I struggle to quiet my pre-Christmas whirling mind. On Christmas Eve, I want so much to find space in my complex life to be still and respond to Jesus, the light of the world. He is the reason for the season, and I want to draw close to his warmth. At our previous church we were encouraged to have all Christmas preparations completed by the afternoon's crib service and adults' meditation. Wonderful idea. Also very difficult.

So hey, if you have found space to read this over the festive season—congratulations! At least none of us has an angel appearing to say what he said to Mary. No wonder she was troubled. How about that for completely upsetting her plans! The Bible is stashed with people like Mary whose lives have been turned inside out by unexpected encounters with God. Churches are filled with them, too. God can be very troubling, as Mary discovered. Yet, whether or not the angel appeared to her in a blaze of light, there was enough light in what he said for her to respond in trust and obedience. He told her that the impossible would be made possible by the Holy Spirit. Once she knew the Holy Spirit was in charge, she was fine.

Whatever God is asking of you this Christmas, be sure that the same Holy Spirit will back you up. Find the light you need in what he says.

'I am the Lord's servant,' Mary answered. 'May it be to me as you have said' (Luke 1:38). How about you?

✣

LUKE 2:6–7 (NIV)

The angels' big moment

While they were there, the time came for the baby to be born, and she gave birth to her firstborn, a son. She wrapped him in cloths and placed him in a manger, because there was no room for them in the inn.

May the peace and joy of Christmas be yours today. May you know something of the excitement of the angels as they burst out of heaven with unrestrainable songs of praise.

The angels' enthusiasm is something of a relief after this incredibly quiet arrival of God's Son. Have a look at Luke's record of the event. Something of an understatement perhaps, given that he knew Jesus' destiny. His account is brief, dignified and to the point. It may be wonderful drama for us, but it cannot have been very nice for Mary to lay her first child in the animals' feeding trough—rather like us driving to hospital to be told there are no beds, we will have to give birth in the cleaner's cupboard. So God slips into the world in a disorganized, almost scruffy kind of way.

It is left to the angels to proclaim the good news. As usual, however, God does the unexpected and chooses some initially terrified shepherds on whom to unleash his jubilant choir. These shepherds were pretty low on the social scale, with not a decent prayer shawl among them. But it fits, doesn't it? God doing it his way, in his time, totally unprecedented. The shepherds are shocked, the angels are ecstatic.

We hear the story and its wonder captures our imagination, woos our hearts. We thrill to the news of God with us, Emmanuel. Like the shepherds, we do not understand everything, yet we want to be caught up in the excitement.

Christmas. God with us. Jesus, the light of the world. Rejoice!

Let the bells ring out!
Let all creation shout!
For a king has been born
Who will bring peace and light to the world.
ANDREW AND WENDY RAYNER

Read John 1:1–9.

✣

LUKE 2:30–32 (NIV)

Revelation light

For my eyes have seen your salvation, which you have prepared in the sight of all people, a light for revelation to the Gentiles and for glory to your people Israel.

Happy Boxing Day! How was yesterday? I hope you found God was with you, however the day went. Perhaps today is an extension of yesterday, with relatives and food still abounding, or perhaps today is leftovers and relaxing. Soon someone will start the 'why-did-we-eat-so-much/buy-so-much?' cry. Soon the bills will come in. The toys will lose their savour.

Isn't it incredible that, in the midst of the mayhem, we know the really good news? We are not dependent on things, food or people to give meaning to our celebrations. Like Simeon in the temple, meeting Jesus for the first time, we have seen something—someone—better. No matter what our circumstances, we have come into contact with truth that changes everything. If you can take some extra 'me time' today to refocus on Jesus, that would be great. If the light theme that has grabbed me is helpful for you, then go with it. Light a candle, or go for a walk and do some electricity-appreciation. Think about the power in the original creation of light, and what it means for Jesus to be named after it. Think about what that means for you.

If your day is just too busy, remember that if God is with us, Emmanuel, then he is with us in everything, not just the spiritual bits. He is with us in the cooking, the caring, the giving, the clearing up, the resting, the talking, the mourning, the rejoicing... Let his light penetrate every aspect of your life, let him be your revelation.

O come, O come, thou dayspring bright,
Pour on our souls thy healing light;
Dispel the long night's ling'ring gloom,
And pierce the shadow of the tomb.
Rejoice! Rejoice! Emmanuel shall come to thee, O Israel.

Enjoy Jesus' light-bringing presence.

✣

LUKE 2:34–35 (NIV)

Switch on!

Then Simeon blessed them and said to Mary, his mother: 'This child is destined to cause the falling and rising of many in Israel, and to be a sign that will be spoken against, so that the thoughts of many hearts will be revealed. And a sword will pierce your own soul too.'

Light does tend to be revealing. It would be nice if the light of Jesus was like a Christmas advertisement—warm, cosy and comforting. But Jesus came into the real world. No sooner has Simeon blessed him and his parents than they are warned of division to come. Jesus will grow to be a truth-revealer. There will be no dissembling with him around. People's reaction to him will be definitive. Not only that, but Mary is in for heart-pain too.

Oh, great. Her baby is not yet nine days old, and poor Mary is warned of future agony. How did she feel? Did the light of that truth feel unwelcome and harsh? Would we have wanted to hear what she heard? We are not told Mary's reaction to these difficult words, but I know I have frequently shied away from the light when it contained a truth I did not want to know. The world can be brutal, even at Christmas. There are times when I want to shut my eyes and keep the light of truth out.

This cannot be a surprise to God. 'Light has come into the world, but people loved darkness instead of light because their deeds were evil,' says John 3:19. The light of Jesus is not always welcome and sometimes we need to be brave to let it in. Yet only the truth of that light will set us free. The nice thing about light is that it only takes a little bit to transform our view. So we only have to be a little bit brave. The light does the rest.

Thank you, Father, for the trouble you went to for us to have the light of life in Jesus. Help us to let him in. Amen

LUKE 2:39 (NIV)

Growing up

When Joseph and Mary had done everything required by the Law of the Lord, they returned to Galilee to their own town of Nazareth. And the child grew and became strong; he was filled with wisdom, and the grace of God was upon him.

Your Christmas may be well and truly over by now. A few turkey scraps perhaps, but that is all. Is it back to work, or entertaining the children? Clearing up the house, writing the thank-yous? For most people, this week is the lull before New Year.

It feels a bit like the above verse. All that build-up, all those ancient prophecies fulfilled, the angels, the star, the stable, the temple; and then back to Nazareth. Everything goes quiet as Jesus is sent home to grow. The rumours die down, the shepherds return to their flocks and the wise men to their countries. King Herod flails angrily, but he cannot find Jesus. Life has gone back to normal. Years pass. Here was Jesus, growing up just as we all have to. But it seems he stood out from the crowd even then, for it was wisdom and grace that people noticed. Not an average description of a male teen, perhaps? He also grew strong—Jesus was not a weed. I love the phrase 'and the grace of God was upon him'. I am not sure exactly what it means, but it sounds wonderful. Folk must have loved being with him.

So what are you going to grow in, now that Christmas is over? A new year approaches. Is this coming year a good one to 'go home and grow'? Often it seems that God gives us a glimpse of the future, as with the excitement over Jesus' birth, and provides a growing time until we are big enough for it. If so, we are in good company. It happened to Jesus.

Read Psalm 130.

Can we choose to grow in wisdom and the grace of God?

✣

ISAIAH 9:2 (NIV)

Arrows of light

The people walking in darkness have seen a great light; on those living in the land of the shadow of death a light has dawned.

Here comes that light theme again. This time it is Isaiah the prophet, looking forward to the one who will come. This is one of many prophecies in the Old Testament concerning the advent of Jesus, his person and his ministry. Like the promise of spring in the middle of winter, Isaiah prophesies a day when darkness will be overcome by light. Even death will be changed by this light, and its awful shadow dispelled. Light brings truth, as we have seen, and also life and hope and vision and growth. Isaiah did not live to see the fulfilment of his prophecy, though he must have longed to. Seven hundred years were to pass before the light appeared. Then thirty years more waiting while Jesus grew. Who remembered the promises surrounding his birth when Jesus finally emerged from obscurity to be baptized by John? Why is God never in a hurry to keep his word? Jesus had thirty years' training for a three-year job. Is life not coming together for you? Are your plans frustrated? This could be training time.

I once heard a riveting explanation by Terry Virgo of the painstaking production of a perfect wooden arrow. The process involves stripping and soaking and steaming and sharpening, to name a few. Each stage sounds very painful for the wood. Some of the processes sound pointless. Sometimes a stage has to be repeated. But at the end is an arrow of perfect weight, size and aerodynamics. Fired by the hands of a master archer, the arrow will hit the target with unerring precision. It has been prepared, and is in the right place at the right time.

Mixing the metaphors completely, the light Jesus brought to the world was similarly hard-won. Extended years of preparation led to intense ministry. If we want to reflect that light, we must trust God's methods too.

Father, your will be done. Amen.

✣

ISAIAH 9:6 (NIV)

The Messiah

For to us a child is born, to us a son is given, and the government will be on his shoulders. And he will be called Wonderful Counsellor, Mighty God, Everlasting Father, Prince of Peace.

Many of us cannot read these words without Handel's Messiah resounding automatically in our heads. Usually associated with Christmas performances, this amazing description of the Messiah cannot be allowed to stay there. For this person is the light Isaiah has promised. Jesus cannot be confined to December: he is for the whole year. Even if you do not know the tune, the glorious richness of Isaiah's words have their own resonance. Don't they describe just the sort of God we always longed for?

Isaiah was writing in a turbulent time in Israel's history, as Assyria was gaining in strength and Israel was generally weakening. The government of his country was far from ideal, and Isaiah must have thrilled to the thought of a royal son like the one promised. But God's plan was bigger and better. His Son would rescue the whole world, not just one nation. The king whom Isaiah foresaw was for all of humanity.

These promises about Jesus are fantastic ones to carry into the new year. They will last for ever, unlike new year's resolutions. Ditch the latter and concentrate on Jesus instead. He is our wonderful counsellor and will act on our behalf. He will encourage and enthuse us. Jesus is our mighty God. He is powerful and will fight evil. He is our everlasting Father who will nurture and care for us. He will always be there, he will adopt us into his family. Jesus is the prince of peace. His hallmarks are justice and wholeness. He breathes his peace on to us.

This is the God we worship. Perhaps one new year's resolution, then: get to know him better as he really is.

The main and central action is everywhere and always what God has done, is doing, and will do for us. Jesus is the revelation of that action.

E. PETERSON, 'INTRODUCTION TO HEBREWS', *THE MESSAGE*, NAVPRESS, 1995

ISAIAH 9:7 (NIV)

A new start

Of the increase of his government and peace there will be no end. He will reign on David's throne and over his kingdom, establishing and upholding it with justice and righteousness from that time on and for ever. The zeal of the Lord Almighty will accomplish this.

So this is it. The last day of the year. Whether we put this year down with relief or regret, let us at least begin next year by renewing our trust in God.

Perhaps part of that is ensuring we carry no unnecessary baggage from this year into the next. If the turning of the year is a new start, then let us pause as we look back. It could be that it is very hard to see evidence of Jesus' government and peace in our lives, let alone his justice or righteousness. It could be that last year saw some wonderful surprises and joys which caused us to thrill at the works of God. I suspect that, for many of us, it has been an uneven mixture of both. So, a quick suggestion. How about jotting down the major things that spring to mind regarding the last year? Then check through, honestly, to see if there is unfinished business to deal with. Are there events to give God an extra bit of praise for? Are there resentments that need releasing? People to forgive? Joys to give thanks for? Be bold—ask God if there are any he wants to highlight. It will probably be the ones we do not expect. I am not suggesting a heavy session, just a clearing of accounts.

Then as we face the new year with a clean slate, can we choose to trust God for the future? No matter what we face, he is here for us, on our side. Whether we can see it or not, his government and his peace are guaranteed in the long-term scheme of things. If our lives belong to Jesus, then his promises belong to us. 'The zeal of the Lord Almighty will accomplish this.'

Happy New Year!

THE QUALITIES OF JESUS

2 CORINTHIANS 3:17–18 (NRSV)

Changed into his likeness

And all of us, with unveiled faces, seeing the glory of the Lord as though reflected in a mirror, are being transformed into the same image from one degree of glory to another: for this comes from the Lord, the Spirit.

The world we live in is very image-conscious—houses and gardens, as well as people, have television makeovers, providing a different style, a different image. And next month we can change it again! Sometimes this kind of process is simply fun, but it can become so important to have the right look that people spend more time and money than they can afford on searching for the right image.

It actually does matter what kind of first impressions we make on the outside. But what about the inside? We can usually see where others need a character makeover! But what are we like deep down? Where do we need to change?

Paul tells the Christians of Corinth that anyone who decides to follow Jesus as their Lord is from that moment being changed into the likeness of Jesus by the Spirit. One day each Christian will stand before God 'conformed to the image of his Son, that he [Jesus] might be the firstborn within a large family' (Romans 8:29).

But we have a part to play in this transformation and Paul wrote about this lifelong struggle to become like Jesus, comparing it to the hard training of the soldier or the athlete. So what can we do to become more like Jesus? How can we learn to answer the question, 'What would Jesus do?' in any situation? One answer is that we can look at what he did and learn from him. Over the next two weeks we will look at some of the stories of Jesus, see how he acted, the qualities he revealed, and ask ourselves whether there is an example to follow.

Lord, thank you for giving me your Spirit to work your transforming power in my life. Help me to do my part to make me more like Jesus.

✣

JOHN 4:3–8 and 1:1–14 (NIV)

Jesus—God and man

So he came to a town in Samaria called Sychar... Jacob's well was there, and Jesus, tired as he was from the journey, sat down by the well. It was about the sixth hour (noon).

In the beginning was the Word, and the Word was with God, and the Word was God. He was with God in the beginning. Through him all things were made... And the Word became flesh and lived for a while among us.

Jesus, tired, sits down on the edge of a well in the midday heat. He does something very ordinary, very human. We all know what it feels like to be tired, hot and thirsty. In the Gospel accounts we catch glimpses of him doing other ordinary things: going to a wedding, sitting down to supper with friends, sleeping at the bottom of a boat. He was a human being. He was like us.

John began his Gospel with the powerful words quoted in our text today, telling us that Jesus is God, the Lord and creator of the universe. How then can we be like him? There is such an enormous gulf between these two views of Jesus, reported by someone who lived and worked with him closely. John knew Jesus as a man and a friend, but he knew he was God.

This is the heart of the Christian faith. We know that in some way beyond our understanding he is both. Someone once said that if he had simply been a man he could not have saved us, but if he had not been a man he could not have died for us. There is powerful assurance in knowing that our Lord has not only divine power and sovereignty, but also human experience and understanding. So we can seek to imitate him in the way he lived on earth, knowing that he is with us by his Spirit to help us.

Read John 1:1–14 and worship him as Lord and Saviour, who has carried the marks of his humanity right up to the throne of heaven.

✣

LUKE 9:10–17 (NIV)

Learning with Jesus

When the apostles returned, they reported to Jesus what they had done. Then he took them with him and they withdrew.

I remember making pastry with a four-year-old, an interesting lesson in patience. Knowing that pastry should not be handled too much was not the best tip for someone who enjoyed the roly-poly part more than any other. But now the four-year-old is an adult, making pastry for her own family. We learn many of our skills by watching, listening and sharing the experience with a teacher. Jesus was a teacher and like the best teachers he 'took them with him'. Whether a student teacher in a classroom, a student nurse on a ward, or an engineering apprentice on the shop floor, most of us learn best by watching someone else and then working beside them.

So the first story we look at is Luke's account of Jesus taking loaves and fishes, a picnic for one, and using them to feed five thousand. As we read this, we can use our imagination to be there with Jesus and learn with the disciples how he does things. Then, whether it's bringing up children, running a youth group, working on a committee, or having responsibility for others at work, we can begin to learn how to be this kind of teacher.

So how did Jesus do it? He listened to them as they told him what they had been doing; he took them with him on his working journey; he suggested that they took action to deal with the problem of the hungry crowd; and then when they were at a loss he gave them a task they could do, organizing the crowd into groups; and then, although the power, authority and the miracle were his, he got them to distribute the food.

Help me, Lord, to be someone who has time to encourage and share as I teach or train. Help me to give time for people to learn in their own way. Give me the patience and love of a true teacher.

✣

LUKE 9:10–17 (NIV)

Being generous

Taking the five loaves and the two fish and looking up to heaven, he gave thanks and broke them. Then he gave them to the disciples to set before the people. They all ate and were satisfied, and the disciples picked up twelve basketfuls of broken pieces that were left over.

Some years ago an anxious young woman at a station asked me for the fare to get home to her grandmother. I didn't know whether to believe her, nor did I have less than a £20 note. I hesitated and then gave it to her. Should I have given her anything? Should I have given much more than her fare? Now I know that I probably shouldn't, because this is a very common ploy to get money. I should have offered to buy her ticket! Generosity is not always easy. Even our regular charitable generosities are measured exactly, with Charities Aid Foundation cheques and Gift Aid forms. No spontaneity and no space to say 'keep the change'!

Today we look again at this familiar story of the feeding of the five thousand, but this time focus on Jesus' generosity. We may not immediately notice just how generous Jesus was, that in his giving he goes further than necessary and ends up with too much! Six times, this event and a similar miracle are recorded and each time the writers record the amount of leftovers!

This overflowing generosity doesn't measure things grudgingly or sparingly, but gives with pleasure and perhaps with a sense of fun. It is the generosity of creation on a slightly smaller scale! This is generosity that does not count the pennies.

But the hidden factor in Jesus' generosity is his perfect relationship of trust with his heavenly Father. If we trust God in our giving—whether money, hospitality or anything else—then we can be generous-minded and open-hearted, giving pleasure, as well as leaving baskets of leftovers.

Help me to enjoy being generous with my money, my time and my life, without counting, but with prayerful thought.

✣

MATTHEW 14:14–18 (NIV)

Being compassionate

When Jesus landed and saw a large crowd, he had compassion on them and healed their sick.

'I know you've had a hard day so I'll put the kids to bed.' Compassion, sympathy, understanding—how heart-warming it is when someone has compassion. From the simple things, like helping get luggage or children into a train, to the more demanding, like taking on the care of an increasingly handicapped friend.

At the beginning of Matthew's account of the feeding of the five thousand, Jesus looked at this large crowd, some sick, and all becoming hungry, having followed him to an isolated part of the lake shore, and had compassion on them. He understood their needs. So he acted. He healed the sick and then he fed them miraculously. He had compassion on them. That was the first step. He had the eyes and ears to see and hear what was happening to other people. The next step was that he had the heart to want to do something about it, and the third step, that he did all he could.

We do not have his clear vision of the needs of others, nor do we have his heart of compassion in such fullness. Nor can we work the same miracles, however much we may long to deal with the suffering that often wrings our hearts. But we can learn to be more aware of others and their needs, when driving, travelling, shopping, working, being with family and friends. It may not always need action, perhaps just a quick prayer for someone. Being aware of people and having a heart of compassion can change lives.

Being compassionate makes demands on us. We know that we sometimes simply cannot find the will to act. We would prefer to find a way out of responding to needs that are very demanding. Our compassion even for those we love can wear thin sometimes. Then we need to turn to him again, seeking his Spirit's power to transform us into being more like him.

Lord, help me to see the needs of others today.

✣

LUKE 18:15–17 (NIV)

Welcoming children

'Let the little children come to me, and do not hinder them, for the kingdom of God belongs to such as these.'

Of course, we all love children and especially babies. That's obvious. But is it? There are many places and times in today's busy world where children in general and babies in particular are out of place, inappropriate, even embarrassing—in the office, on a rush-hour train, in a seminar. More women are choosing not to have children and some couples see children as simply a disruption of a comfortable lifestyle. They make a lot of noise, demand long-term attention and restrict freedom.

There are a number of groups who are treated as inappropriate or in the wrong place—mothers of small children often suffer from embarrassed unspoken rebukes in public places. But the elderly and the disabled can also be made to feel unwelcome, out of place or embarrassing because they need extra consideration in a busy world.

Out of place? Absolutely not, said Jesus. They are to be encouraged: let the mothers bring them right into the centre of the group. The disciples were, I hope, the ones really embarrassed as Jesus held and blessed these babies and children.

But this wasn't just a rather touching and heart-warming interlude. Jesus was still teaching, even as he held a child. The babies were not only welcomed for their own sakes, but also to reinforce the truth that unless we receive the kingdom of God like a child we will never enter it. So we should perhaps look hard at the children we know and meet; we should welcome them and begin to learn the lessons that Jesus was teaching. No pretence? No artificiality? But simplicity, innocent trust, lack of self-importance. Jesus welcomed children. We should do the same—and learn from them.

Lord, help me to welcome children for your sake, and to learn from them. Help me, too, to welcome into fellowship all those who are pushed to the fringes as embarrassing or out of place.

✣

LUKE 8:40–56 (NIV)

Having time for people

Then a man named Jairus, a ruler of the synagogue, came and fell at Jesus' feet, pleading with him to come to his house... As Jesus was on his way, the crowds almost crushed him. And a woman was there who had been subject to bleeding for twelve years.

How do you manage your time? This morning I drove half a mile to the dentist, because I hadn't the time to walk. The washing is still in the machine because I haven't had the time to get it out. I'm glad it's raining because I haven't the time to water the garden. I haven't time to stop.

So reading this chapter again, I was struck by the way Jesus stopped and made time for those who needed him. How would I cope with the sudden need of a stranger that required me to stop where I was going, cancel what I was doing, and spend as much time as it takes to help them? I know that if this happened to me I would feel cornered, resentful that I could not keep to my crowded timetable for that day.

Jesus stops, listens to the anguished cry of Jairus, whose daughter is dying, and then on his way to Jairus' house, stops again for the women with the haemorrhage. He gives her his full attention, does all that is needed to restore her and heal her, and then moves on to give Jairus and his daughter his undivided attention.

I pray that God will use me, but in my busyness I do not always let him. Many of us need to ask ourselves where our priorities are. Is it more important that a child is washed, dressed and fed (in a hurry!) than played with, sung to, hugged? Is it more important that cheques are put in the bank, and the house tidied, than a lonely friend is invited in? This is not everyone's problem, but it is certainly mine. I need Jesus' help to start developing Jesus' priorities.

Lord, help me to get my priorities right today.

✣

MATTHEW 8:1–4 (NIV)

Loving the unloved

A man with leprosy came and knelt before him and said, 'Lord, if you are willing, you can make me clean.' Jesus reached out his hand and touched the man.

People with leprosy were excluded from the social life of the community. This harsh exclusion was part of the Old Testament law that helped to limit the spread of contagious diseases. The woman with a twelve-year haemorrhage we read about yesterday would also have been excluded. That would mean that anyone—family or friends—would be considered unclean if they were touched by her. Such people had to live away from others and were not allowed to attend synagogue or social events.

Jesus broke these laws; he 'ate with tax collectors and "sinners"'; he spent time with the socially excluded; he reached out his hand and touched the man with leprosy; he put his arm round those who were shunned. He broke social convention to meet the down-and-out, the disabled, and the beggars. He touched the dead body of Jairus' little girl, and a widow's only son, even though the dead, too, were 'unclean'. He healed and restored them so that they could go back into their communities to be included in the social life around them. He told them to go to the priests for the medical examination that would show they were healed and could go back to family and friends.

I once pushed a friend round our town in a wheelchair and I

became aware that many people who knew us both spoke to me over his head. He was being excluded, although others did not realize they were doing it. Who is excluded from your circle of friends, from your church fellowship? Those with learning difficulties? Those with difficult personalities? Those housebound?

Lord, if I really want to follow you, then I have to follow you in this. Help me to be willing to move out of comfortable fellowship and to reach out to those on the edges, who are left out.

✣

LUKE 6:12–16 (NIV)

Learning to pray

One of those days Jesus went to a mountainside to pray, and spent the night praying to God. When morning came, he called his disciples to him and chose twelve of them.

Jesus was about to decide on the twelve men who would be his closest disciples. So he went away to a quiet place and spent the night in prayer. This was a significant moment and much would depend on his choice. This night of deep, focused prayer matched the importance of the decision.

But we may wonder why Jesus needed to do this. He was one with his Father in ways that are beyond our understanding. Every moment of his life was focused dependence and communication with God. Only that moment on the cross when he touched the depths of separation would that communication falter. Yet he went out into the hills for a night of prayer.

Jesus shows us the importance of special times of prayer for important decisions. Most of us recognize this need and seek this kind of deep prayer for guidance and wisdom for big decisions. But the ongoing walk of daily prayer, talking to the Lord, can be the point of greatest struggle.

Prayer fits awkwardly into a busy life. The very word 'prayer' resonates with slowing down, sitting still, being alone, shutting our eyes. It is not about quick responses and one-line e-mails; it doesn't fit with crowded trains, demanding children, fussing colleagues. Prayer ends up swept into hasty getting-up and sleepy before-lights-out times.

But that is exactly what Jesus' life was like—full of crowds and clamour, endless demands, dusty roads and temporary homes. So maybe we should practise the presence of God as Jesus did—praying about each day as it happens, the decisions, the joys and disappointments, the individuals we meet, our work—quick prayers, short prayers, but a real attempt to communicate with the Lord in the middle of a busy world.

If we want to follow Jesus, then we really do need to follow him in this as well.

✣

MARK 9:2 (NIV)

Being a friend

Jesus took Peter, James and John with him and led them up a high mountain, where they were all alone. There he was transfigured before them.

The other day I investigated the website that aims to bring old school friends together. I looked at the names of some of the girls I knew once and was overwhelmed with memories. I have failed to keep up with any of them, even though, with one or two, the foundations for a lifetime's friendship were laid. Friendship is often a casualty of modern life, where mobility and busyness make the effort of keeping up difficult. The regrets come later.

Jesus seems to have had a wide circle of friends who travelled with him, with an inner core of the twelve disciples. Several times he singled out the three who were closest to him, Peter, James and John, and took them to be with him for special times. So they were there when his glory as the Son of God shone out, and when he prayed in anguish as he faced the cross (14:33).

As we look at his friendship with Peter in particular, we can see that Jesus had a far closer relationship with friends than he had with his family, who did not seem to have understood his ministry and were not followers until after the resurrection. 'Who are my mother and my brothers? Whoever does God's will is my brother and sister and mother', he says at one point (Mark 3:31–34). For the many who remain single and who are far from family, this can be an encouragement to build real friendships.

He was also committed to his friends, even when they failed him. He knew Peter would deny that he knew him when he was arrested. But at the first opportunity he restores and forgives Peter. Honesty, truthfulness and forgiveness are important in true friendship. So is encouragement and empowering. Jesus does not just forgive Peter but he trusts him with the leadership and pastoring of the new church.

Why not contact an old friend today?

✣

MATTHEW 4:1–11 (NIV)

Learning humility

Then the devil took him to the holy city and had him stand on the highest point of the temple. 'If you are the Son of God, throw yourself down.'

Straight after Jesus had been baptized and had heard the voice of God affirming him as his Son, he was led into the desert to face temptation. Can this lonely spiritual battle teach us how to follow him?

The tempter begins twice with the words, 'If you are the Son of God'. He is suggesting that if Jesus has the authority and power to perform miracles, then he should do so and turn stones into bread, demonstrate that he is divine so that all can see, and enjoy being Lord over all the 'splendour' of this world.

Jesus does have power; he shows that many times—in healing, in quieting a storm, in breaking a loaf to feed thousands and in teaching with authority. But he does not use his power for himself; he does not make people believe in him by stunning them with a very visible show of power; he refuses to take a short cut to being the Lord of all. He knows that he has to take the humble servant route, through death to glory. He will not be tempted to use power to take the easy way.

Anyone who has any kind of power—bosses, parents, teachers, the rich, the influential—faces this kind of temptation. Even evangelists and preachers can use eloquence and atmosphere to overwhelm. We find it difficult when people don't seem to know who we are or talk to us as if we are not very important. We are greedy for status and appreciation. But not insisting on our rightful place at the banquet is a life-changing quality. Jesus chose not to grasp his rightful position, but gave up the glory of heaven to live on earth. Until we learn that this is the way, we will not understand the enormous gulf that Jesus bridged in the incarnation and on the cross.

Read Luke 14:7–11.

✣

MATTHEW 26:36–42 (NIV)

Facing suffering

Going a little further, he fell with his face to the ground and prayed, 'My Father, if it is possible, may this cup be taken from me. Yet not as I will, but as you will.'

Most of us at some time in our lives have to face suffering. And suffering comes in different forms. Jesus faced a cruel death, and shrank from it. He also endured betrayal, denial and abandonment by his friends, mob violence, the casual brutality of soldiers, false witnesses and injustice for political reasons.

All over the world, 'Please don't let this happen to me' rings out over and over again. When faced with the unfairness and injustice of much suffering, our cry is, 'Why?' There are often no satisfactory answers and human suffering can be a huge stumbling-block to faith in a God of love. But here in the Garden of Gethsemane, Jesus' anguished prayer for a way out and on the cross, his cry, 'Why, my God, have you left me alone?' is part of human suffering. Our Lord knows what it is like.

Jesus' death is the most important event in the history of the world. It is God's plan for salvation, his way of dealing with human sin and rebellion. But it also means that the Lord we serve walked through suffering and death to vindication and resurrection. He calls us to take up our cross and believe that we too will rise to be with him in glory.

Sometimes we bear the suffering of our own and others' sin, but often we do not know why suffering comes. Jesus shows us that suffering can be redemptive, turned to good, although not always and not easily. Suffering can teach us lessons about ourselves. It can give us better understanding of others. It can drive us to fight for a better world, to seek cures for disease and to fight injustice and hunger.

We have a Lord who knows what suffering means, and walks with us through the valley of the shadow of death.

MATTHEW 8:18–20 (NIV)

Learning to live with little?

'Foxes have holes and birds of the air have nests, but the Son of Man has nowhere to lay his head.'

We never hear of Jesus going to his own house. He stays with friends; he borrows a room in someone's house for his last meal; he tells a would-be disciple that he doesn't have a bed of his own.

There are other things he lacked. He never married. He never reached middle age. He seems not to have had any money, but a common purse, provided with funds by followers, for his and his disciples' needs. He had little privacy unless he went out at night into the hills. 'Do not store up for yourselves treasures on earth,' he said, 'for where your treasure is, there your heart will be also.' He lived a full, perfect, wholly holy life without most of the things we take for granted.

If only I were married. If only I had a better job. If only I were healthy. If only I lived in a better place. We all live with longings that cannot be fulfilled, but can destroy our happiness and our peace with God, if we let them. Jesus shows us that it is possible to live a full and purposeful life, with rich friendships and a close relationship with God, with little earthly treasure.

The way we respond to 'handicaps'—to limitations on our lives — is more important for a full life, than the 'handicaps' themselves. If our hopes and dreams are only for material things, then we are bound for disappointment and regret. But true peace and true happiness depend on our relationship with Jesus, who said, 'In this world you will have trouble. But take heart! I have overcome the world' (John 16:33). Take heart and enjoy what we have, put aside anything that might lead us away from holiness and know that one day all the riches of his glory will be ours.

Read Romans 5:1–5.

JOHN 21:4–14 (NIV)

Breakfast with Jesus

Early in the morning, Jesus stood on the shore, but the disciples did not realize that it was Jesus... Jesus said to them, 'Come and have breakfast.' None of the disciples dared ask him, 'Who are you?' They knew it was the Lord.

Oh, what a beautiful morning! Sunrise beside the lake, and Jesus gets a small fire going so that the freshly caught fish can be grilled for breakfast. The disciples stumble ashore and join him to eat. Here is another very human moment, idyllic, peaceful and simple.

Only there is a difference. The relationship has changed. This is the risen Christ. He died and was buried. They are certain of that, but not yet fully sure of just who he is now. There must have been amazement, disbelief and a huge growing joy ever since he came back from the dead. How can anything go wrong again?

He cooks for them, cares for them and reassures them, particularly Peter. But soon he will leave them and they will never see him again. There will be fear, persecution, martyrdom and exile, but there will be the exhilaration of preaching the gospel in the Spirit's power and seeing the Church grow and spread. It will all be worthwhile.

But for now, on this quiet morning round the fire, they realize once and for all that he is indeed the promised Christ, risen from the dead, but he is also still their friend, teacher and brother, who serves them breakfast. There is no one else to follow, no other example to copy. He is the only Lord, the only Saviour, our vision, our hope and our example.

High king of heaven, when battle is done,
Grant heaven's joy to me, O bright heaven's sun,
Christ of my own heart, whatever befall,
Still be my vision, O ruler of all.

GAELIC, EIGHTH CENTURY, TRANSLATED BY ELEANOR HULL

JESUS AND HIS DISCIPLES

MARK 1:20 (GNB)

An exciting start

As soon as Jesus saw them, he called them; they left their father Zebedee in the boat with the hired men and went with Jesus.

Recently I went to a lovely wedding, where the beautiful English bride was marrying a charming Dutchman. We all glowed in their reflected happiness, and wished them well, especially since the new wife would have to get used to living in another country, and learning a new language. This didn't appear to bother her, though—she would follow her new husband because she loved him, and deal with any difficulties using the strength that love gave her.

James and John must have felt something rather similar. To be prepared to leave their families, their jobs, their security, and follow Jesus into the unknown must have demanded much more than just curiosity or a thirst for adventure. They were the next generation of the family business, and their father was going to miss them. But for something as special as this it was worth it.

I wonder if our relationship with Jesus is still like that of the young bride or the new disciples, fresh and exciting, with every day bringing thrilling discoveries? Or has it settled down into boredom and duty, with a feeling that something important is missing? If that's the case, then to do nothing is to allow something glorious to fade away. After all, Jesus didn't say 'Follow me, and I will fill your life with interminable meetings' or 'Follow me and I will teach you how to sleep through the sermon'!

If we keep close to Jesus, though, we will feel the same sense of excited anticipation that the disciples knew. They walked with Jesus every day, they discussed, prayed, argued, suffered, laughed and failed in his presence, and marvelled at the things they saw him do. Perhaps today, we could talk the day through with him, as events unfold, and look at his world with a sense of wonder at what he shows us.

Help us to be eager to follow.

✣

MARK 1:17 (RSV)

Take a risk

And Jesus said to them, 'Follow me and I will make you become fishers of men.'

I doubt if Simon Peter and his brother Andrew had any idea what Jesus meant by this, or how he was about to turn their lives upside down. They knew, though, that to refuse his invitation would be the biggest mistake they could make. So they accepted the challenge, and began to let him transform them from unremarkable fishermen into his confident and capable agents.

Today's reading was the text for the sermon at my confirmation service, when I was made a full member of the church. I was 13, and my most vivid memory of the service was that I was wearing what I regarded as an unflattering dress, and looking particularly dumpy. My faith didn't really ignite until my last week at school, when I was challenged by a group of friends. If I really believed that Jesus was raised from the dead, and was therefore alive now, what difference did it make to me? I struggled with this all night, because I was convinced that if I let God have some control in my life, he'd send me as a missionary to South Africa, and I didn't feel up to that!

But I finally had to take the risk, just as the disciples did. As it turned out, I think God knew that I wasn't missionary material! He's had some challenging things in store for me, but all in some way 'good'. There are times when we say a resounding 'No' to God, for fear of him leading us into the unknown, lacking confidence in ourselves and in God. But God knew what the disciples were capable of, and he knows what we can become too. He can see the gold buried deep within us, even if we can't, and he would love us to trust him enough to let him guide us into our future.

Is there something that God is wanting to lead you into?

✣

MATTHEW 9:9 (GNB)

Unconditionally loved

Jesus left that place, and as he walked along, he saw a tax collector, named Matthew, sitting in his office. He said to him 'Follow me.' Matthew got up and followed him.

Matthew was not used to good people actually talking to him. He'd got used to being ignored, avoided, pointed out to the children as an example of someone gone bad. He worked as a customs official, something no Jew who wanted to obey all the rules about purity could do, so he was despised as unpatriotic. But then, he wasn't poor as so many others were—he'd made his choice, and he could live with it most days, as long as he didn't think about it that much.

He'd heard of Jesus, of course, and he'd even dreamed of lurking anonymously at the edge of the crowd to listen. Then Jesus turned his world inside out: 'Matthew, follow me.' What on earth was going on?

Jesus didn't say, 'Matthew, if you make a stupendous effort to reform, prove that you're a new man, then I'll let you sneak in at the back.' Matthew was in his office—he was still doing his job, an unreformed character—when Jesus called him. He was called first, and reformed later.

We often get this the wrong way round in our lives. A lovely lady once told me that she prayed a lot for other people, but wouldn't ask for anything for herself, as that would be presumptuous as she wasn't a good enough person. We need to learn that God sees not just what we are, but what we can become, and that it's he who changes us, and not us by our own efforts. Whatever we are at the moment, we are good enough for God. So if you are disappointed in yourself, if you feel you are always getting it wrong, remember that Jesus put no preconditions on his call to Matthew—and Matthew got up and followed him.

Thank God that he loves us as we are.

✣

LUKE 9:1–2 (NRSV)

Relying on God

Then Jesus called the twelve together and gave them power and authority over all demons and to cure diseases, and he sent them out to proclaim the kingdom of God and to heal.

When I was a student, I was talked into going on a mission in Hull. The churches there had been working towards this for a long time, planning and praying, as had the students. We eventually descended on this unsuspecting town, filled with a mixture of enthusiasm and terror, but determined to do our bit for God, and leave no soul untouched. I marvel now at the patience and generosity shown to us by the mature and forgiving Christians of Hull, as we babes in the faith either blasted our way through all doubt, or shrunk away in a corner trying not to be noticed! We learned a vast amount about ourselves, and the need to rely totally on God.

Jesus knew what was good for people, which is why he sent the disciples out before they probably thought they were up to it. I can hear them asking for more time to study, or pleading that they were too inexperienced for anyone to take them seriously. But we learn from our mistakes, and the best way to get closer to God is to rely on him for help. We are much more comfortable doing things we know we can do, trusting only in our own ability, and leaving God out of it. We need to tackle the difficult stuff, for which he alone can give us strength. Or if we are stuck with doing something we've done lots of times before, then we need to make a special effort to hand it over to God, to let him make it seem new. If we pray for a new challenge, we need to be aware that God answers prayer!

Pray for God's strength for someone (maybe yourself) facing a difficult challenge.

✣

MARK 6:30–31 (NRSV)

Take a break—if you can!

The apostles gathered around Jesus, and told him all they had done and taught. He said to them, 'Come away to a deserted place all by yourselves and rest a while.' For many were coming and going, and they had no leisure even to eat.

Do you recognize this scenario? The disciples had been sent out by Jesus, all had gone amazingly well, and now they were so busy they could hardly think. Success breeds success—you only have to give one good talk and the phone never stops ringing with requests for more! You only have to be a good listener to one needy soul, and somehow the whole world thinks you have the time and ability to listen to them! The phone always rings at meal times, because that's the only time you're in, and all of a sudden you're resenting all these demands on you and wishing you'd never got involved in the first place.

Jesus knew the value of a time apart, and he taught the disciples to at least try to build some space into their lives. He was good at finding the quiet place to be alone. But if you read on a little, these verses are the lead-in to the feeding of the five thousand. The crowd wasn't going to leave these wonderful people alone that easily, and they rushed on foot round the lake to reach the other shore before Jesus and the disciples got there. Instead of complaining about them, Jesus taught them, and fed them. There is a difficult balance to be maintained here, and we need to be flexible. Jesus and the disciples did manage at other times to have time alone, to rest and to relax. But when faced with people in need, Jesus showed by example what to do. Our task is to try to get the balance right, and to enjoy the busyness of life as well as the stillness.

Lord, teach me to enjoy what life brings, and to keep my life in balance.

✣

LUKE 9:23–25 (NRSV)

The cost of discipleship

Then he said to them all, 'If any want to become my followers, let them deny themselves and take up their cross daily and follow me. For those who want to save their life will lose it, and those who lose their life for my sake will save it.'

No one could accuse Jesus of not giving it to them straight. Not a great way of enticing people to be disciples, we may think—no promises of good health, happy family life, promotion at work, or plenty of money. But the disciples were all prepared to try it, and go down the road of possible suffering, self-denial and surrender to God. At the end of Peter's life, tradition has it that he asked to be crucified upside down, because he was not worthy to meet the same death as his Lord. Had it all been worth it for the disciples? We need only to open the Bible on any page of Acts to find that it was!

But how seriously should we take Jesus' words today? We may not be asked to face persecution, but self-denial isn't too nice either! As I write this, my husband is climbing the highest mountains in England, Scotland and Wales, in 48 hours, with an intrepid group of (younger and fitter) volunteers, to raise money for youth work. This has involved fitness training—going up and down our three flights of stairs 15 times a night—and now climbing in the cloud and rain. I'd hate it! But they wouldn't be able to do this without the training, and that's what we must do as disciples. Every little act of saying 'no' to our desire to put ourselves first, 'no' to our resentment of others, 'no' to our fear of commitment, is an act of training towards the goal of finding our truly glorious life in God.

Lord, help me to see if there is something I should be working on in my training.

MARK 9:5–6 (GNB)

Putting your foot in it

Peter spoke up and said to Jesus, 'Teacher, how good it is that we are here! We will make three tents, one for you, one for Moses, and one for Elijah.' He and the others were so frightened that he did not know what to say.

Peter brings hope to those of us who writhe in embarrassment at some of the stupid things we've managed to say. Here was a completely mind-blowing incident, where Jesus' clothes had become dazzling white, and he appeared to be talking to the long-dead Moses and Elijah, representing the law and the prophets—a great visual confirmation of who Jesus was. In this situation, most people would keep their mouths firmly shut! But not Peter. If there was an awkward silence, Peter was just the man to fill it. He made the totally inappropriate offer to build three tents for Jesus, Moses and Elijah. Maybe Peter was trying to make permanent a vision that could be only temporary, or maybe he was once more speaking first and thinking second!

Have you had similar times when what you've just said has made you feel stupid? For those of us who have problems remembering people's names and faces, there's the classic, 'Could you just remind me of your name, your face looks so familiar?' 'Certainly, it's Jenny—you had dinner with me last month.'

Then there's the old favourite, 'It's lovely to see new people in church.' 'Actually I'm not new, I've been coming for 20 years.' Do you wonder how God could possibly have patience with someone who can get it so wrong? Then remember that Jesus built his church on Peter.

Perhaps you have been on the receiving end of some well-meaning but unintentionally hurtful comment? We are sensitive beings and easily hurt. Remember that despite Peter's ability to put his foot in it, Jesus still loved him, and saw the good inside.

Help me to forgive myself when I say stupid things, and to have patience with others.

✣

MARK 9:14–20 (GNB)

Back to reality

A man in the crowd answered, 'Teacher, I brought my son to you because he has an evil spirit... I asked your disciples to drive the spirit out, but they could not.'

Jesus, Peter, James and John had just come back from the 'mountain top' experience of the transfiguration, and immediately found argument and failure. The disciples left behind had been attempting to heal an epileptic boy, and were making a mess of it. Back to reality with a dull thump! Have you noticed how often this happens? You've just been to a really inspiring talk, and come home ready to set the world alight, only to find that the cat's been sick, or the oven hasn't turned itself on, or your daughter thinks she's failed her exams. It's easy to leave the world behind when we're singing uplifting hymns, but reality is waiting to engulf us as soon as it can!

The disciples had to face this too. Living every day with Jesus, they still couldn't escape real life, and now their failure to heal the epileptic boy was giving the scribes ample opportunity to belittle them, and cast doubt on Jesus' choice of them.

So what's the answer when the world swamps us with its ordinariness? How do we cope when we're interrupted every few minutes, and all the good things we planned to do that day just fail to happen? How do we recapture our closeness to God when the dinner is burning and the phone is ringing? The mountain-top moments may not happen often, but recalling them when life gets tough can help to refresh us and give us confidence. We just have to get on with life, remembering that Jesus and the disciples knew all about tough living—God is as close to us in everyday life as he is on the mountain-top.

Try to remember the times when you felt that God was especially close.

✣

MARK 10:35–37 (GNB)

What gives us status?

Then James and John, the sons of Zebedee, came to Jesus. 'Teacher,' they said, 'there is something we want you to do for us.' 'What is it?' Jesus asked them. They answered, 'When you sit on your throne in your glorious Kingdom, we want you to let us sit with you, one at your right and one at your left.'

James and John, together with Peter, formed the inner circle of Jesus' disciples. They were always there at important moments, and maybe thought of themselves as being rather special. They'd given up a lot for Jesus, and done their very best to do what he wanted. So surely, when all worked out well in the end, some reward was in order? This was not some unrealistic pious group of devout characters, but a group of ordinary people just like us, with natural ambitions. They believed in Jesus' greatness with all their might, and they wanted some recognition for their devotion.

James and John received the gentle reply that only God could sort out the end times, and that in the meantime, the ones who were the greatest were the servants of others. Wow! That turns the world's values upside down, doesn't it? Our marks of status, like our shiny new car, our good job, our smart clothes, our responsibilities in church, our being popular, might give us confidence but are not what makes us great in God's eyes. It's what's inside —our attitudes towards others, our desire for their good, our willingness to put other people first. On that basis, however successful we may seem, we have a lot further to go. Even James and John, who listened to Jesus daily, hadn't got it right.

Then what about ambition? God has given us abilities in order to use them, and as long as we know where our true status lies, then we're free to show the world that Christians are good at things too!

Help me, Lord, to remember where true greatness lies.

MARK 14:29–30 (GNB)

Peter's denial

Peter answered, 'I will never leave you, even though all the rest do!' Jesus said to Peter, 'I tell you that before the cock crows twice tonight, you will say three times that you do not know me.'

Peter the enthusiast, the impetuous, the man of action, the leader, was about to meet his biggest test. Over-confident perhaps, and certainly unprepared for the terrible fear and danger he was about to encounter, but totally devoted to his Lord, and in theory anyway, prepared to risk everything for him. Peter was one of the two who followed Jesus, who tried to stay close despite the risks, whilst the other disciples faded into the night. So Peter started off well.

Do you remember the disgrace of the cricket captain who had to admit that despite being a much respected and admired Christian, he had been involved in taking bribes to fix matches? We hear of cases where the church treasurer has been less than honest with the finances or where the organist has run off with the vicar's wife. And it's not just something that happens to other people. We all have the possibility of over-confidence, of taking the easier way out of trouble, of manipulating the truth a bit if it makes life easier, of lashing out without thinking, of ignoring our principles.

And what makes it worse is that Peter had been warned, so he should have been on his guard. Sometimes we are so caught up in the present, that we find it hard to stop and look objectively at what we are doing. But take heart. Jesus did still found his church on this glorious failure of a man, and sometimes through failure we start to see ourselves with more realism and humility. Then Jesus can get to work on the real person, and not an imaginary superhero we could never really be.

Lord, help me not to be crippled by my failures, but to know they give you a way of re-making me.

✣

JOHN 21:15–19 (NRSV)

Peter's second chance

When they had finished breakfast, Jesus said to Simon Peter, 'Simon, son of John, do you love me more than these?' He said to him, 'Yes, Lord; you know that I love you.' Jesus said to him, 'Feed my lambs.'

I know of an upright, gracious man whose daughter got involved with drugs, and was arrested in a remote country on suspicion of drug dealing. He braved the hazardous journey out to visit her, stood by her, and welcomed her back into the family home when the charges were eventually dropped. He glows with joy and pride when he talks about her, how she's trying to start afresh, and how wonderful it is to be re-making their relationship. That's how God is with us.

Peter had probably tried to put his denial of Jesus to the back of his mind, pretending to himself that it didn't matter that much. But Jesus knew that Peter needed to face his failings and really experience forgiveness, right in the core of his being. So when the right time came, Peter was given his chance. Peter had to look into the eyes of Jesus, and say boldly that he loved him, three times over to mirror the three denials, three times over so that the experience became real and not just in his head. We can believe theoretically that we're forgiven, but we need really to experience this, like the daughter did when her father arrived at her cell, or like Peter when he looked straight into Jesus' eyes.

Forgiveness has consequences though. Peter was to 'feed my lambs'—to look after those who would be caught up into this life-changing movement, to tell them what had happened to him, to assure them that God's love was for them too, and that it was never too late to start again.

In a time of quiet, try to look into the eyes of Jesus. Know that he sees you as you really are, let him forgive you, and give you a fresh start.

✣

JOHN 20:24–29 (NRSV)

Thomas the outsider

So the other disciples told him, 'We have seen the Lord.' But he said to them, 'Unless I see the mark of the nails in his hands, and put my finger in the mark of the nails and my hand in his side, I will not believe.'

Thomas was not with the others when Jesus first appeared. Maybe he needed to have some space on his own to grieve for his Lord. Now he had a whole week of the other disciples talking non-stop about what the appearances of Jesus meant, whilst he felt out of it, isolated and confused.

It's easy to feel an outsider, and it hurts. I remember being driven home by the headmaster from school camp when I was ten because I'd caught mumps. The poor man had to put up with a weeping child for many hours. I was not particularly upset by the illness, but was mortified that I was missing out on what all the others would be doing. We can forget how difficult being an outsider is, and need to be reminded. Remember when you were a child in a new school, or an adult moving to a new area, or a newcomer in church?

We often label Thomas a 'doubter' as if doubt was something to be ashamed of. But Thomas was being honest: he knew that he couldn't feel convinced unless he'd had the same experience as the others. He didn't give up, opt out, shrink into himself or go back home! Thomas stayed where he felt most close to Jesus and talked to the others about what he was feeling. He didn't pretend to be all sorted out when he wasn't. He persevered and waited. And what a reward he got! Jesus knew what Thomas needed, and Thomas came through in the end with the greatest possible statement of faith—'My Lord and my God!'

Look out for anyone who seems to be an outsider. Can you help them feel more at home?

✣

ACTS 2:32–33 (GNB)

Transforming power

God has raised this very Jesus from death, and we are all witnesses to this fact. He has been raised to the right-hand side of God, his Father, and has received from him the Holy Spirit, as

he had promised. What you now see and hear is his gift that he has poured out on us.

Here was Peter, who a few weeks before had been afraid to admit that he was a follower of Jesus, now giving the first Christian sermon to a crowd of over a thousand people. He was arguing persuasively and authoritatively, without any thought of his own safety, or of his lack of experience in public speaking. His message came straight from the heart, and his heart had just been set ablaze by the Holy Spirit. Now he knew the power of God within him and there was no stopping him!

It's very fitting that it was Peter who gave this sermon—the man who was never short of a word, a natural leader and spokesman. Yet Peter in his wildest dreams would never have imagined that he'd be up on his feet, exposed to public scrutiny.

The Spirit was a gift the disciples sorely needed. They'd seen their risen Lord, they'd got the head knowledge, but then what? They needed something to set them alight inside. Their questions must have been the same as ours today. How can we be different from our old selves, how can we have confidence, how can we live lives which show we know God in a special way?

We, like the disciples, have been given the gift of the Spirit, even if we've not experienced it in as dramatic a way as they did. We need to use this power, and not be afraid. It's when we risk using the gifts the Spirit gives, as Peter did, that we give him the chance to show us what he can do.

Help me to let the power of the Spirit grow in me.

PROMISES FROM JESUS

LUKE 11:5–7 (NIV)

Questions of prayer

Suppose one of you has a friend, and he goes to him at midnight and says, 'Friend, lend me three loaves of bread, because a friend of mine on a journey has come to me, and I have nothing to set before him.' Then the one inside answers, 'Don't bother me. The door is already locked, and my children are with me in bed. I can't get up and give you anything.'

Our church has recently completed a congregation-wide survey on prayer. The awkward questions ranged from favoured positions, frequency and style to ways in which God communicates to us—very comprehensive and very challenging. Unfortunately, I scanned my copy on one of those 'is-God-listening?' days. I had no idea how I was going to answer the detailed questions. To me, God felt shut up behind some very formidable doors just then, and I had no confidence that he would even hear me knocking.

I suspect we all have times when prayer flows naturally and times when it does not. Some of us try to emulate prayer models which do not suit us. Sometimes life hurts too much to concentrate. Sometimes we wonder if God is occupied and unavailable, as in the opening scenario of Jesus' parable. This midnight request was pushing the boundaries of even Middle Eastern hospitality, so Jesus knew that the natural sympathies of his listeners would be with the man closed up for the night.

Is it all too easy to ascribe a similar reluctance to God? When the compiled results were available from our church survey, I saw that our approach to prayer is very much that—our approach. We may experience real and often profound frustration in our stumbling attempts to connect with the Almighty, but God is not like us. The survey revealed a kaleidoscope of praying practices and bore witness to a glorious variety of God's responses. Perhaps if we started more often with his agenda and his ideas for prayer, then we could short-circuit our difficulties.

Lord, teach us to pray.

Read Luke 11:1–4.

LUKE 11:8 (NIV)

Pray and pray

I tell you, though he will not get up and give him the bread because he is his friend, yet because of the man's boldness he will get up and give him as much as he needs.

The idea of boldness here carries with it persistence and perseverance. Jesus' hero gets what he wants because he keeps going. He is prepared to risk his friendship by being a bit of a nuisance, but it works. He gets his bread.

All of us have times when we feel inconvenienced by others. I suspect that most of us would try to avoid being the source of inconvenience. It has been said that women are relationship orientated and are perhaps more motivated by this than men. I am sure this is not universally true, but I must admit that my husband finds it impossible to understand why, when I am on the telephone to ask a friend a simple question, I have to find out how the family are, what the news is, how she is feeling and so on. A two-minute phone call is never that! I would have phrased the late-night plea in this parable very carefully.

How does this affect the way we approach God? I wonder. Do we ever catch ourselves checking up on our relationship with him, feeling hesitant, wondering about his response? There's nothing wrong with sorting out things that need it, but Jesus is encouraging boldness and persistence in prayer. What would militate against that in our own personal prayer life? What internal blocks dissuade us from approaching prayer with confidence? Is there anything that, even today, would hold you back from a good talk with your heavenly Father?

We all have our different battles, and perhaps that is why Jesus tells the parable. He knows what God is really like and does not want us to miss out because of our limited understanding. It is OK to be bold. It is OK to expect.

Take the risk of giving prayer some quality time—today.

Read Hebrews 4:14–16.

✣

LUKE 11:9 (NIV)

Prayers and answers

So I say to you: Ask and it will be given to you; seek and you will find; knock and the door will be opened to you.

Right, says Jesus. If persistent knocking on a reluctant friend's door will yet bring results, let us apply that to your prayer. First, can you really imagine God being reluctant? Second, he is more than your best friend. Third, the bread you are after is of a different batch altogether. We are into another league here. We are dealing with a lavish creator God who even knows the number of hairs on your head (Matthew 10:30). We are talking about the sustainer of the universe (Psalm 8), the one who loved the world so much that he gave up his only Son to rescue it (John 3:16). Keep things in perspective.

This is the God who responds to our longing with assurances that it will be met. The contrast between the grudging friend in the parable and our generous God could not be greater. When we stop and consider the vast richness of all he has made, how can we possibly suspect him of stinginess?

We still do, though. Well, I do. I assign to God the same small-mindedness of which I am often guilty, and think he will act accordingly. I suspect he will mete out assistance if he has the time. I need to look again at the words of Jesus and take them at face value. There is no proviso or condition to this sequence: 'Seek and you will find.' I have been encouraged by some friends who have recently become Christians. They have searched and they have found. They did not know God and now they do. The seeking was not easy but they now have a priceless treasure. Wherever we are on our life's journey, the principle is the same. God wants to be found.

Do not be outdone by the man in the parable. Put your heart into it and find what you need.

Read Luke 18:1–8.

✣

LUKE 11:10 (NIV)

Prayer promises

For everyone who asks receives; everyone who seeks finds; and to everyone who knocks, the door will be opened.

These are amazing promises. Jesus tells us that the basis to our prayer life is an expectation that we will receive what we ask for. We are to build the foundation for our prayers on this understanding. God will give. He will be found. He will be welcoming. We will get what we are looking for.

However, I do not know how you react to these wonderful

promises to prayer, but I venture to suggest a hitch. Why, when it all sounds so simple and glorious, does it not always work? Before you write me off as heretical, let me explain. I quite understand that these promises follow the first utterance of the Lord's Prayer, and that we must see them in context. My husband's not receiving the motorbike he prayed for is not a big theological problem. It was low on the list of priorities for 'your kingdom come', right? But you cannot be a Christian for very long before you hit some big unanswerables on this prayer business. There are things that must surely be within 'your will be done', which refuse to happen—or happen when we do not want them to. The child who is killed. The loved one who does not respond to God's love. The marriage that breaks down. The war that will not end. The pain. These things seem to fly in the face of receiving all you ask. Indeed we would not ask for them. They open huge debates about the nature of God, the world, the devil and humanity.

Jesus lived in the same world and yet he still insisted that we would find what we long for. He does not leave us pat solutions, but instead invites us to tussle with reality, all the while building on his promises.

Father, give me right foundations and right understandings. Amen

Read 2 Samuel 12:15–23. How do you understand the concept of God's will?

LUKE 11:11–12 (NIV)

Trusting prayer

Which of you fathers, if your children ask for a fish, will give them a snake instead? Or if they ask for an egg, will give them a scorpion?

I have never been to the Holy Land but would dearly love to visit one day to see if my overactive imagination is anywhere near the mark. I want to find out if my picture of Jesus standing near the water, addressing the crowd, could be fitted into a real landscape. This scorpion comment is precisely the sort that sends my mental pictures into overdrive. There is no way that such a ridiculous suggestion would have been met with anything else than laughter, and suddenly there I am, surrounded by ordinary people in unfamiliar garb. The children are running round the back, the cynics are clustered just in front of them, the hurt are squeezing down the side, the curious are all ears... and suddenly a ripple of laughter from all as Jesus reminds them of their common humanity.

Of course they know how to feed their children! How, then, implies Jesus, could God know any less? Of course their children, startled from their games into listening, know they can trust their parents for provision. How then can we grown-ups expect any less from our heavenly Father?

Of course we are just like them, in need of reassurance. Jesus' understanding of humanity echoes down the centuries and hits the mark. We too need encouragement to trust God completely for all our needs. We too need his impeccable logic. How could God provide in any less a way than we do? How could he be anything less than the perfect parent? Yet we need to clasp these words close to our souls in the face of a hard world that would tell us they are not true. In the sight of all that would discourage us, we must learn that God is to be trusted and is exactly who he says he is.

'You prepare a table before me in the presence of my enemies. You anoint my head with oil; my cup overflows' (Psalm 23:5).

✣

LUKE 11:13 (NIV)

Intimate prayer

If you then, though you are evil, know how to give good gifts to your children, how much more will your Father in heaven give the Holy Spirit to those who ask him!

A bit of Gospel comparison here. Nothing too heavy, in case you are reading this first thing in the morning and, like me, it takes you a while to come round. Matthew's Gospel also records the teaching about asking and receiving, but he tells us that God will give us 'good gifts' instead of the Holy Spirit (Matthew 7:11). There was a time when I could easily grasp Matthew's version—everyone can envisage good gifts—but I was not sure about the Holy Spirit. A while and some gentle theology later, I came to appreciate that the Holy Spirit is just about the best good gift you can get.

So when Jesus talks about us receiving the Holy Spirit in answer to our asking, he is promising us more than we can imagine. He is not setting up a slot-machine kind of trust where we drop in the request and God duly pays out. God is looking for relationship. He wants us to experience his love for us, because there is nothing else like it; and he wants us to love him back, because there is nothing to equal that either. Getting our foundations for prayer fairly stable becomes a springboard for a friendship with God that is totally unique to each one of us. The unanswered problems do not disappear, but as we discover that God is totally trustworthy, we can trust him for the things we do not understand.

All of this sounds excellent and to be desired. If you are anything like me, however, there are moments when heaven feels almost tangible and moments when the whole thing feels impossible. Sometimes it is by sheer decision of the will that we come to God at all, and at other times no one can get us away. Prayer is nothing if not interesting.

Keep on going! Stuck for prayer? Try a psalm.

✣

MATTHEW 6:6–7a (NIV)

Secret prayer

But when you pray, go into your room, close the door and pray to your Father, who is unseen. Then your Father, who sees what is

done in secret, will reward you. And when you pray, do not keep on babbling like pagans.

So, prayer. We have Jesus' own teaching on prayer as a basic inspirational structure; we have parables to encourage us and promises to build on. Over the next few days, we will pick up on different aspects of prayer to which Jesus draws our attention.

If you have ever been discouraged by someone's seeming expertise in prayer, take heart. Jesus has no time for those who prayed to show off. Dare I say that I have occasionally wondered if a particular prayer was truly addressing God, or rather aiming to impress the rest of us? That sounds judgmental, yet Jesus raised the subject! Prayer is not about flowery language or popular techniques. Prayer is about honesty and relationship. So if you catch yourself longing to spout a few choice phrases at the next prayer meeting, it might be better to keep quiet until you get home. Trying them out alone with God should soon sort out whether they are coming from your heart or your ego. Take a leaf out of Jesus' book. He often withdrew from the crowds to pray alone (for example, Matthew 4:23). He would get up early, or stay behind late. He always prayed before major decisions. I would love to have eavesdropped on his conversations with God. No wonder the disciples were fascinated and asked to be taught to pray. They could see how important and special it was to Jesus.

Different personalities will find different ways of praying appropriately. I am learning not to copy others but to find my own style. Your relationship to God is just yours, so find what is right for you. Gather ideas from others and experiment, then enjoy exploring your unique pattern. Remember that God himself will reward us for our efforts, so go ahead—discover what that means.

Father, teach me to pray.

✣

MARK 11:15–17 (NIV)

Prayer first

Jesus entered the temple area and began driving out those who were buying and selling there. He overturned the tables of the money changers and the benches of those selling doves, and would not allow anyone to carry merchandise through the temple courts. And as he taught them, he said, 'Is it not written: "My house will be called a house of prayer for all nations"? But you have made it a den of robbers.'

Can you imagine the chaos? Mark describes the scene with typical understatement, but this was no polite disagreement. Jesus drove out the merchants—in his version, John tells us he used a self-plaited whip (John 2:15)—and tipped up tables. This outer court of the Gentiles was already a noisy, busy place. Would-be worshippers haggled over the price of a sacrificial dove, merchants touted for business, lambs bleated, money clanked and ordinary folk jostled their way through. Suddenly there is a disturbance near the doors and in strides Jesus, causing mayhem as he flings tables to the floor. Birds fly free of crushed cages, money cascades on to people's feet, sellers escape as he approaches. Why doesn't anyone stop him or question him? Isn't it awesome as he marches through, breathing authority and anger?

The Jewish leaders concluded that he was way out of line, but Jesus' priorities were clear. This was his Father's house. It was built for prayer, not for people's greed and extortion. It was not just the inflated prices for worship necessities, but the human-centred atmosphere that Jesus was objecting to. This temple was a holy place of pilgrimage for all, a place to meet with God.

As the Holy Spirit leads us into a warm and intimate relationship with God, it does not mean we are to treat casually things that he takes seriously. Would we have noticed the mixed-up priorities in the temple that day? Is the challenge to ask God to help us to see things as he sees them?

Would you have supported Jesus' actions?

Read Micah 6:6–8.

✣

MATTHEW19:13–14 (NIV)

Children's prayers

Then little children were brought to Jesus for him to place his hands on them and pray for them. But the disciples rebuked those who brought them. Jesus said, 'Let the little children come to me, and do not hinder them, for the kingdom of heaven belongs to such as these.'

There is no doubt that Jesus' prayer life was something special. It sprang from a unique relationship with God and it made things happen. Small wonder that parents wanted to bring their children to him for prayer. Perhaps the disciples thought the children insignificant—hardly pivotal to the exciting opening up of Jesus' ministry and extraordinary teaching. As usual, Jesus turned human perception on its head. He welcomed the children and gave them quality time. He told off his disciples for getting the wrong end of the stick and declared to all that the children had special access to the kingdom of heaven.

So he set a precedent for us—on the one hand, the obligation to pray for and bless our youngsters; and on the other, actually to strive to be like them. Having taught us to pray for God's kingdom, he now encourages us to approach this kingdom with the dependent, trusting and sincere attitude of a child. Children generally have no choice in being dependent. We grown-ups easily forget that we are dependent too. Yet coming to God on any other basis is illogical, for we are dependent for our every breath on the one who made us. Some of us struggle with the illusion of our independence, and find that it can get in the way of trusting prayer. Watching my daughter climb on to her father's lap for a snuggle reminds me again of the principle. To paraphrase our parable: if earthly fathers can give hugs that well, how much more wonderful can one from our heavenly Father be?

'Where were you when I laid the earth's foundation? Tell me, if you understand' (Job 38:4).

Pour out your heart to God, your Father. He understands you better than you do.

✣

MATTHEW 5:44–45 (NIV)

Praying for persecutors

'But I tell you: Love your enemies and pray for those who persecute you, that you may be children of your Father in heaven. He causes his sun to rise on the evil and the good, and sends rain on the righteous and the unrighteous.'

This has to be one of the most challenging things Jesus ever said. The desire for justice and vengeance seems deeply embedded in humanity, and is surely the prime cause for many of the world's conflicts. The fate of nations turns on the principle of revenge for past wrongs. Jesus challenges us at the deepest level when he commands us to pray for our enemies. I know I am not alone when I react to this with hesitation. 'But Lord, those actions were inexcusable...'; 'But Lord, that was so unfair...'

We all have an inbuilt fairness monitor, biased in our own favour. Even for small slights, we struggle to let the perpetrators off the hook. For Jesus to ask us to pray for those who have hurt us, whether in a minor or major way, seems patently unfair. Surely God is a God of justice? Yet Jesus says we must pray for those who have injured us. I think this is incredibly difficult. The hurt is real. The injustice is obvious. To pray for blessing demands that we forgive and release our demands for vengeance. Yet on the few times when I have battled through to obedience on this one, I have discovered—eventually—a remarkable healing for my own sore spirit. Laurens van der Post explains the effect of forgiveness on his fellow confinees in a Japanese prisoner-of-war camp, when they extended it towards their captors:

*The tables of the spirit would be strangely and promptly turned and we would find ourselves without self-pity of any kind, feeling deeply sorry for the Japanese as if we were the free men and they the prisoners—men held in some profound oubliette of their own minds (*The Night of the New Moon, *Penguin, 1986).*

Is forgiveness a feeling or an action?

Read Matthew 6:14–15.

✣

MARK 9:26–29 (NIV)

Fast and pray

The spirit shrieked, convulsed him violently and came out. The boy looked so much like a corpse that many said, 'He's dead.' But Jesus took him by the hand and lifted him to his feet, and he stood up. After Jesus had gone indoors, his disciples asked him privately, 'Why couldn't we drive it out?' He replied, 'This kind can come out only by prayer and fasting.'

OK, so if we take this story at face value, it could seem pretty wild. The boy reacted to Jesus' ministry so dramatically that the onlookers thought he had died. This was not a quiet, subtle prayer moment, it was a major deliverance session. Some of us might find the whole concept of spirit invasion and its subsequent banishment hard to swallow, but Jesus obviously did not. He dealt with the situation quickly and calmly, and reassured his frustrated disciples that they had been up against a tough situation.

Sometimes things are like that. Sometimes it seems we hit a deadlock in a situation, and no matter how hard we pray, it just will not shift. We battle on, but feel up against insuperable odds. Frustration sets in, and we are tempted to get discouraged. Well, we are not alone. The disciples obviously felt the same. They had done everything they could think of, and still the boy was not better. Then along comes Jesus to rescue them.

The disciples would have been used to the concept of fasting (Matthew 6:16), and Jesus clearly expected them to exercise this particular discipline. Here he implies that it released an extra shot of power that was just what was needed. Perhaps fasting is already part of your worship pattern, but if not, I recommend you give it a try. It is not always easy, but it sorts out your priorities immediately. It can clear the channel between you and God for those resistant situations, and focus your attention on what really matters.

Father, teach me your ways. Give me the courage to try something new if you want me to. Amen

✣

LUKE 22:40 (NIV)

Pray and stand

He said to them, 'Pray that you will not fall into temptation.'

Just as Jesus repeated his desperate prayer to God that there might be a way other than the cross, so he also exhorted his disciples at least twice in the garden to pray that they would not fall into temptation.

Yet while he was wrestling with deep anguish, his friends had collapsed with exhaustion and sorrow, and were sleeping. It is very easy to condemn the disciples for not standing with Jesus in his hour of need, but would we have done any different? Surely we too would have been confused by Jesus' increasing agitation, and scared by the escalating tension of the night. Besides, he was the strong one: we leaned on him. What did he mean by temptation?

Jesus knew all too well what trials the disciples would face in the ensuing days, and only wanted to prepare his friends. It's interesting that he picked this particular angle on prayer for the days ahead—rather than, say, praying that they would be delivered from evil. The disciples would certainly be hounded and threatened by the authorities, but Jesus' main priority was that they would stand the test and keep their faith.

How often do you pray that you will not fall into temptation, when faced with difficult situations? I must admit that my first prayer is more likely to be, 'Lord, get me out of this!' But Jesus urges us instead to pray that we will not fall—into despair, into discouragement, into hopelessness or lack of faith. He wants us to stand, and not give in to an easy way out if we know it is wrong, or if it will damage others. Sometimes choosing not to listen to temptation is very hard, and we may need the support of a good friend or two. Perhaps that is why we are to pray that we will not fall—before it hits us.

Thank you, Lord, that we can handle this together. Amen

Read Luke 22:31–34.

✣

JOHN 17:20 (NIV)

Jesus, prayer and you

My prayer is not for them alone. I pray also for those who will believe in me through their message, that all of them may be one,

Father, just as you are in me and I am in you. May they also be in us so that the world may believe that you have sent me.

If you have never read John's account of Jesus' prayers for his followers before his crucifixion, now is the time. John 17 is so wonderfully reassuring. Jesus prays for himself, his disciples, and then... us. He prayed that we also would be caught up into the glorious union that is Father and Son and good news and unity with each other—something so special that it seems hard for Jesus to put it into words.

It is good to know that we were there in that original prayer, when Jesus was entrusting all he really cared about to his Father. Jesus only prayed because he knew the power of prayer and knew that his Father would listen. As we draw our fortnight of focus on prayer to a close, I hope that you have been encouraged. Wherever you are in your prayer experience, keep going, and do not fear to try something new. The trouble with writing these notes is that inevitably I challenge myself, probably more than anyone else. So I will join you in a renewed approach.

In case we still need any more convincing, how about this: university psychologists have published the results of a survey among 474 students which claims that daily prayer wards off depression.

*We measured depressive symptoms, anxiety and self-esteem and found people who prayed daily or often were more likely to report lower depression, lower anxiety and higher self-esteem than those who hardly ever prayed. They were, however, unable to explain where the power of prayer came from. (*The Times*, 12 November 1999)*

So, now that it is official, how can we resist?

Dear Father, set my prayer life alight by your Spirit. Teach me to pray. Amen

JESUS AND THE CROWDS

LUKE 2:10–14 (NIV)

Promises to the crowds

But the angel said to them, 'Do not be afraid. I bring you good news of great joy that will be for all the people. Today in the town of David a Saviour has been born to you: he is Christ the Lord... Glory to God in the highest, and on earth peace to those on whom his favour rests.'

Familiar words. It's almost impossible to separate them from the aroma of roasting turkey, the rustle of presents, or the unforgettable atmosphere of a church lit and decorated for Christmas.

However, when these words were first spoken, no one had yet thought of Christmas. Did the angels know they would be quoted so often? This glorious moment when heaven broke through to announce the new order was nothing to do with red and green candles. This was a message of freedom, declared to everyone. This affirmation was for the whole of humankind. Hey people, God likes you! He is sending his Son who will save you! Isn't that the best news ever? There will be joy and peace for everyone! Then the angels burst with excitement into sky-blazing praise of God.

Joy, peace, salvation, favour, God's glory—what a mandate. God promised all this through Jesus. As Jesus began his public ministry some 30 years later, were there any in the gathering crowds who remembered these promises? As we take a few days to join the crowds, bear in mind these clear promises of God. The people who gathered to Jesus could look for the good stuff, for real good news. There would be no need for anyone to feel reticent or ignored. This great joy was for all people. Every person who came to hear what this new rabbi was saying had the same opportunity. The good and great promises of God, fulfilled in this man, offered to you.

Ever feel just one of a crowd? Jesus does not see you that way. No one is left out in 'all'.

Read Luke 4:14–21. Jesus knew what he had come for.

✣

MATTHEW 9:35 (NIV)

The crowds begin

Jesus went through all the towns and villages, teaching in their synagogues, preaching the good news of the kingdom and healing every disease and sickness.

It really is not surprising that Jesus attracted crowds. Can you imagine yourself among them? There were other itinerant rabbis of course. But the word was out that Jesus of Nazareth was different. For a start, he had this amazing authority that made you want to listen for more (Matthew 7:29). He was not afraid of opponents and had a cavalier attitude to the laws which ordinary folk struggled to keep. Why, one Sabbath he dramatically healed a woman during his own teaching slot. Then he took to task those who criticized him for 'working' on the Sabbath. It was the talk of the town and the crowd was delighted with the wonderful drama. The healings, well, they had to be seen to be believed. It was astonishing to watch him make people better. It made you ask the question—who is he? (Matthew 12: 23). Somehow he made you feel closer to God and want to praise him for the wonderful things you were seeing and hearing (Luke 18:43).

Small wonder, then, that the crowds grew. The question is, if you had been there, would you have joined them? Would you have left your housework and rushed to hear him when he came to town? Or would you have been too busy? Would you have grabbed a sick friend's hand and hurried through the dusty streets, hope rising as you saw a space at the front of the crowd? Or would you have dallied alone at the back, in case nothing happened? Would you have listened attentively to his surprising stories, wrestled with the difficult bits, but come back for more? Or would your mind have wandered to the prospects for next market day?

Then, as now, we are so human, with so many mixed motives. What do you come to Jesus for, and do you trust him to be there for you?

✣

LUKE 4:42–43 (NIV)

The crowds persist

At daybreak Jesus went out to a solitary place. The people were looking for him and when they came to where he was, they tried to keep him from leaving them. But he said, 'I must preach the good news of the kingdom of God to the other towns also, because that is why I was sent.'

Once people got a taste for all Jesus was offering, they wanted more. They chased after him when he looked for some space, and hung on to him when he wanted to leave. Most of them were wonderfully ordinary folk. Certainly the teachers and Pharisees joined in, as the stir Jesus created demanded their attention. The powerful people were there. But the majority were the ordinary folk of Galilee, mesmerized by a teacher they could understand and respond to.

Jesus did not call the Jewish religious leaders together to proclaim his mission and ask for their endorsement. He patently did not use the social, political or religious structures of the day to give his message clout. He never responded to the seductive trappings of power.

Given the questionable security of human power structures, this is good news. Jesus stood alone, not dependent on any human institution. He was exclusively obedient to his Father in heaven. He shared the good news of the kingdom with everyday people and excluded no one who wanted to listen. He was honest about the demands of the kingdom, but only the religious leaders earned his explicit condemnation (Matthew 23)—an awesome challenge for those with similar responsibilities today.

He chose his disciples from among the ordinary Jews. He was particularly close to Peter, James and John. He was the son of God walking the hills of Judah, but he was normal. His friends were normal. He invites us, as ordinary humans, to be his friends today.

Dear Lord Jesus, some days I feel ordinary, some days I feel great, and some days I feel distinctly weird. Thank you that you invite me to be your friend every day. Amen.

Read John 15:15–16.

✣

MATTHEW 9:36 (NIV)

Jesus' attitude

When he saw the crowds, he had compassion on them, because they were harassed and helpless, like sheep without a shepherd.

Jesus' attitude to the multitudes that surrounded him was consistent. He had compassion. He had compassion when they were hungry, and the miracle of the feeding of the five thousand ensued. He had compassion when they were ill, and healed them. He told a riveting story about a compassionate father who ran to embrace his prodigal son, and set the scene for many of us to return to our heavenly Father in the same way. Jesus saw people's struggles, had compassion and acted in love. No wonder the crowds followed him.

There are some heartwarming accounts of individuals who stand out from the crowd. Many of them—oh yes!—were women. There was Peter's mother-in-law, healed of a fever, and Jairus' daughter, rescued from death. There was the oh-so-brave woman who touched the edge of Jesus' cloak. In touching him she broke levitical laws, as she was ceremonially unclean from her illness and a woman at that. But Jesus responded with compassion, acknowledging her healing and uniquely calling her 'Daughter'.

Each person was treated with the utmost dignity and compassion by Jesus. They must represent so many other encounters Jesus had which were not written down. So many discovered that Jesus really did bring good news, joy and peace. It is so encouraging that even when the people broke through cultural and religious boundaries to get to him, they all received the same treatment. I have a theory that it was the women who had more courage in this than the men. Think of the Canaanite woman, begging for her daughter's restoration (Mark 7:24–30), or the lady lavishing tears and perfume on Jesus' feet in the middle of a meal.

Each one refused to stay away. Each one received Jesus' compassion.

Whether you feel near or far away from God today, do not let anything keep you from coming closer.

✣

JOHN 7:12–13 (NIV)

Whisperings

Among the crowds there was widespread whispering about him. Some said, 'He is a good man.' Others replied, 'No, he deceives the people.' But no one would say anything publicly about him for fear of the Jews.

Nothing new here. Nothing new about the way some people will respond readily to Jesus, while others will judge and condemn. It was fair enough that people should have asked searching questions as to Jesus' identity. They did not have the benefit of hindsight as we do. When we meet Jesus it can only be as the risen Christ, gloriously alive in the here and now. Then, the Jews had to struggle with explosive issues. Was he the Messiah, the Promised One? Did he really do these remarkable healings by the power of God? What did he mean when he claimed to be the bread of life? No separation of synagogue and state then, no question of Jesus being an irrelevance. If he was the Messiah, the political implications would be cataclysmic. Likewise if he was not.

These were enormous questions. Yet it seems Jesus was most able to respond to those who set all their agendas aside and simply came to him in honesty, need and openness. These were the ones who received his compassion. The others, the scribes and Pharisees who tried to catch him out with their cunning, rendered themselves blind to Jesus' true nature. They were so anxious about the political implications and so enmeshed in their religious structures that they could not relate. Were they cynical and hardhearted or just misguided? Perhaps both. But we all know people who seem incapable of enthusiasm for anything except their own point of view. They seem to have forgotten that good news, joy and peace really do exist. How could the ruling Jews not see the calibre of person Jesus was? Eventually they influenced even the crowds to betray Jesus and call for his death.

Are you free to respond with open-hearted simplicity to Jesus? Treat yourself to some 'me time' to do just that today.

Read Matthew 18:2–10.

✣

MATTHEW 28:16–20 (NIV)

Doubt in the crowd

Then the eleven disciples went to Galilee, to the mountain where Jesus had told them to go. When they saw him, they worshipped

him; but some doubted. Then Jesus came to them and said, 'All authority in heaven and on earth has been given to me... And surely I am with you always, to the very end of the age.'

I find these words some of the most remarkable in the Bible. Did you spot them? That little phrase, 'but some doubted'. How on earth did they do that? These were the guys who had travelled the road with Jesus. They knew him so well. They had eaten food he provided out of nowhere. They had spoken to those he had healed. They had been empowered by the Holy Spirit to do the same. Then they had tumbled from excitement into terror as the forces ranging against this unpredictable, unownable teacher closed in. They ran when he was arrested and hid when he was crucified. They thought that was it. They would never see him again. Back, somehow, to tax collecting and fishing.

Then another emotional twister as he appeared to them in a risen body. Wow! Back on line again, but in a whole new dimension!

So how did they doubt? They saw what so many of us wished we had seen, and yet they doubted! How could they disbelieve even the evidence of their own eyes? Is it why God so often withholds himself from us today when we are begging for a sign? Is this why he does not reveal himself clearly to the world in general? Perhaps it would not make any difference.

The miracles did just what Jesus had predicted. To those who chose to believe him, they gave even more reason to believe. But for those determined to deny him, the miracles made little difference. Some things just have to be believed to be seen.

PHILIP YANCEY, *DISAPPOINTMENT WITH GOD* (MARSHALL PICKERING, 1995)

Dear Father, have mercy on us. We want to see, and worship. Amen

✣

JOHN 6:66–67 (NIV)

The crowds leave

From this time many of his disciples turned back and no longer followed him. 'You do not want to leave too, do you?' Jesus asked the Twelve. Simon Peter answered him, 'Lord, to whom shall we go? You have the words of eternal life.'

If yesterday's verses included one of my most puzzling phrases, today's contain one of my favourite. When life seems at its bleakest and faith at its lowest, there is always that indisputable awareness that Jesus is it. There is nowhere else to go, no one else to turn to. No one else offers words of eternal life. I guess different scriptures grab different people but I have returned countless times to Peter's words and found in them the steadying security I need.

Yet the occasion that prompted Peter's declaration must have been such a sad one for Jesus. His ministry had attracted all those wonderful, excitable, enthusiastic crowds, eager to receive his compassion. But as soon as Jesus began to say truths they did not want to hear, their commitment fell away. This must have been much harder for Jesus than facing up to his enemies in the crowds. Opponents are one thing, but friends who desert are another. Though he never wavered, or watered down his message, it must have been heartbreaking for Jesus to see his friends unable to digest the bread of life he was giving them.

The parallels are obvious. Do we stay the course when the terrain gets rough? Do we too try to take the bits of Jesus we like and leave the rest? Are we determined to stick by Jesus because we know his are the words of eternal life, no matter how unpalatable?

I imagine that those who turned away returned to their lives in disillusionment. Perhaps they criticized Jesus robustly to ease their emptiness. Perhaps they were quiet and sad. Surely many must have wondered why life was never quite the same again.

Dear Father, I worship and praise you for Jesus. How could anything compare to him? Amen

Read Revelation 7:9–17.

LEARNING FROM JESUS

MARK 1:35 (GNB)

Space to pray

Very early the next morning, long before daylight, Jesus got up and left the house. He went out of the town to a lonely place, where he prayed.

Most mornings I wake early and stay comfortable and warm under the duvet knowing that the alarm won't go off for at least another hour. Some of those mornings, as I slowly gain consciousness, the unsolved worries of the day before flood into my mind and I lie there struggling to be positive about the day ahead. Occasionally one of these 'worry mornings' has coincided with my husband needing a lift to the station to catch an early train to London, so I have taken our two dogs up to the common for a walk. At first light, the air is fresh and clear, the birds are singing and no one else is around. There I walk and talk to God about my family, my fears and the beauty of his world. And when I get home those worries have mostly disappeared. Why don't I manage to do that every morning?

Jesus often took himself away to a quiet place to pray. Early in his ministry he had begun to teach and to heal the sick—news of this had spread quickly in Galilee and people came from all directions to see him. He had been with the crowds all day and had gone to the home of Simon and Andrew for the night. But the crowds still came and gathered in front of the house with sick people for Jesus to heal. Can you imagine how it must have been, with the constant buzz of conversation and the pleading of people for his help? There would have been little sleep for those in the house that night.

Yet we read in Mark 1 that when Jesus had been under pressure he went away to a lonely place to pray. He gave himself space in a busy, pressured life to spend time with his Father. I get hassled by the demands I feel people make on me—yet they are nothing compared to the demands people made on Jesus.

Help me to follow the example of Jesus and find my own 'lonely place' to talk with God and receive his peace.

Read Mark 1:29–39.

✣

MARK 2:17 (GNB)

All welcomed

People who are well do not need a doctor, but only those who are sick. I have not come to call respectable people, but outcasts.

Jesus had called Levi, a tax collector, to follow him—which he did without any hesitation. Tax collectors were not socially acceptable people in those days. Later, when Jesus and his disciples were having a meal with Levi and some of his friends, they incurred the disapproval of some local Pharisees. Jesus overheard them criticizing him for actually eating with the outcasts of Jewish society.

This story reminds me of an incident that happened a long time ago in church in the middle of a large housing estate. The curate had noted how many teenagers hung around the streets in the evenings just kicking their heels as there was nowhere for them to go. He decided that the church should do something for them and hired an empty shop to turn into a coffee bar and meeting place. The church supported this venture with finance and prayer, while the youth group turned up faithfully each night to serve coffee and talk to the teenagers who came along in their leathers and heavy boots.

The curate, in time, invited some of them along to the evening service—and they came! They arrived as we were finishing the first hymn. Downstairs was full, so they clattered loudly up the wooden stairs into the circular gallery of our lovely modern church. The congregation were by now sitting down, some peering round to see what all the noise was about. This was not a familiar environment for the lads in the gallery, so they shuffled and giggled in embarrassment. Disapproval flowed up to them from the respectable congregation (who had indeed been praying for their conversion). They didn't come again... I think Jesus would have been sitting up there in the gallery with them.

Help me, Lord, to see others as you see them, and to treat everyone I meet today with true courtesy and respect.

Read Mark 2:13–17.

✣

MARK 4:33 (GNB)

Teaching in parables

Jesus preached his message to the people using many other parables like these; he told them as much as they could understand.

I am a teacher, and I enjoy nothing better than being able to spend time teaching primary school children. Mostly, but not always, they enjoy finding out about all sorts of things. I remember going on a fungi hunt in the local woods with two top classes at our school. Over 60 children plus teachers and mums returned to school with an immense booty of assorted fungi. For the next couple of hours, the school hall was abuzz with groups of children searching through books, identifying and recording. By the end of the day, we all knew about the poisonous ones, the ones that were harmless and those that were edible. They learned as much that day as a seven-year-old could understand. Good teachers know just how much their pupils are able to understand, leaving them interested and wanting to find out more later.

Jesus knew just how much the crowds who followed him around could and could not understand. So he taught them in parables—interesting stories in themselves, yet with far more meaning to those who were ready to hear about the kingdom of God. In my classroom, a firm favourite with small children was the parable of the good shepherd. 'Please tell us the story of the lost lamb again,' they would plead. Every child knows what it is like to be lost, and their eyes would get bigger and they would hold their breath as they heard how the silly lamb got further and further away from home! Then, when the good shepherd left all the others and went to find that lost lamb, a cheer would go up and the relief in their smiling faces would sometimes bring a tear to my eyes. I hope that some of those children, who are now adults, will have kept that story in their minds and have a more mature understanding of the unconditional love our heavenly Father has for each one of us.

Pray today for all Christian teachers in our schools—especially those with responsibilities for RE.

Read Mark 4:1–20.

✣

MARK 4:37–38 (GNB)

Peace in the storm

Suddenly a strong wind blew up, and the waves began to spill over into the boat, so that it was about to fill with water. Jesus was in

the back of the boat, sleeping with his head on a pillow. The disciples woke him up and said, 'Teacher, don't you care that we are about to die?'

Two years ago I was lying awake contemplating the day ahead. We were in Chile—a country I had been interested in through missionary friends for many years, but never expected to visit. As I dozed, I became aware of a deep rumbling underground—rather like the heavy goods trains going through the tunnel near my home when I was a child. Suddenly I was wide awake, the light in the ceiling began to swing around, the furniture jumped and creaked—an earthquake! My first reaction, when I realized what was happening, was to shake my husband, lying peacefully beside me. How could he be asleep when I was scared and not sure what to do?

Well, it wasn't a huge earthquake, and the house didn't fall down —but I can understand how the disciples felt to see Jesus sleeping peacefully when they were sure they were all about to drown.

Jesus brought peace in that storm—outward peace, in that the wind and waves became calm; but he also gave them inward peace, because he was awake and with them in the boat.

Life is full of storms of one sort or another. Exams, unemployment, illness, waiting for an operation, anxiety, depression—the list seems endless. It is at these times we need to remind ourselves that Jesus is with us in the boat and he can bring peace in the middle of whatever 'storm' we are facing. Spend a few moments remembering anyone you know who is suffering in any way and pray that he or she will experience the peace that only Jesus can give.

A promise to learn by heart: 'Peace I leave with you, my peace I give you… Do not let your hearts be troubled and do not be afraid' (John 14:27, NIV).

Read Mark 4:35–41.

✣

MARK 10:13–14 (GNB)

A welcome for children

Some people brought children to Jesus for him to place his hands on them, but the disciples scolded the people. When Jesus noticed this he was angry and said to his disciples, 'Let the children come to me, and do not stop them, because the Kingdom of God belongs to such as these.'

I am sure the disciples normally welcomed the presence of children as they travelled around. But they knew Jesus was tired, and they were trying to protect him from the demands small children can make.

Jesus must have known why they were trying to keep the children away from him, that they had the best of intentions for him, but it says here that Jesus was angry. Anger is a strong word. Maybe we, too, need to feel angry about the fact that today only a small percentage of children are 'brought to Jesus'. Most children are growing up in a world that teaches them a confusing set of values—that you have to be tough to be a hero, you have to be better than anyone else to achieve anything, you have to be slim and beautiful (if you are a girl!), you need to be rich and famous to be a successful person. Yet Jesus said, 'The Kingdom of God belongs to such as these.'

Jesus clearly loved children. What were the attributes of children that Jesus would have been referring to when he said, 'The Kingdom of God belongs to such as these'? The children brought to him were probably very young, and nearly all toddlers are trusting, confident of receiving love and care from others. Babies and toddlers are on the receiving end of everything; they are not expected to earn a living! Similarly, our place in the Kingdom of God is not something we can earn by leading a godly life—our place is there because it is freely given to all those who come like a child, with nothing to offer, to Jesus.

Spend time praying for the children you know. Ask that nothing will prevent them from being part of God's kingdom.

Read Mark 9:36–42.

✣

LUKE 12:6–7 (GNB)

No one is forgotten

Aren't five sparrows sold for two pennies? Yet not one sparrow is forgotten by God. Even the hairs on your head have all been counted. So do not be afraid; you are worth much more than many sparrows!

I have become quite fond of sparrows! They are cheeky, noisy, busy little birds and they have taken over my bird-table. About 20 at a time hop busily around, demolishing every scrap of food put out—every now and then conducting noisy arguments in the clematis climbing all over the fence. There is one who has a white feather on his wing, but all the others look exactly the same as each other—same markings, same size, same chirping call. I wouldn't know if it was the same group of sparrows coming to the table each day, or even if one was missing. Yet Jesus said that not one sparrow is forgotten by God.

Jesus realized that his disciples were living in fear of the Pharisees and the teachers of the law because he had accused these powerful people of being hypocritical. He said that they were full of violence and evil, and that they neglected justice. The crowds that always followed Jesus heard the hard words he had for the Pharisees, and from then on the Pharisees were his bitter enemies—and the disciples were afraid. This is when Jesus told them about the sparrows. Surely the God who looked after every single sparrow would be able to look after them. 'You are worth more than many sparrows,' Jesus assured them.

So I am reminded of this fact whenever I look at the sparrows. And when I'm sad, or lonely, or anxious and depressed, I am reminded that

God—almighty God—cares for me. I, too, am worth more than many sparrows.

A verse to learn: 'Leave all your worries with him, because he cares for you' (1 Peter 5:7).

Read Luke 12:22–31.

LUKE 13:34 (GNB)

His protective love

Jerusalem, Jerusalem! You kill the prophets, you stone the messengers God has sent you! How many times I wanted to put my arms round all your people just as a hen gathers her chicks under her wings, but you would not let me!

There was a great commotion among the birds at the bottom of our garden last week. A sparrowhawk had swooped down and taken one of the young sparrows that have learned to fly and are noisily beginning to fend for themselves. I was sad to be reminded how fragile life is—most of the time I want to feel that this world is a safe place for all living creatures, and especially for those I love.

When children are small and always in your sight, you can protect them, pick them up when they fall down, cuddle them when they are unhappy. But children grow up—they have to venture out into a world you know can be dangerous and harmful in many ways. And they don't always follow the way you would choose for them. You don't have to be a parent to experience the pain of seeing those you care for rejecting what you know is best for them and causing themselves and others unhappiness.

Here in this verse from Luke's Gospel, Jesus shows how he longs to protect the people of Jerusalem from the harm that will come from their rejection of God's love for them. 'How many times I wanted to put my arms round all your people, just as a hen gathers her chicks under her wings, but you would not let me.' What a wonderful picture of the selfless nature of Jesus' love for each one of us!

Jesus experienced the pain of rejection from those he loved and wanted to care for. He is still being rejected by his children today—and yet he still goes on offering this warm love and care to each one of us.

Thank God for his caring, protective love; pray for those you care for, that they too may experience this love.

Read Romans 8:31–39.

MIRACLES OF JESUS

LUKE 7:20–23 (NIV)

The miracles of Jesus

So he replied to the messengers, 'Go back and report to John what you have seen and heard: The blind receive sight, the lame walk, those who have leprosy are cured, the deaf hear, the dead are raised, and the good news is preached to the poor.'

Today we begin two weeks thinking about the miracles of Jesus. Most of the recorded miracles involve healing of one kind or another, and in our verse, Jesus himself lists all that has been happening. He is responding to John the Baptist, who is having some doubts that Jesus really is the promised Messiah. John had preached to large crowds, calling them to repentance and telling them that the Messiah promised in the Old Testament had come. He pointed to Jesus, a carpenter's son from Nazareth, saying that the Messiah would baptize with the Holy Spirit and would come with the fire of judgment (Luke 3:16–17).

Some wondered how an ordinary man, not one with proper religious authority, who lived down their street, whose brothers and sisters were around, could be the king promised by God. John expected something far more dramatic than Jesus' everyday gentle approach. So he sent his disciples to ask Jesus himself, and Jesus replied, 'Go back and report what you have seen and heard.' These are signs of the coming of God's kingdom. This is what Isaiah the prophet said would happen (Isaiah 61:1).

As we walk beside Jesus in the next two weeks, watching him as he performs many different miracles, we see people in every kind of need coming to him, and in every situation he heals in the way that is best for them. Sometimes quietly and privately, sometimes in public places, sometimes praising their faith, sometimes forgiving them first. Above all, we see that no individual, however lowly or marginalized, is unworthy of his love and attention. They have only to recognize their own need and he responds.

Help us to know you better, Lord, as the king who will come again in splendour with fire, but also as one who comes with concern for our ills and healing for our hearts.

MATTHEW 4:1–11 (NIV)

Miracles he did not do

After fasting for forty days and forty nights, Jesus was hungry. The tempter came to him and said, 'If you are the Son of God, tell these stones to become bread.'

If you won the lottery, what would you spend the money on? If you had the power to perform miracles, what would you change? Jesus had the power to do anything, but there were lots of miracles he chose not to do. Here in the desert he was tested by the devil, who suggested he use his power to make stones into bread because he was hungry. But Jesus refused. Then he was tested again and invited to do something very spectacular and very public, to throw himself down from the temple. Then everyone would have to believe in him.

But he would not use his powers for selfish purposes, nor would he compel people by spectacular performances to believe in him and follow him—no magic conjuring tricks, no use of power to punish people. The crowds often said to him, 'Do it again! If you just do something really exciting once more, then we will follow you.' But his miracles were quiet ones on the whole: walking on water, but only his disciples were there; feeding thousands of people, but only with bread and fish, and those on the outskirts of the crowd had to be told what had happened. Some of those healed were warned not to tell people, perhaps to protect them from harassment.

Even on the cross Jesus was scoffed at by watchers who thought he couldn't save himself. We know that he could have, but would not. He shows us what God is like and calls us to love him and follow him because we want to, not because we are compelled by power and miracle.

Did you think of what you would do with a multi-million lottery win, or with the power to perform miracles? I suspect that even if we intended the best, we would still do more harm than good.

Father, help me to recognize and resist temptation.

✣

MATTHEW 4:23–24 (NIV)

Signs that point to God

Jesus went throughout Galilee, teaching in their synagogues, preaching the good news of the kingdom, and healing every disease and sickness among the people.

Five times Matthew sums up Jesus' ministry with a couple of 'snapshot' verses like these two, so we know that Jesus healed many people, sometimes spending time with a crowd of sick people, all of whom he healed. When I began to think about writing these notes, I decided to list all the miracles in the four Gospels, and I discovered something surprising.

Lots of people were healed. Matthew lists many different kinds of sickness in verse 24: severe pain, demon possession, seizures and paralysis, and to those we can add blindness and deafness. But the Gospel writers chose only a few of these healing miracles to describe in detail—Matthew about fourteen; Mark mainly the same ones as Matthew, but fewer of them; Luke a similar number but including four that no one else mentions. John, writing a very different kind of Gospel, tells us that Jesus did many miracles, but only records four healing ones. The one miracle that is in all the four accounts is not a miracle of healing, but Jesus feeding the crowd of five thousand.

Even more surprising is that the most amazing miracle of all—bringing people back from death—is frequently mentioned in the lists of healings, but while three Gospels tell us the story of the daughter of Jairus, only John describes the raising of Lazarus, and only Luke the dead son at Nain.

The reason for this selection seems to be that they were not just writing up fantastic tales. These events, the miracles—both healings and others—are important signs, pointers, to help the reader to understand who Jesus is and what God is like.

He still heals. In every fellowship group of Christians there are miracles of healing, sometimes breath-stopping, amazing ones, but also slow, deep healing of hurts and wounds from the past, of addictions and of the regrets and resentments of past sins.

Read Acts 2:22.

✣

MARK 2:1–11 (NIV)

Healed and forgiven

Which is easier: to say to the paralytic, 'Your sins are forgiven,' or to say, 'Get up, take your mat and walk'?

A friend of mine spent some time in a ward of men who had spinal injuries. Several would never walk again. Mostly their injuries were self-inflicted, usually when drunk. One had driven his motorbike into a wall, killing his passenger. His greatest need was to find forgiveness, from those whose lives were devastated, and also for himself. That torment was sometimes greater than the need to walk again.

Was this paralysed man lying in front of Jesus carrying so great a burden that he longed for peace and forgiveness more than anything else? If so, Jesus sensed that need and told him he was forgiven.

There is a turmoil of emotions almost hidden in this brief story—the friends desperate to get the man to Jesus; the tormented and paralysed man himself; the mean-minded reaction of the religious leaders; and in the middle, Jesus, with calm, quiet authority, who knew what they were all thinking. 'Why does this fellow talk like that? Only God can forgive.'

Yes, only God can forgive our sins. Jesus shows them that he has that authority by healing the paralysed man as well as forgiving him. Supposing he had been forgiven but not healed, would he be so restored to peace that that would have been a miracle in itself? Forgiveness is a powerful healer. Finding forgiveness from Jesus, and in our turn forgiving others, can have a powerful effect on our mental and physical health. The most completely 'whole' people are not always the ones who are physically fit.

Dear Lord, thank you for giving me healing and hope, forgiveness and peace. Amen

✣

MATTHEW 8:14–15 (NIV)

Healed and encouraged

He touched her hand and the fever left her, and she got up and began to wait on him.

Before he stepped out into the evening to meet the sick and to heal them, Jesus ate supper in Peter's house. Peter's mother-in-law was in bed with a fever. Jesus went to her, touched her, her fever left and she got up to help with the supper. Such a simple story in just two verses. As you read it, think yourself into the scene—imagine you are there. What comes into your mind? When I read it I remembered an evening when the young people's group met in our house. My mother was staying with us, 89 years old, frail and rather confused. One of the boys in the group went into the living-room, knelt by her chair and chatted to her.

It is so easy to be busy and happy in our different groups, in church or out, whether it's a coffee morning, a young people's Bible study, or Jesus and his disciples having a meal. We may simply not notice those on the edge, just in the shadows, ignored, not part of the group. Jesus noticed, went, touched and healed. The young boy made my mother feel included, excited that there were young people in the house, so that she talked about them afterwards. He encouraged her to be part of the group.

But the story doesn't end with the healing. Peter's mother-in-law got up and helped. In a way we need to move on from miracles, from excitement, from the attention we get when we are ill, from times of inspiration and encouragement. We are healed and saved, encouraged and made strong again, for a purpose. Sometimes we can talk too much about what has just happened, enjoy the excitement for too long.

Help me, Lord, to encourage others with the encouragement that has come from you, and to draw in those who feel left out, as you have drawn me.

✣

LUKE 8:40–56 (NIV)

Healed and given new life

Then the woman, seeing that she could not go unnoticed, came trembling and fell at his feet. In the presence of all the people, she told why she had touched him and how she had been instantly healed. Then he said to her, 'Daughter, your faith has healed you. Go in peace.'

I wonder whether you skip these notes some days, or just read the notes quickly and don't open the Bible at all. But this story of Jesus healing an older woman and a young girl really needs to be read slowly, thoughtfully and with imagination, reconstructing the scene. Only that way do we notice small points that may carry just the word from the Lord for us today.

Notice how Luke repeats the twelve years: twelve years of loving family life for Jairus' daughter, about to emerge into womanhood; twelve years of misery, hopelessly searching for a cure, disabled and socially excluded as unclean, for the older woman. How long those twelve years must have seemed for the woman; how speedily they passed for Jairus' family.

Luke shows us desperation breaking down barriers. The woman, a source of pollution, dares to emerge into a public place and then reveal her secret to a crowd which includes the synagogue leader. Jairus himself has to overcome barriers to approach Jesus, the healer that so many synagogue rulers disapproved of.

Jesus turns his total attention to each one who needs him, dealing with them differently—a public recognition of healing for the woman; a family protected from publicity for the girl come back from the dead.

Both these two were brought back from death. Jesus said, 'I have come that they may have life, and have it to the full' (John 10:10). We too are given new life in him—a life to live for him on earth, given back to us in conversion, and the promise of eternal life with him for ever.

Help me, Lord, to live life to the full for you.

✣

LUKE 7:11–17 (NIV)

Healed out of compassion

When the Lord saw her, his heart went out to her and he said, 'Don't cry.'

It's difficult to think of anything more wonderful than to know that the almighty and sovereign Lord looked at a widow who had just lost her only son and, his heart full of sympathy, said, 'Don't cry.'

The Gospel writers record a number of occasions when Jesus spent time with women, talking to them, teaching them and healing them. This widow is the fourth we have focused on. In some ways, if he had wanted to reach the people of influence and power, he certainly wouldn't have bothered with women. But he turned away from the rulers, the religious leaders and the teachers of the law. They thought they were right and he was wrong, that they were important and he was not.

Jesus responded to those who knew their need. Most of those he healed were in real distress—those with handicaps that meant they could only beg; those excluded from social life like those with leprosy; and now a widow with a dead son.

Jesus, his disciples and a large crowd approach the town of Nain and at the gate they meet another crowd—a funeral procession. With people jostling and bustling in opposite directions, in the middle of the confusion, Jesus comes face to face with the distraught mother, left alone, facing poverty and loneliness. 'Don't cry,' he says.

He touches the stretcher, once again cutting through taboos by touching a dead body. Is that why everyone stands still? In that moment of surprise, he brings the son back to life so that he sits up and talks. Just as Jesus did with Jairus' daughter, he gives him back to his mother. It is almost as if Jesus and the woman, with her son, are on their own, while round them the two crowds stand amazed and 'filled with awe'.

Let me share your heart of compassion, Lord. Help me to care when others cry. I may be able to offer very little, but I can tell them about you.

✣

JOHN 9:1–12 (NIV)

What have I done to deserve this?

As he went along, he saw a man blind from birth. His disciples asked him, 'Rabbi, who sinned, this man or his parents, that he was born blind?' 'Neither this man nor his parents sinned,' said Jesus, 'but this happened so that the work of God might be displayed in his life.'

Here is a simple story that gets more and more complicated as it proceeds. This blind man prompts the disciples to ask a very important question. What caused this man to be born blind? Did he sin or did his parents? Jesus tells them that because something bad has happened, we must not presume that it is a direct result of that person's sin. Punishments and rewards are not regularly given to those who deserve them in this world. If they were, then everyone would be good in order to avoid nasty things happening!

The Bible's answer is that in general sin and suffering are with us because the world has fallen away from its right and true relationship with God, so that everything is spoilt. But sometimes life is very unfair and it is difficult to cope with gross unfairness. I once worked in a big London hospital. A woman, diagnosed with MS, desperately wanted a baby. She was told that having one might well make the condition worse, but she went ahead. She produced her baby, her MS was not affected, but the baby died, an unexplained cot death. It was the first time I had come face to face with something that seemed desperately unfair.

I know these things happen. I also know and believe with all my heart that the Lord is loving and compassionate, and that one day in heaven we will understand. The blind man was healed, but I also know that not many are miraculously healed today. Most of us will have to find the strength to live through the dark times of suffering we or those we love have to endure.

Lord, help me to trust you whatever happens, however unfair life seems to be.

✣

JOHN 9:13–41 (NIV)

Who is really blind?

Jesus said, 'For judgment I have come into this world, so that the blind will see and those who see will become blind.'

Jesus makes a mud pack, puts it on the blind man's eyes and tells him to go and wash in a nearby pool. Immediately, for the first time in his life, he can see. His parents and neighbours then get involved in a series of increasingly acrimonious scenes with the Pharisees and elders of the synagogue. Jesus has healed on the Sabbath; that is against the law, unless the need is desperate. 'He cannot be from God for he does not keep the Sabbath,' some of them say. Others can see the silliness of saying this, when a man born blind has just received his sight back. In the end the man chooses not to join in insulting Jesus, so he is thrown out of the synagogue.

Jesus hears about this and immediately goes and finds him and helps him to see, not just with his eyes, but with faith, that he has been healed by God. 'Lord, I believe,' he says, and worships Jesus.

The ones who are blind are those who refuse to acknowledge their blindness and insist that they can see the truth, denying Jesus, the light of the world.

Lord, I was blind: I could not see
In thy marred visage any grace;
But now the beauty of thy face
In radiant vision dawns on me.
W.T. MATSON (1833–99)

✣

JOHN 2:1–11 (NIV)

A miracle with wine

The master of the banquet tasted the water that had been turned into wine. Then he called the bridegroom aside and said, 'Everyone brings out the choice wine first, but you have saved the best till now.' Jesus thus revealed his glory, and his disciples put their faith in him.

This, the first miracle that John records, seems a surprising way for Jesus to reveal his glory. If we know the story well, we can lose the impact of such an amazing act. Jesus goes to a wedding and when the wine runs out rather early in the celebrations, he makes water into wine—not rough table wine, but wine that is rated the best; and not one glass each but, if we have the measurements right, around 600 litres. Enough for as long as it was needed.

We are told what Jesus and his mother said to each other, and what Jesus said to the servants, but we do not know what they were thinking, and cannot guess the tone of voice being used. But Mary tells the servants to do whatever Jesus says, and they obey, filling the huge ceremonial jars to the brim with water. Then, in even more daring obedience, they fill a jug with what was definitely water a few minutes ago and take it to the man in charge of the banquet. I hope the servants got some wine too.

Jesus gives us wine, wine as part of a joyful banquet, a feast we begin here when we become part of his kingdom, and will go on with when we sit down to the wedding feast in heaven. It is his promise that as we remember his death and break bread and drink wine together in Christian fellowship, we are in communion with all the millions of saints who will feast together in heaven. Underlying all we do as we follow him and he walks beside us through our lives is the deep, underlying joy of knowing that we are wedding guests at a wedding feast that will never end.

Spend some time thinking about what it means to be a guest at that great wedding feast in heaven.

✣

JOHN 6:1–15 (NIV)

A miracle with bread

Jesus then took the loaves, gave thanks, and distributed to those who were seated as much as they wanted. He did the same with the fish.

Jesus has attempted to get away from the crowds to be on his own with the disciples, but they have followed him round the lake. He reacts with compassion, and plans to use his life-giving and love-driven power to feed the crowd and to illustrate an important truth. He knows they need to eat, and he knows what he is going to do. He asks Philip, one of the disciples, a simple question. 'Where shall we buy bread for these people to eat?' Philip knows that it is impossible. Andrew spots a boy with five loaves and two fishes. So Jesus takes them, gives thanks and feeds the crowd.

This miracle has many echoes. The Lord rained down bread from heaven to feed the people of Israel in the desert (Exodus 16:4). At the last supper, Jesus takes bread, gives thanks and breaks it, saying, 'This is my body' (Mark 14:22). Did the disciples remember this meal of bread and fish beside the lake, much later on when the risen Lord invited them out of their fishing-boats to an early-morning breakfast of fish and bread, beside the same lake? (John 21:12).

Just after feeding this crowd, Jesus tells them that he is the bread of life, saying, 'He who comes to me will never go hungry and he who believes in me will never be thirsty.'

How would you have reacted to the miracle and then to this man saying he was the source of life—the only satisfying source of nourishment? Some of those around were not convinced: 'We know his mother, his family,' they said; 'how can he say those things about himself?'

We praise you, Lord, that, in feeding the five thousand, you showed your power and your compassion and above all your willingness to give anyone who asks, the bread of life. There is nowhere else for us to go for food.

✣

JOHN 11:17–46 (NIV)

A miracle of life

Jesus said to her, 'I am the resurrection and the life. He who believes in me will live, even though he dies; and whoever lives and believes in me will never die. Do you believe this?'

Like the story of the man born blind, John tells this miracle of Lazarus being raised from the dead at great length. There are many issues, including some difficult questions, in this moving and emotional passage. There is so much in it that we would honestly need several days to take it all in.

An ordinary death: Lazarus, a loved friend of Jesus and his disciples, is sick. His sisters, Mary and Martha, send desperate word to ask Jesus to come, but Jesus delays going, long enough for Lazarus to die. 'This is for God's glory,' he says, 'so that God's Son may be glorified through it.'

An extraordinary promise: Martha meets Jesus on his way into their village, four days after Lazarus' death and, in her anguish, expresses her passionate 'If only...' If only Jesus had been there in time. Jesus gently draws out of her what she believes about life after death, and then makes the great promise, 'He who believes in me will live, even though he dies.' How many, many times has that statement been said over millions of coffins! How many of those who have heard it have really believed it?

An amazing miracle: Weeping at their distress, Jesus goes to the tomb, prays to his Father that those watching will now believe he has come from God, and calls Lazarus out.

A terrible response: Many of those who saw what Jesus had done put their faith in him, but some go to the Pharisees and tell them what Jesus had done. They plot to kill him.

Lord of miracles, I believe; help my unbelief. You alone are the resurrection and the life. Keep me safe with you and bring me to your everlasting kingdom.

JESUS AND LAZARUS

JOHN 11:17–19 (NIV)

The body of Christ

Many Jews had come to Martha and Mary to comfort them in the loss of their brother.

Jerusalem was not far from Bethany. To visit Martha and Mary at the time of their bereavement was a natural thing to do for first-century

Jews—part of their culture. It is not so natural for us now. We live in an individualistic society. Grief, loss, hardship of any kind are considered personal things. Besides, it is easier not to get involved. What would we say? What if we said the wrong thing?

Maybe we can learn something from the example of those first-century Jews. Jesus calls us to love our neighbour—and that includes the friend who has just lost her child or whose husband has walked out on her. But what can we say? Religious platitudes often do more harm than good. Sensitivity is called for and the willingness to be God's ears and hands as well as God's mouth. Just being there, showing that we care, can make a world of difference. We can show our care by offering practical help, taking the children to school, doing a pile of ironing... Being God's hands can take many forms.

After my father had died, many of my friends knocked on my door just to give me a hug. Then they went again. It was all I could cope with. Others came and said, 'We don't know what to say, but we share your pain because we love you.' What more did they need to say? Others helped in practical ways. A number of my friends prayed for me every day. A bookmark with the following text, given to me at that time, has meant a lot to me: the people who just sat and wept with me, holding my hand, they were the people who helped.

'We are the body of Christ. By one Spirit, we were all baptized into one body. Let us then pursue all that makes for peace and builds up our common life.'

ALTERNATIVE SERVICE BOOK 1980

✣

JOHN 11:20–29 (NIV)

If only...

'But I know that even now God will give you whatever you ask.'

If only he had left home a bit earlier, then he wouldn't have had that terrible accident. Or, even worse, if only I had not kept him, he would have left a bit earlier. These kinds of reproaches are often heard from those who are bereaved. They cannot believe that their friend or relative is really dead, so they come up with reasons why it should not have happened. It's a natural but not a helpful reaction.

Martha does not stop at accusing Jesus. In the second sentence, there is a glimmer of hope, maybe even a hidden request: 'Not all is lost, for God will give you whatever you ask. Go on, ask!' Martha is desperate, yes, but also full of faith. She knows that her 'if onlys' will not bring Lazarus back to life. Only Jesus can do the impossible and work a miracle. Martha is sure of that.

What do we do when faced with loss? Do we complain, feel sorry for ourselves, try to wish it away? Or do we turn to the one who can work a miracle?

Martha had asked her question. Now she had to wait. How would Jesus react? Would he say, 'I will raise Lazarus from the dead, right now'? Or would he say, 'Sorry, can't help you here'? In fact, he says neither of those things, but that is not the point. Martha could do nothing more but trust God for the outcome. She can't have found that easy. It would have been easier to revert to more 'if onlys'. Asking God and then trusting him involves risk, and is one of the biggest challenges of the Christian life. But it is worth taking on this challenge. Go on, ask!

'And we know that in all things God works for the good of those who love him, who have been called according to his purpose' (Romans 8:28).

⁂

JOHN 11:23–27 (NIV)

I believe

'I am the resurrection and the life. Those who believe in me will live, even though they die.'

What a statement! It was not unusual for Jews to believe in the resurrection. It was an item of dispute for some—the Pharisees believed in the resurrection, the Sadducees did not. Martha will have been familiar with traditional Jewish belief on this subject. In fact, her instant response to Jesus' initial question (v. 24) reflects this belief. But Jesus' statement goes much further. He does not comfort Martha by pointing at the resurrection in some distant, unobtainable future. He says instead, 'I am the resurrection—and I am standing in front of you.' Resurrection and life here and now, through Jesus, and in the face of death, with Lazarus lying in the tomb, dead and buried. Traditional Jews would have been shocked by Jesus' claim. Not so Martha. She answers by affirming her belief and acknowledging that Jesus is the Christ: 'Yes, Lord, I believe you are the Christ.'

We might be almost too familiar with the message of the gospel. Let us not forget how radical it was in Jesus' day and still is in our day. Be honest—are you not afraid of death? It is not something we like to think about. We might simply be afraid of what might happen tomorrow, never mind death. Whatever may happen tomorrow, however long we might live on this earth, one thing is certain: Jesus is the resurrection and the life. We will live, even though we die. He offers us life in abundance (John 10:10). We can have real life, now, through him.

Jesus has not promised us an easy, pain-free life. He makes no promises to Martha at this stage. She questions him no further but goes back inside the house to call Mary. Martha has shown her extraordinary faith and her recognition of who Jesus is—the Christ, Messiah, Saviour of the world.

Take time today to place all your worries into Jesus' hands and thank him for giving you life in abundance.

✣

JOHN 11:30–36 (NIV)

Being real

Jesus wept.

He wept. In public. And he was a man. How embarrassing. Simon, a vicar, well respected, admired by many, one who seemed to 'have it all together', had to interrupt his sermon. It was one of the first sermons he had preached since the death of his mother. He paused and wept. His congregation respected him even more after this sermon. Simon had shared a part of himself that otherwise often remained hidden. He was grieving, suffering, hurting. He was real.

As women, we are often better at showing our emotions than those men who were told, 'Boys don't cry' when they were little. Yet even for us it can be difficult to be open about what goes on inside. For years, I did not want to admit how I really felt, not even to myself. Too painful, too dangerous. I might lose control. Well, when I did lose control, and tears came, what a relief it was. Those who knew respected me more, not less. They had seen the real Kristina and they liked her better than the pretend one they had seen before. There is nothing wrong with emotions. Why do we think we have to pretend we can cope with everything all the time? Who are we trying to fool? Of course, there are times in life when we just have to grit our teeth and get on with the task at hand. Work needs to be done, children need to be cared for, dinners need to be cooked, even when we feel like hiding in a corner and crying. But these times of pulling ourselves together need to be balanced with times of letting go. Jesus was not afraid to be real. Try it! You will be surprised.

We can only be real if we are not afraid of other people's reactions. Pray that God will give you the inner security that comes from knowing that you are his beloved daughter.

✣

JOHN 11:37 (NIV)

But...

But some of them said, 'Could not he who opened the eyes of the blind man have kept this man from dying?'

But why...? But how...? Why not...? Could you not...? How could she...? Jesus must have been exasperated by those questions—many of them asked in order to trap him. Whatever their motives, there were always people who knew exactly what he should have done. Even as he was hanging on the cross, there were those who sneered at him and explained what they would have expected him to do (Luke 23:37; Mark 15:29).

'If your Jesus is such a wonderful God, why didn't he intervene in the war in Kosovo?' 'Why is there such poverty in Africa when God loves everybody?' Or, closer to home, 'Why didn't he heal little Johnny of his cancer?' You might have heard such questions from your non-Christian colleagues, friends or members of your family. These could be genuine concerns but more often than not, people just use them as 'proof' that God cannot be who we know he is—our loving Father and the maker of the universe, omnipotent and omnipresent. It is hard to know how to respond and requires a lot of sensitivity as we often don't know what is behind the questions. Do they serve as excuses not to deal with the message of the gospel, or do they cover up other, deeper questions? It is often worth probing to find out why the original question was asked.

Being a Christian is not always easy. We will meet people who reject the good news of Jesus and who will sneer at us and reject us because we are followers of Christ. We should not be surprised at that. We are called not to respond with the same rejection but to show Jesus' love by our words and our lives.

'The ways of the Lord are right; the righteous walk in them, but the rebellious stumble in them' (Hosea 14:9).

✣

JOHN 11:38–41 (NIV)

The glory of God

Then Jesus said, 'Did I not tell you that if you believed, you would see the glory of God?'

Martha has just affirmed her belief that Jesus is indeed the Christ. Now, a few minutes later, she seems to have lost all faith. When Jesus stands in front of the tomb and asks for the stone to be rolled away, she does not expect a miracle. Quite the opposite: 'By this time there will be a bad odour, for he has been there four days.' What has happened to her faith? Was it not genuine?

Her faith was genuine enough. However, she found it hard to see beyond the obvious, to go below the surface of the meaning of Jesus' words. She had difficulties connecting her faith in the Christ to everyday life. Yes, Jesus was the Son of God. But would that change anything right now?

Jesus is still the resurrected Christ. Does that make a difference to our lives? Can we see beyond the obvious and get a glimpse of the 'bigger picture'? Martha did not realize that Lazarus had to die to reveal the glory of God. We often don't understand what has happened, don't understand how God could have let this happen, don't understand how our daily worries, big and small, might fit into God's plan. May I suggest that sometimes, more often then we think, events happen in order to reveal the glory of God?

Martha did not (yet) know the outcome. If she had, she would not have worried about the smell from the body of Lazarus. We often cannot know the outcome of events. What we can know, however, is that Jesus' life, death, and resurrection make a difference to our lives. And we can be part of events that reveal the glory of God. What a privilege!

For yours, Lord, is the power, the glory and the majesty, for ever and ever. Amen.

✣

JOHN 11:43–44 (NIV)

New life

'Lazarus, come out!'

God definitely has a sense of humour. Can you imagine Lazarus coming out of the tomb, probably more hopping than walking, possibly bumping into things because the grave clothes tied his legs together and obscured his vision? This is a comical and at the same time awesome scene. Lazarus had experienced the depth of death and had come back to life again. How must he have felt, stumbling out of the tomb? Overwhelmed? Confused? Maybe even reluctant to come out? I think there is one thing we can be certain about: life after this experience would never be the same again. Lazarus had been given new life, a second chance here on earth. But let him speak for himself:

'I heard his voice calling me. It was not a loud voice, but, how can I say it… it sounded urgent, compelling. I knew I had to obey it. There was no doubt about that. I wasn't quite sure where I was, it was all dark. I got up and found that I could hardly move! My legs were bound together and so I moved forward with some difficulty. Half shuffling, half hopping, I moved towards the voice calling me. It became lighter around me but I still could not see. There were other people there, not just him. I stood there, trying to listen to what the voices where saying, trying to make sense of it all. Finally, after what seemed like a long time to me, a hand gently started to take away what had bound me. I could see, I could move, I could walk again. I saw people around me and they were weeping. I saw plants, trees, the sky—it was all so beautiful. And I saw Jesus, looking at me, just looking at me.'

Could this not be a description of somebody coming to Christ? What can we do to take away what binds others? What binds us?

Reflect on what Martha would have felt at this point.

EASTER

JOHN 1:29–36 (RSV)

The Lamb of God

The next day [John the Baptist] saw Jesus coming toward him, and said, 'Behold, the Lamb of God, who takes away the sin of the world! ... I myself did not know him; but he who sent me to baptize with water said to me, "He on whom you see the Spirit descend and remain, this is he who baptizes with the Holy Spirit." And I have seen and borne witness that this is the Son of God.' The next day again John was standing with two of his disciples; and he looked at Jesus as he walked, and said, 'Behold the Lamb of God!'

Most of us don't like to think about lambs going to be slaughtered—perhaps herded into lorries, frightened and sometimes thirsty. We choose our lamb in tidily butchered joints in the supermarket and eat it roasted with redcurrant jelly or mint sauce. The slaughter of lambs isn't part of our thinking. But it was very much part of Jewish thinking and when John the Baptist spoke about the Lamb of God the people would have thought immediately about the lambs that were killed in the temple and the Passover lambs that were killed and eaten at the Feast of Passover.

The people must have been puzzled if they really thought about what this strange prophet was saying—pointing to a man and saying, 'Behold, the Lamb of God.' They wouldn't have understood, not until much later, when the Lamb of God had died on the cross for the sin of the world and the eleven apostles had gone out into the world to preach the good news about the forgiveness of sins and the death of Christ. Sin is a difficult subject to think about and not a fashionable one. But whether we like it or not, it is present in our world, and it is a killer. It destroys relationships and lives like a polluted and poisoned river of hate.

When you listen to the news today, consider how many of the news items are events caused by human sin. Then consider the words of Jesus: 'Out of the heart of man come evil thoughts, murder, adultery, fornication, theft, false witness.'

✣

EXODUS 12:1, 3, 5–8, 11–13 (RSV)

The Passover

The Lord said to Moses and Aaron, 'Tell all the congregation of Israel that… they shall take every man a lamb… Your lamb shall be without blemish… and you shall keep it until the fourteenth day of this month, when the whole assembly of the congregation of Israel shall kill their lambs in the evening. Then they shall take some of the blood, and put it on the two doorposts and the lintel of the houses in which they eat them. They shall eat the flesh that night, roasted… It is the Lord's passover. For I will pass through the land of Egypt that night, and I will smite all the firstborn in the land of Egypt, both man and beast; and on all the gods of Egypt I will execute judgments: I am the Lord. The blood shall be a sign for you, upon the houses where you are; and when I see the blood, I will pass over you.'

Yesterday for my Sunday lunch I had roast lamb, and as I smelt it cooking, and then ate it, I thought about the Israelites eating their Passover lambs first on the night of their exodus from Egypt, and then through the years at every Feast of Passover.

There is a cost to living, and for us to live, other living things than ourselves have to die (whether animal or vegetable). There is also a cost to forgiveness. 'The wages of sin is death' (Romans 6:23)—a spiritual death which is a broken relationship and separation from God. For the relationship to be put right again, the one who was sinned against has to bear the pain of the sin and offer love and friendship to the sinner. Every sin against another person or creature is a sin against God, and after he had committed adultery with Bathsheba and had her husband murdered, David cried out, 'Against thee, thee only have I sinned.' And it is only God who can forgive sin and take it away in the ultimate sense. He does it by taking the pain of it into his own body and holding out the arms of love to the sinner. But there is a terrible cost.

Behold the Lamb of God, who takes away the sin of the world.

✣

ISAIAH 40:9–11 (RSV)

The good shepherd

Get you up to a high mountain, O Zion, herald of good tidings; lift up your voice with strength, O Jerusalem, herald of good tidings, lift it up, fear not; say to the cities of Judah, 'Behold your God!' Behold, the Lord God comes with might, and his arm rules for him; behold, his reward is with him, and his recompense before him. He will feed his flock like a shepherd, and he will gather the lambs in his arms, he will carry them in his bosom, and gently lead those that are with young.

When many of us read these words from Isaiah, we hear inside our heads the marvellous aria from Handel's *Messiah*. As I listen to it now (in my head) my heart lifts up with delight that this is our God and through the words we can do what Isaiah told us to do: 'Behold your God!' When we look, we see God as a shepherd who looks after the flock, and who loves it so much that he dies for it. That is what Jesus said. He spoke about the nature of God by using all the Old Testament imagery that came out of their pastoral, sheep-keeping culture.

The other day when I was looking out of my study window at the Shetland sheep who live three fields away, the owner came out and separated one sheep and its lamb from another mother and baby and gave to each pair a little heap of food. Special food for each one, and the shepherd knew just what they needed. The Lord who is our shepherd can make any circumstances of our life into nourishing food for our soul, however bitter it tastes to eat. We can know the presence of God with us in all our circumstances and then every moment can be a sacrament in which we know and encounter the living God who creates us and loves us.

'His reward is with him.' 'Fear not, Abram, I am your shield; your reward shall be very great' (Genesis 15:1).

✣

EZEKIEL 34:10–11, 15–16 (RSV)

The wrathful shepherd

Thus says the Lord God, Behold, I am against the shepherds; and I will require my sheep at their hand, and put a stop to their feeding the sheep; no longer shall the shepherds feed themselves. I will rescue my sheep from their mouths, that they may not be food for them. For thus says the Lord God: Behold, I, I myself will search for my sheep and will seek them out... I myself will be the shepherd of my sheep, and I will make them lie down, says the Lord God. I will seek the lost, and I will bring back the strayed, and I will bind up the crippled, and I will strengthen the weak, and the fat and the strong I will watch over. I will feed them in justice.

The other day on television I saw a gentle-faced mongrel dog that was so thin it could hardly stand. Its owner had starved it and beaten it and kept it tied up—and the RSPCA had rescued it. I felt very angry with the owner.

There is a school of thought in Christianity which says that God never gets angry. But the Bible and our own experience tell us how false that belief is. The wrath of God is the other side of the coin of the love of God. How could a loving person not be implacably opposed to actions that hurt and destroy? The loving person doesn't stop loving the person who does harmful and hurtful things—but love wants the sinner to repent and turn away from his or her sin and be forgiven.

Ezekiel spoke out the wrath of God against the shepherds of Israel—the teachers and leaders who were supposed to be looking after the people of God. But they weren't: they were looking after themselves. There was a religious hierarchy which was disgracefully failing in its task. So the God who passionately minds about the welfare and the happiness of the sheep would come and do the job himself.

Think about the nature of the God whom we worship. Reflect on the wrath of God, and why he gets angry. Then reflect on the love of God, and the actions that a good shepherd takes in looking after the flock. Turn your response into prayer.

✣

JOHN 6:52–56; 10:10–11 (RSV)

Eating the Lamb of God

The Jews then disputed among themselves, saying, 'How can this man give us his flesh to eat?' So Jesus said to them, 'Truly, truly, I say to you, unless you eat the flesh of the Son of man and drink his blood, you have no life in you; he who eats my flesh and drinks my blood has eternal life, and I will raise him up at the last day. For my flesh is food indeed, and my blood is drink indeed. He who eats my flesh and drinks my blood abides in me, and I in him.' ... 'I came that they may have life, and have it abundantly. I am the good shepherd. The good shepherd lays down his life for the sheep.'

Jesus' hearers would have been horrified. They were forbidden to eat animal blood—let alone human blood or human flesh. Their scriptures told them the truth that 'the life of the flesh is in the blood' (a truth it took hundreds of years for the medical profession to discover) and their whole sacrificial system was about creatures being killed and their blood drained out—sometimes poured out on to the earth and sometimes sprinkled over the people.

What Jesus did on that first Maundy Thursday evening was to set up for all time the great sacrament of the Eucharist, or Holy Communion—and to eat his flesh and to drink his blood was to share in 'the benefits of his death and passion'. 'In Christ God was reconciling the world to himself, not counting their trespasses against them, and entrusting to us the message of reconciliation,' wrote Paul in 2 Corinthians 5:19. In 1 Corinthians he said that 'Christ, our paschal lamb, has been sacrificed. Let us, therefore, celebrate the festival' (1 Corinthians 5:7–8). Every service of Holy Communion looks back to that Passover night when Jesus set up the sacrament—and to his death on the cross which is at the heart of it.

Think about the nature of the one whose body and blood you eat and drink in the sacrament. Think about the paschal lamb, sacrificed and then roasted and eaten with bitter herbs. Think about the Lamb of God, who had come to Jerusalem to be slaughtered to take away the sin of the world.

ISAIAH 53:3–7 (RSV)

The sin bearer

He was despised and rejected by men; a man of sorrows, and acquainted with grief; and as one from whom men hide their faces he was despised, and we esteemed him not. Surely he has borne our griefs and carried our sorrows; yet we esteemed him stricken, smitten by God, and afflicted. But he was wounded for our

transgressions, he was bruised for our iniquities; upon him was the chastisement that made us whole, and with his stripes we are healed. All we like sheep have gone astray; we have turned every one to his own way; and the Lord has laid on him the iniquity of us all. He was oppressed, and he was afflicted, yet he opened not his mouth; like a lamb that is led to the slaughter, and like a sheep that before its shearers is dumb, so he opened not his mouth.

Christianity is the only religion in the world which tells us of the suffering God—and the God who suffers is the only God there is. The first Christians recognized in Jesus the suffering servant of the Lord whom Isaiah wrote about. In Acts 8 the Ethiopian eunuch is reading Isaiah 53 and wondering who the prophet is writing about, and beginning with verses 7 and 8 Philip 'told him the good news of Jesus'.

It says in Isaiah 53 that the suffering servant of God bore our griefs and our sorrows and that God laid all our sins upon him. That means that every individual can know the forgiveness of God through the sin-bearing of the Lamb of God who takes away the sin of the world. Yet although he takes away our sin he doesn't take away our griefs and our sorrows. He bears them but that doesn't mean that all the pain is his and that our pain disappears. It does mean that in our sorrow we can know the presence with us of the suffering Christ, suffering with us.

Hold in the presence of God anything that is making you sad and sorrowful and just stay in silence for a few moments. Then hold in his presence the sadness of another person or another situation and pray for that.

✣

LUKE 15:1–7 (RSV)

He looks for the lost one

Now the tax collectors and sinners were all drawing near to hear him. And the Pharisees and the scribes murmured, saying, 'This

man receives sinners and eats with them.' So he told them this parable: 'What man of you, having a hundred sheep, if he has lost one of them, does not leave the ninety-nine in the wilderness, and go after the one which is lost, until he finds it? And when he has found it, he lays it on his shoulders, rejoicing. And when he comes home, he calls together his friends and his neighbours, saying to them, "Rejoice with me, for I have found my sheep which was lost." Just so, I tell you, there will be more joy in heaven over one sinner who repents than over ninety-nine righteous persons who need no repentance.'

Two couples I know have both lost one of their children. The son of one has died. The daughter of the other has left home to 'live it up' with men, sex, drink and drugs. A prodigal daughter—and for her parents her loss is the same as if she were dead. Both couples have other children—just as the man in Jesus's story had other sheep, 99 of them. But they didn't fill the place of the one who wasn't there any more. The first couple know that one day they will see their son again, because he was a Christian. For the parents of the prodigal daughter it is a sort of living death. Both sets of parents are waiting, not knowing what will happen in the future. The parents of the son who has died can wait in hope for the resurrection morning. The parents of the prodigal daughter can wait in hope too, because they know what God is like.

In this much-loved chapter 15 of Luke, Jesus tells us about three things that are lost—a sheep, a coin and a prodigal son. God is the Father who waits for his son to come home again, and then runs out to meet him with his arms wide open. Then there is great rejoicing, because 'this your brother was dead, and is alive; he was lost, and is found.'

What are you waiting for in hope?

✣

REVELATION 5:6–10 (RSV)

The Lamb upon the throne

And between the throne and the four living creatures and among the elders, I saw a Lamb standing, as though it had been slain... and he went and took the scroll from the right hand of him who was seated on the throne. And when he had taken the scroll, the four living creatures and the twenty-four elders fell down before the Lamb, each holding a harp, and with golden bowls full of incense, which are the prayers of the saints; and they sang a new song, saying, 'Worthy art thou to take the scroll and to open its seals, for thou wast slain and by thy blood didst ransom men for God from every tribe and tongue and people and nation, and hast made them a kingdom and priests to our God, and they shall reign on earth.'

Today we shall hear the story of the first Easter morning, and listen to the glorious words which tell us about the resurrection of Jesus Christ from the dead and the joy and bewilderment and disbelief of those first disciples. But the resurrection of Christ happened once in time—and his appearances and his empty tomb were events experienced and seen by the ones who were there in the beginning. For us the present reality is not that today Jesus rises again from the dead but that he rose on that first Easter morning.

It was the risen Christ whom John saw in the series of visions that form the book of Revelation. Earlier in this vision John has been weeping, because he has seen a scroll sealed with seven seals containing God's future plans for the earth, and no one has been found worthy to open the scroll. But John is told not to weep, because 'the Lion of the tribe of Judah, the Root of David, has conquered' so he can open the scroll. Yet when John looks he sees a Lamb. The purposes of God can go forward, but only because the Lamb has been slain and Christ has died for the sin of the world.

Crown him with many crowns,
The Lamb upon his throne;
Hark! how the heavenly anthem drowns
All music but its own:
Awake, my soul, and sing
Of him who died for thee,
And hail him as thy matchless King
Through all eternity.

MATTHEW BRIDGES (1800–94)

PART TWO

Learning to live God's way

When I ask children how they are getting on with friends in the school playground, they explain the ups and downs of friendship—who is talking to whom; who is included and who gets left out; who joins in and who keeps themselves to themselves.

We can ask ourselves the same question about our relationship with God. How are you getting on with God? Are you still having a conversation or have your prayers become a monologue? Do times together bubble with life or are they dull and dry? Is God involved in all of your life, or is his influence restricted to Sundays and church meetings?

In the next set of readings, we will be turning our attention to living God's way—quite the opposite of Frank Sinatra's famous song, 'I did it my way'. We don't learn to live God's way by following a set of rules. Instead, as we fall in love with Jesus, we find our lives begin to change. We want to please him, so we put his teaching into practice. As Jesus said, 'Those who love me will obey my teaching. My Father will love them, and we will come to them and make our home with them' (John 14:23, NIV).

How do you respond to Jesus' love for you? If you want God to change you as you use this series of notes, start by inviting him to do just that—to change you. As you take time to read the suggested Bible passage each day, invite God to speak to you through it and to go on speaking through the day, bringing to mind words or thoughts that help you to get to know Jesus better.

Expect a dialogue, not a monologue. When God speaks, sometimes it's a deep impression; very occasionally he uses audible words.

Keep track of your conversation with God by writing a few notes. Then, from time to time, review what God seems to have been saying, ideally with the help of a godly friend who can help you to discern what God is saying specifically to you. There will be a mixture of your own thoughts and God's words to you. Look for the recurring themes and use the Bible as a plumb-line. If God is speaking to you, he will not contradict what he says in scripture.

ISAIAH 61

ISAIAH 61:1–13 (NIV)

Sent to the poor

The Spirit of the Sovereign Lord is on me, because the Lord has anointed me to preach good news to the poor. He has sent me to bind up the broken-hearted, to proclaim freedom for the captives and release from darkness for the prisoners, to proclaim the year of the Lord's favour and the day of vengeance of our God, to comfort all who mourn, and provide for those who grieve in Zion.

God is on the move in this chapter. The Sovereign Lord has anointed and sent someone, somewhere. Who? Where? Well, that *someone* will preach good news. That someone has the authorization and power of the Spirit of the Almighty God. So who is this someone? In Luke 4:16–22, Jesus claims this reading about himself—he is the someone who brings good news.

But let's not stop here! As believers in Jesus, *we* have that someone dwelling within us. We have the Spirit of God upon us! We also are authorized in the power of the Spirit to preach good news. We also are 'anointed ones'. And it is you and I who are being sent.

Now, I don't know about you, but I get pretty nervous when *someone* is sending me—to do anything! To be sent to preach good news to the poor… I don't know. Preaching demands courage. Simply being around the broken-hearted brings me pain—and a terrible sense of helplessness. Is there really release from the prison of fear? And how can I comfort those who mourn? Just watching the six o'clock news leaves me emotionally fatigued.

On our own we can do little. But it is not ourselves, or our own power, or our own good news that we bring. We bring the *someone* who was sent. We bring Jesus in the Spirit of the Sovereign Lord.

Jesus, you know our fear and disbelief that the good news will even make a dent in the world around us. Anoint us with the Spirit of the Sovereign Lord to proclaim and believe the good news. In the middle of our own poverty, give us courage to be sent. Amen

✣

ISAIAH 61:3 (NIV)

From ashes to beauty

... and provide for those who grieve in Zion—to bestow on them a crown of beauty instead of ashes, the oil of gladness instead of mourning, and a garment of praise instead of a spirit of despair.

This whole chapter of Isaiah is about change. Change from ashes to beauty, from mourning to gladness, from despair to praise, from what was to what is, from what is to what is 'becoming'.

But change is entangled and entwined with loss; and loss is enmeshed with grief. Whether we grieve the loss of the good of what was or smart from the sting of what happened, change and grief walk hand in hand. Here God is saying that he will provide for those who grieve. His provision will transform ashes to a crown of beauty. Ashes—black, dirty, put on the head in Isaiah's time to represent mourning. Ashes—the result of fire and burning. Ashes—having no resemblance to what was burned. Ashes in our lives. Where have yours come from? Things stripped away prematurely? Experiences that it is a relief to have in the past? But Isaiah says that our ashes will be changed to a crown of beauty.

Suddenly our images shift—to jewels sparkling in the light, to dignity and splendour. Stop for a minute and imagine the ashes of your life. See those dark, dirty ashes blackening your head being transformed into jewels and splendour. See yourself standing tall and straight with that effervescent crown replacing those ashes.

Isaiah continues this wonderful imagery of transformation. The oil of gladness will replace mourning. Oil, a different symbol. Oil, running over our head, anointing us for a new identity of gladness instead of mourning—new beginnings. And not only a crown and oil but a resplendent gown of praise, falling from our shoulders to our feet, enfolding our whole body. A gown that dispels that dull listlessness of despair. A gown that explodes praise from the very core of our being.

Thank you, dear Jesus, for giving us designer clothes of praise, for crowning us with beauty, for lifting us into gladness. Today give us grace to see how you provide for us in change and in our grieving.

ISAIAH 61:3 (NIV)

Oaks of righteousness

They will be called oaks of righteousness, a planting of the Lord for the display of his splendour.

I am looking out of my window as I type this. The sun is shining on beautiful, big, old trees in the park across the road. They are absolutely majestic. And yet there is a gracious gentleness as these elegant trees bend and dance in the wind, revealing light undertones of their leaves. Tended, planted, cared for by municipal gardeners, these magnificent trees display splendour.

Isaiah says that the poor will be called oaks of righteousness. Those whose wounds have been bound up and nursed back to health. Those who are released from their dark prisons. Those who have been comforted in their mourning. Those who have been crushed and bruised by life, they will be called oaks. Oaks with deep roots, strong trunks, majestic in form and dimension.

Not just any old oaks but oaks of *righteousness*. But what on earth does 'righteousness' mean? Well, it has to do with 'right-relatedness'—to God, to ourselves, to our neighbour. It is about how we treat one another through our actions and through our thinking. It is God himself who is cultivating us to be in that right relationship. Like the gernaiums on your windowsill or those busy lizzies in your favourite garden corner, you are delighted in—'a planting of the Lord'.

As I pause and look out of the window again, these wonderful trees seem to be somehow drawing me into a larger, more grand and cosmic relationship. They drag me out of myself and connect me with the world around me. As 'oaks of righteousness' we have the elegance, the splendour and the graciousness of the Spirit of the Sovereign Lord upon us that draws others into that cosmic splendour of God.

'For as the soil makes the young plant come up and a garden causes seeds to grow, so the Sovereign Lord will make righteousness and praise spring up before all nations' (Isaiah 61:11, NIV).

✣

ISAIAH 61:6 (NIV)

A royal priesthood

And you will be called priests of the Lord, you will be named ministers of our God.

We have a wonderful declaration in this verse: you will be called priests of the Lord, you will be named ministers of our God. This chapter of Isaiah began by focusing on the poor, the broken-hearted, the captives, the prisoners and those who mourn and grieve. The focus then shifted to restoration and rebuilding of ancient ruins. And now we have new identity for those who have received the good news, for those who have been bound up, freed, released and comforted. Priest of the Lord. Minister of our God. A new calling; a new name.

These restored cities and rebuilt ruins require new leadership built on character and calling. The Sovereign Lord anointed his people and gave them a new identity along with the new calling: 'a chosen people, a royal priesthood, a holy nation, a people belonging to God, that you may declare the praises of him who called you out of darkness into his wonderful light' (1 Peter 2:9). No longer captive, prisoner or poor but priest of the Lord and minister of our God.

Priests and ministers in deed and in word. Loving, caring, and serving the broken-hearted, the captive and prisoner, those who mourn and grieve. Young and old. Strong and weak. Powerful and marginalized. Those who are lovable and those who are not. Those who smell of Harrods and those who smell of sewage.

We have the Spirit of the Sovereign Lord upon us. As priests and ministers we can bring Jesus to our neighbours and to our cities, or we can hide Jesus in the bottom left-hand drawer of our desk or leave him lifeless in the pew at church. I wonder what difference it would make if each one of us really understood our new identity as priests of the Lord? Or if we lived out our new name—ministers of our God?

Sovereign Lord, how often we live in the shadow of the old names and old identities—broken-hearted, prisoner, mourner. Give us strength and desire to live out our new name and our new identity as your priests and your ministers. Amen

✣

ISAIAH 61:7 (NIV)

Bent and crooked

Instead of their shame my people will receive a double portion, and instead of disgrace they will rejoice in their inheritance; and so they will inherit a double portion in their land, and everlasting joy will be theirs.

The first time she came to the store-front community centre, she backed in. With her back to the wall she began to make her way around the centre—around the tables where people were having coffee, around the shelves and racks bursting with second-hand clothes—until she got near to where I was making soup for lunch.

She was bent and crooked. I learned later that she was 51, but she looked 81. She was unkempt and wary. But she kept coming back. She began to help me make soup. She seemed to like that.

Several months later, as we were talking, she seemed quite agitated. She seemed to want to ask me something—to do something. Finally, she asked me if I would teach her how to write. Well, I was delighted to do that. Starting the next day, she came in 15 minutes before we opened the centre to learn to write.

I will never forget the day she wrote her name for the first time. She glowed with the delight of a child. I thought she would burst.

Then things began to change very rapidly. She stood taller and straighter. She had her hair cut. She started wearing lipstick. She dressed differently. Laughter erupted from her. She was a transformed woman. She brought her husband and family in. We eventually met seven of her eleven children. Not being able to write had shamed her for years. Being able to write her name replaced her disgrace with dignity.

And so it is with 'the poor' of Isaiah 61. The good news has been proclaimed. The captives have been released into new identity and wholeness. Those who mourn and grieve have become oaks of righteousness, rebuilding and restoring places long devastated.

'Instead of their shame my people will receive a double portion, and instead of disgrace they will rejoice in their inheritance… and everlasting joy will be theirs.' Thank you, Sovereign Lord.

ISAIAH 61:10 (NIV)

My soul rejoices

I delight greatly in the Lord; my soul rejoices in my God. For he has clothed me with garments of salvation and arrayed me in a

robe of righteousness, as a bridegroom adorns his head like a priest, and as a bride adorns herself with her jewels.

Our eldest daughter got married several years ago. One of my favourite memories around the preparations was going shopping for her wedding dress. I was absolutely stunned as she shed her blue-jeaned California Birkenstock look and emerged a silk-draped bride, beautiful and radiant. She took so naturally to yards of silk dress and demure veil—as if she was made for this.

Just so, we have been made to receive the Lord's garments of salvation and robes of righteousness. In these verses it's not just the bride but both bride and bridegroom who are created to wear the Lord's garments, bringing both to a new status before God and before the world. These celebration clothes speak a message of salvation and hope. They are tailor-made for the priests of the Lord and ministers of God of verse 6.

I have an even earlier memory of shopping with both my daughters for new summer dresses. They were about eight or nine. When one of them put on a lovely little dress, she burst out of the fitting-room and began to dance and twirl around the dress racks, around the assistants and around the customers—to everyone's delight. It was spontaneous delight, a rare moment in our world of a natural expression of joy.

Such a natural, spontaneous response seems absolutely appropriate for us when we realize that we are clothed with a priestly wardrobe of salvation and *haute couture* of righteousness. Take a minute to see yourself dressed in these wonderful robes. Now, in your mind's eye, give yourself permission to delight in the Lord and let your soul rejoice as you dance around the room in joy.

Sovereign Lord, release us into joy. Set our feet dancing as we delight in you. Open our mouths that our lips may speak your praise. Amen

TRUST

PSALM 37:1–8, 34–40 (RSV)

Trust

Commit your way to the Lord; trust in him, and he will act.

The book of Psalms, the great hymn book of Jewish scripture, is a mirror for all our human emotions. These encouraging words from the Psalm 37 are pithy and precise. So easy to say, yet oh, so difficult to enact!

When I am feeling insecure, vulnerable or generally frustrated, it helps me to recall and meditate on those people whose faith I admire. One of those people in my life has been Jan, who, with her husband, responded to God's call to serve with the Mission Aviation Fellowship. This meant giving up a good job, leaving a nice area, training at a Bible college and then leaving family and friends to live for Jesus Christ in a vast African country.

Over the years they have experienced wonderful blessings, adventures and the joy of truly making a difference to people's well-being, both physically and spiritually. There have also been times of disappointment, discouragement and uncertainty for their future. Through all these things, this brief verse from Psalm 37 has sustained Jan, anchoring her faith and motivating her commitment. Here is a family truly committed to the Lord. Their trust has been a powerful witness and the Lord has been seen to act in so many unexpected ways.

Too often I suppose I'm not prepared to trust implicitly—it's as if I feel I need to help the Lord along, to engineer opportunities for his presence to operate. I'm so grateful he has touched my life with people like Jan, for it not only underlines my need for (as the hymn writer put it) 'a childlike, praying trust', but I am inspired by their shining faith.

I am thrilled to hear and see the Lord's work being done, and it spurs me on to look afresh at how my own life has been guided and nurtured.

Dear Lord of all, today, as your trusting and eager child, I commit myself and those I love into your eternal keeping. Amen

✣

PSALM 139:7–10 (NIV)

Trust—held fast

Your hand will guide me, your right hand will hold me fast.

Clay is a great medium for self-expression. It also offers a good excuse to make a fine mess, all in the name of art. I was once in a group where we were encouraged to portray a recent experience in clay. We then had to look at each other's efforts and guess what they represented. I guessed that the model I looked at was somebody caged and held against his or her will.

The young man who created the model was, at that time, helping out at a school for children with severe learning and mobility problems. He told us that one afternoon there was great excitement because the school was given a trampoline. Of course, the children could not use the apparatus on their own, so members of staff climbed on with each child to hold them safe. In order that adults and children kept safely to the middle of the trampoline, they painted a large cross in the centre. So, far from representing imprisonment, this model recreated a loving gesture of security and happiness. My judgment had been so wrong.

Many people make wrong judgments about the teaching of Jesus. They suspect the Bible of being a book of restricting rules. In reality, the Bible shows us how ordinary, often anonymous men and women found themselves supported and loved by God like the children in the arms of their carers on the trampoline. They did not need to understand; they just knew they were being supported and kept safe.

Let's pray for situations we have to face where we long to know that Jesus is going to be right there with us, holding us, encouraging us and loving us through them.

Lord, whatever happens, I know I'm safe with you. Amen

⁘

PSALM 44:6–8 (NIV)

Trust—in God

I do not trust in my bow, my sword does not bring me victory.

Over and over again the inspired writers of scripture make plain the fact that people of God are people of peace. The painful, unlearned lessons of history reveal that trust in weapons of destruction always brings tragedy and tears. We are nevertheless a world dominated by weapons of indescribable evil. Whether we are watching pictures of terrified schoolchildren or the victims of teenage gun madness in America, or seeing victims of landmines, given a high profile by the late Princess Diana, we feel utterly helpless. It seems that the more ingenious we become, the more inhumanely we behave.

The humble psalmist, who only had his bow and sword, recognized their shortcomings. Weapons themselves cannot give us moral victory and weapons will always have unwanted side-effects. But God asks us to depend on him and be part of a world which cares for its inhabitants and shares its vital resources. God does not want us to live in fear, tension and international turmoil.

It's tempting to say that the world was less complicated in biblical days, but the Old Testament graphically records many wars between nations. In all history we can be certain of two things. One, human nature has not changed and, two, nor has God. Our God is the same God in whom millions have put their trust in times of conflict. We, in our time and place, are called to put our faith in Christ before weapons. It's so hard for us to do this because we are conditioned to be self-reliant. This self-reliance steers us away from God, away from the law of love to the worship of ourselves.

Try praying the wise words found in Proverbs 3:5: 'Trust in the Lord with all your heart and lean not on your own understanding.'

✣

JOHN 14:1 (NIV)

Trust—when anxious

Do not let your hearts be troubled. Trust in God; trust also in me.

A friend of mine has two sons. They each followed hobbies that they called exhilarating but their mother called downright dangerous! The older son went pot-holing and the younger white-water canoeing. Not being a serious sportsperson of any variety, I cannot begin to see the attraction in these high-adrenaline pursuits. Yet I know that thousands of people find fulfilment in pushing mind and body to the limit. It's their 'fun'.

I'm told abseiling is fun, too. Somehow I can't imagine myself dropping over the edge of some cliff or building for fun, but I've been fascinated to watch other people do it. It's amazing what trust they have in the one who holds the rope at the top. They trust that person with their life.

We all go through experiences which make us feel as though we are going over a cliff of some sort and at these times it is pretty hard to trust the one above us. And yet the Old Testament is peppered with God's promises to be with his people in every situation. Jesus gave words of encouragement to his disciples: they could trust God and they could also trust Jesus, God's Son.

Once 'over the top', the abseilers can no longer see the hands that hold them safely, but they know they have not been abandoned. In one of his hymns, Charles Wesley wrote, 'Give me the childlike, praying trust.' It's only when we learn to trust our Lord in this way that we shall know ourselves held secure in eternal hands. Then we will experience the peace that Jesus promised (John 14:25–27) and be able to enjoy the adventures of life.

Lord, I'm a gold medallist when it comes to anxieties. Help me today, hold me, and teach me how to trust in your strength and power. Amen

⁜

GENESIS 28:10–22 (NIV)

Trust—on life's journey

When Jacob awoke from his sleep, he thought, 'Surely the Lord is in this place, and I was not aware of it.'

Jacob comes across as the Old Testament 'sly guy'. We see his equivalent in many a modern soap, deceitful, thieving and scheming, yet likable with it—a salutary reminder that there is good in the worst of us and bad in the best of us.

Into the middle of the Jacob saga fits the story of the prophetic dream. Jacob wakes up to realize he has had a spiritual encounter with God. As we read of him in a fluster of reverence and guilty conscience, it's amusing to note that Jacob just couldn't resist trying a quick deal with God. If God would look after him then he, Jacob, would worship God and even offer God one tenth of his possessions! It's very tempting to feel superior to Jacob, to look down our noses at his brash audacity; but haven't we all, at some point in our lives, slipped into bargain mode with God ? If he will do such and such, then we will promise to do this and the other thing. The more desperate we are, the more eager we are to make commitments.

Now Jacob was honest enough to admit he'd gone to sleep without giving God a thought. Even so, he woke with a definite awareness of God's presence. This experience was a turning point for Jacob. From that moment he began the journey of spiritual discovery, a journey through baffling difficulties and heartache, from self-sufficiency to dependence and trust in God.

It's a long journey for each of us but Jesus waits to accompany us all the way.

Jesus, I will trust you, trust you with my soul: I'm tired and worn and hopeless, only you can make me whole.

PSALM 18:1–2 (NIV)

Trust—for refuge

I love you, O Lord, my strength… my God is my rock, in whom I take refuge.

Having spent most of my life in the West Country, I feel a great affinity with the rugged landscapes of Dartmoor and Bodmin Moor. The windswept swathes of grass and heather are dominated by the great boulders and identified by the various tors. Some say it is a bleak and forbidding landscape but more people find it a place of strength, of solace even. There is something so reassuring in the grandeur and the knowledge that the hills have been as they are for thousands of years. Somehow these wild places trigger our respect for the miracles of nature.

Not only have these same triggers been evident to the ancient authors of the Psalms but the whole idea of strength and stability creeps into our own language and we are proud to speak of relationships as being 'rock-solid'.

A Victorian hymn writer with a wonderfully Victorian name, Augustus Toplady, was walking in the Mendip Hills when he was caught by quite a violent thunderstorm. As he sheltered in the vast rock-face of Burrington Coomb, he felt that God was protecting him. Afterwards he wrote the hymn 'Rock of Ages, cleft for me, let me hide myself in thee'. There is a beautiful modern hymn which also speaks of God as 'my hiding-place... whenever I am afraid, I will trust in you'.

It is wonderful to know that we are not alone. We can run to our God for 'shelter' and we can 'hide' in his strength. In an ever-changing, complicated and sometimes frightening world, God is our rock.

Read Psalm 121.

✣

ROMANS 8:38–39 (NIV)

Trust—for the future

For I am convinced that neither death nor life, neither angels or demons, neither the present nor the future... nor anything else in all creation will be able to separate us from the love of God that is in Christ Jesus our Lord.

I shall always be grateful to the woman who sent me a beautiful card which said simply, 'Look back with gratitude, look forward with hope and look upward with confidence.' I placed it in the kitchen where I would see it many times a day.

None of us is immune from crises of one kind or another, and when we feel overwhelmed by problems or loss, looking back seems to pile on the recrimination, the regrets and the tears. We can become so bowed down and stressed that we have no energy left to look forward, let alone look upward. Yet move forward we do. Life goes on, and in the end, it takes us along too. In our own time we rejoin the world to find that time has begun the process of healing.

It's then that in looking back we realize we can be thankful and praise God for the miracle of memory. But we mustn't just look back, craving for what used to be. We must face the untouched, unfolding future, not with an unrealistic optimism, but with a confidence and trust in God. Paul's letters were messages of hope, just like the little card in my kitchen.

Why not try it for yourself? Take time to look back with gratitude, look to the future with hope and you'll find you are able to look upwards with confidence to your loving creator.

'For I know the plans I have for you,' declares the Lord, 'plans to prosper you and not to harm you, plans to give you hope and a future' (Jeremiah 29:11).

SECURITY IN CHRIST

PSALM 121 (LB)

Looking to God, our Rock

Shall I look to the mountain gods for help? No! My help is from Jehovah who made the mountains! And the heavens too! He will never let me stumble, slip or fall. For he is always watching, never sleeping. Jehovah himself is caring for you! He is your defender. He protects you day and night. He keeps you from all evil, and preserves your life. He keeps his eye upon you as you come and go, and always guards you.

I don't have to spend much time in front of commercial TV to see that the advertisers of financial products are preying on our increasing concerns about our own security and the security of those we love. We are offered plans to protect our possessions, our holiday plans, our health, our earnings, our loved ones if they are bereaved; to provide for school fees, home improvements, an idyllic retirement and pensions, luxury extras that we can only dream of... and even our own funerals!

If we are not careful, we can be lured into thinking that our own security is purchasable if we can only earn enough money to cover the cost. However, we need to wake up and remember that the only certain thing in life is our Father God who loves us. He is more dependable than all the man-made products that we are persuaded to believe in. The psalmists describe God as 'a rock'; he is the immovable object that holds us steady and secure whatever life brings.

If we give our lives to Christ and live for him every day, we are like those who build on that Rock (Matthew 7:24): our foundation becomes God himself. But Jesus never said that those who build on the rock would be free from trouble; he said, 'Though the rain comes in torrents, and the floods rise and the storm winds beat against his house, it won't collapse, for it is built on rock' (Matthew 7:25).

The next set of readings will remind us of some eternal truths that, as God's children, our security is ultimately in none other than him.

Lord, realign our vision, that we may look only to you.

⁘

ROMANS 8:1–14 (LB)

Free from condemnation

So there is now no condemnation awaiting those who belong to Christ Jesus. For the power of the life-giving Spirit—and this power is mine through Christ Jesus—has freed me from the vicious circle of sin and death.

Much of our personal security comes from knowing that we are accepted by the people who surround us every day, especially those who say they love us. However, many of us experience ongoing condemnation, though it may be low-level and not expressed verbally. As women, we have a tendency to think we are 'not good enough' and we can easily feel criticized. If this happens enough, it produces the insecurity and lack of self-confidence that affect our ability to handle everyday situations and give of our best. Ultimately such a situation can lead to a life of irrational fear.

Jesus came to show us that our personal security should not be built on what other people think or say about us, or even on what we think about ourselves. Our personal security should be based on Christ's redeeming love for us. God made us who we are; he made each one of us special. If God loves us, we must learn to love ourselves and not allow ourselves to listen to the condemnation of our own hearts or of other people.

Although we mess up our lives, make mistakes and are in need of improvement, we can know God's acceptance and forgiveness for ourselves through Jesus' death for us. Whatever our emotions tell us, our mind should constantly remind us that we are of value to God, and that we are not condemned by him for who we are or what we have done: we are accepted and forgiven. Then we allow the Holy Spirit to begin to recreate us and we have the chance to grow into the person God intended us to be, secure in our knowledge of Jesus Christ.

Spend some time in quiet confession, allowing the Holy Spirit to minister God's love, acceptance and forgiveness to your heart.

✣

ROMANS 8:26–30 (LB)

God has every day under control

And we know that all that happens to us is working for our good if we love God and are fitting into his plans.

One of my favourite films is *Parenthood,* which follows the joys and sorrows of bringing up children from the simultaneous point of view of four generations of parents. Towards the end of the film, the great-grandmother tells the distraught father that life is like a rollercoaster—it goes up and down, seemingly out of control—but what a ride, and how much preferable to the carousel that merely goes round and round!

The Christian life can seem more like a rollercoaster than a carousel: the 'up' times are glorious but it can seem like only a minute before you are plunged down, hurtling into a dark tunnel or swung round in a direction that was completely unanticipated, leaving you feeling dizzy and sick.

I never feel more insecure than when I have to accompany our children on theme park rides. Then I hold on tight, shut my eyes and tell myself that the designer of the ride has it all worked out so that the car stays on the rails and you end up safely in the exit bay when the whole terrifying experience is over. In the same way, when my Christian life seems to be all ups and downs, full of unexpected situations or just plain dark and frightening, I remind myself that I can feel secure, because whatever is going on around me God is in control.

When life is hard and complicated, it can be impossible to see how God can bring any blessing out of the difficulties we are experiencing—but he can, and we must believe it and trust the situation to him. It is also important to notice that God works things out for our good if 'we love him and are fitting into his plans'. If we are not walking in obedience, then we have no one to blame for our problems but ourselves.

Lord, may I know I am secure in you, despite outward circumstances.

✣

ROMANS 8:36–39 (LB)

Never separated from God's love

For I am convinced that nothing can ever separate us from his love. Death can't, and life can't. The angels won't, and all the powers of

hell itself cannot keep God's love away. Our fears for today, our worries about tomorrow, or where we are—high over the sky, or in the deepest ocean—nothing will ever be able to separate us from the love of God demonstrated by our Lord Jesus Christ when he died for us.

I don't need to read the gossip magazines to see how fragile relationships have become these days. I just need to look at the people around me, in the church and in the community. Adults and children are separated from those they love or the love they need by bereavement, imprisonment, violent crime, jobs that involve a lot of travelling and relational breakdown that ends in divorce. Even those who live in apparently happy families can, in reality, be living lonely lives, putting on a brave face for the outside world.

There is one relationship that remains secure despite the fickleness of human nature and the tragedies of life, and that is the love of God. Whatever happens to us, we can be secure in the knowledge that his love is eternal, constantly present in our lives, and that no one and nothing can take it away from us.

When we can't or don't feel that love, it is not because God has withdrawn it from us, it is because we have withdrawn ourselves from him. The Father is there, waiting with arms open wide for you to run into them. You may say your sin is too big or circumstances are too dark for the Father's love to reach you. Not true! The passage tells us that because Jesus took our punishment, nothing can separate us from the love of the Father. Corrie ten Boom once said that no pit was so deep that Jesus was not deeper still. I challenge you to reach out in your circumstances and see that he is there, loving you despite everything.

Remember today that nothing can ever separate you from his love.

✣

MATTHEW 6:31–33 (LB)

The Lord provides

So don't worry at all about having enough food and clothing. Why be like the heathen? For they take pride in all these things and are deeply concerned about them. But your heavenly Father already knows perfectly well that you need them. And he will gladly give them to you if you give him first place in your life.

As the mother of four children who seem to need increasingly more food and increasingly expensive clothing, it can be a great temptation to worry about what the family are going to eat or how I am going to be able to afford shoes, uniform and sports equipment, never mind the fashion items. I then start plotting all sorts of projects and plans that might bring in a few more pounds, and before I know it I have left what I know to be God's will for my life and found myself floundering around in ever-decreasing circles.

Jesus said that if we decide and actively seek to give him first place in our lives and spend our time doing what he wants us to do, whether that be paid or voluntary, he will provide all the things that we need, when we need them. Our everyday security is to be in him, not in our own worrying and attempts to control a difficult situation.

The Lord recently challenged me as to which was better, 'a job for life' or 'a life'. The former would have been more secure in worldly terms, but left me exhausted and no use to my family. The latter involved following God's calling on my life, even though it would not provide much in terms of financial income for quite a long time to come. The Bible encourages us to 'choose life' (Deuteronomy 30:19), to do what the Lord is calling us to do, because we can rest secure in the knowledge that he will provide for our physical needs.

Lord, help me to actively seek your kingdom and to trust you for the food and clothing I worry about. Amen

⁜

JEREMIAH 29:10–14 (LB)

God has planned our future

For I know the plans I have for you, says the Lord. They are plans for good and not for evil, to give you a future and a hope. In those days when you pray, I will listen. You will find me when you seek me, if you look for me in earnest.

I thought it was just people like me, whose children were now all at school, who wondered what they were going to do with the next chapter of life. I was wrong. I recently met a woman who had taken early retirement. Now she had finished cleaning her house and catching up on family and friends, she was seriously seeking the Lord about how she should spend her time, and asked us to pray for her, that she might hear the Lord clearly.

This woman was not at all insecure. She had not lost meaning and direction in life because she no longer had a job to give her identity and income; she knew that the Lord had something special planned for her and said that the Lord was miraculously stretching her finances. In the same way, we do not need to be insecure about what our future holds for us, because the wonderful thing about new chapters in life is that the Lord knows what he has planned for us in them right down to the last detail (Psalm 139:16). What's more, his plans are for good and not evil: they are filled with hope.

The exciting bit is listening to the Lord and following his directions step by step as we enter into each new day of the life he has given us. We don't need to worry that we won't hear him clearly, because he has promised that when we enquire of him, we will hear a voice behind us saying, 'This is the way; walk in it' (Isaiah 30:21, NIV).

Thank you, Lord, that with you things don't just happen, but are planned according to your good purpose. Help us to listen to the directions you are giving us.

✣

2 CORINTHIANS 12:9 (LB)

The Lord is our strength

[The Lord said] 'I am with you; that is all you need. My power shows up best in weak people.' Now I am glad to boast about how weak I am; I am glad to be a living demonstration of Christ's power, instead of showing off my own power and abilities.

Much of our security is wrapped up in the level of self-confidence we have when we are asked to do something different or a difficult task. If we think we are capable and can do a good job, we tend to be more self-confident and get on with things. My experience is, however, that the majority of women are exactly the opposite: we lack self-confidence and feel that we are incapable of performing responsible tasks. This is the very opposite of the truth, but most of us prefer to believe the lie.

The key here is not to depend on our own self-confidence, but to depend on the Lord and let him be our confidence. 'For (we) can do everything God asks (us) to with the help of Christ who gives (us) the strength and power' (Philippians 4:13). In challenging situations, the Lord can take our weaknesses and use them to his glory if we are willing to trust him. The people that stand by and watch us will then see that the strength with which we are performing our task is not of our own making, but an empowering of the Holy Spirit… and that changes lives.

I was recently asked to speak at a conference abroad—and not in English but in the language I have been studying for three years. I felt that the Lord had given me a special message to share, but I was terrified of delivering it. A friend from our church prayed that my weakness would make the message even more powerful and that the Lord would be my strength and confidence. And the Lord was just that. When our security is in Christ, he changes the lives of those we reach out to.

Lord, be our confidence in the tasks you set for us.

✣

2 TIMOTHY 1:6–9 (LB)

No need to fear

For the Holy Spirit, God's gift, does not want you to be afraid of people, but to be wise and strong, and to love them and enjoy being with them. If you stir up this inner power, you will never be afraid to tell others about our Lord.

Recently I had to sit an oral foreign language exam. I found it hard to believe the level of anxiety that the anticipation of the exam was beginning to produce in me. I felt very challenged by this and became determined to have a relaxed attitude and try to enjoy getting to know my 'interrogators'.

'Are you nervous?' one of them asked. 'A bit,' I said, 'but not as nervous as when I had to address a gathering of five hundred people in your country in your language last week!'

'So you are thinking that there is not much only two people can do to you!' said the other. Then I spent twice as long as scheduled, talking to them about praying in the power of the Holy Spirit for those in need and how God was moving in their nation.

This experience was quite an eye-opener: two strangers recognized that I had no need to be afraid. Due to their comments, I realized that God had changed my perception of myself as well as my perception of what he was able to achieve through me, to the extent that I could feel secure in a difficult situation. We really don't have anything to be afraid of from the people we deal with from day to day.

If we are secure in our knowledge of who we are in Christ, I believe that the light of Jesus can't do anything except stream out of our words, actions, attitudes and bearing. We will not be afraid, because God's perfect love casts the fear out of our lives; we can confidently be the beloved children of God that we were designed to be.

Lord, change our perception so that we can face every situation secure in the knowledge of your love.

✣

HEBREWS 4:14–16 (LB)

Mercy when we need it

Jesus the Son of God is our great high priest who has gone to heaven itself to help us; therefore let us never stop trusting him… Let us come boldly to the very throne of God and stay there to receive his mercy and to find grace to help us in our times of need.

The times I feel the least secure are when I have made a silly mistake and I have to go and put things right with someone. It can be very frightening, going to see someone to apologize. I find all sorts of worries whizzing round in my head: 'What if they slam the door in my face? What if they listen but won't accept my apology? What if…?'

The wonderful thing about God the Father is that we have constant access to him through Jesus, never mind what it is we are coming to say sorry about. Today's verse tells us that Jesus is there in heaven to help us: he makes it easier for us to come into God's presence. We can therefore be secure in knowing that we can find mercy and forgiveness in the courts of heaven whenever we need it. There is no need to fear that God will slam the door in our face.

We all fail, but the Lord is committed to ensuring that we grow into the people he intended us to be. He has promised to 'keep right on helping you grow in his grace until his task within you is finally finished' (Philippians 1:6). Jesus actively encourages us to continue in our walk with him. Perseverance is the mark of a true disciple and is the discipline by which we eventually learn the truth of God's nature and experience the security that brings real freedom (John 8:31–32). God doesn't give up on what he has started in us, and we mustn't give up on ourselves.

Lord, may I never forget that I have the security of knowing that you are always there when I fail; that you will pick me up, dust me down and set me back on the path to eternal life.

JOHN 3:10–21 (LB)

A secure eternity

For God loved the world so much that he gave his only Son so that anyone who believes in him shall not perish but have eternal life. God did not send his Son into the world to condemn it, but to save it. There is no eternal doom awaiting those who trust him to save them.

Our two older children have suddenly started to ask how they can be sure that they are going to heaven. Whether you are young or old, the answer is the same one that I keep telling them: if you have asked Jesus into your heart, have confessed your sin and are trying to live for him every day, then you can be secure in the knowledge that you have a place in heaven with Jesus.

Jesus sends his Holy Spirit to live in our hearts. He is like the receipt you are given when you order something that will be collected later: he is our security, our assurance of heaven. If we keep listening to what the Spirit is saying in our hearts, rather than listening to the doubts that the devil whispers in our ears, then we will remain secure in the knowledge that we have decided to follow Jesus and that we have eternal life.

'But how can I be really sure?' they say. There is no way to make your place in heaven any more sure than by taking God at his word and trusting that what he has promised is true; and he does not break his promises. However, I have told my children that if they are not completely sure they belong to Jesus they should ask another Christian to listen to their prayer of commitment, or come forward in church and make their decision public before witnesses. Then there is something a little more tangible to hold on to when they begin to doubt that they really belong to Christ.

'For I know the one in whom I trust, and I am sure that he is able to guard safely all that I have given him until the day of his return' (2 Timothy 1:12).

PSALM 112 (LB)

A portrait of security

Such a (wo)man will not be overthrown by evil circumstances. God's constant care of (her) will make a deep impression on all who see it. (She) does not fear bad news, nor live in dread of what might happen. For (she) is settled in (her) mind that Jehovah will take care of (her).

This psalm pulls together all the aspects of our security in God into one complete picture, and shows us that this security is part of what we should be as a whole person. Our security in Christ should be a natural expression of our relationship with a loving God in every area of our lives, not just in one part or another. I felt that the person described in this psalm fitted the bill perfectly and I have changed the personal pronoun in the passage quoted, so that the description hits closer to home for us as women.

The psalm describes a person who fears and trusts the Lord. The secure Christian fears nothing and no one but the Lord; she understands that nothing life can throw at us is to be feared, and nothing that the world tempts us to trust in is as trustworthy as the assurances we are offered by the Lord.

This psalm also indicates that security in Christ is not an excuse for thoughtless and reckless behaviour. The secure Christian woman is 'settled in her mind' because she knows, from head knowledge and from experience, that the Lord will take care of her, and she directs her 'business' accordingly, whether that is at home or in the marketplace. It is only then, when our focus is fixed on living for God's glory, that we obtain the acknowledgment that our worldly self-worth used to crave and demand (v. 9). However, by this stage of our spiritual growth, we know that the glory is the Lord's, not our own, and we redirect the praise to him.

Read the psalm again, changing the pronouns to 'I' or 'my'. Ask the Lord to deal with any discrepancies that the psalm points out in your life.

PHILIPPIANS

PHILIPPIANS 1:6 (RSV)

God is with us

And I am sure that he who began a good work in you will bring it to completion at the day of Jesus Christ.

I remember a time when I doubted that there was anything of worth in me. My self-esteem was at rock bottom, and everything I was trying to do seemed to be going wrong. I felt a huge responsibility as a Christian to pull myself together and get on with living the victorious life. But I couldn't convince myself that I was worthy, or even able, to do that.

What helped me to stop being overwhelmed by my own inadequacies, and to start focusing on what God could do, was this verse at the beginning of Paul's letter to the Philippians. It made me see my situation in an entirely new light.

If God had given me the work to do, then I could be confident that he was at least as keen as I was myself that it should be done! It was my responsibility to be obedient and faithful, but it wasn't up to me to ensure that everything would turn out all right. This realization proved to be the beginning of a greater acceptance of myself as a beloved child of God, no matter what I was managing to achieve at any time. I started to believe that my identity rested on who God said I was, not on what I was doing, nor even on what I thought about myself.

Also, I began to understand that I should live more fully in the present, without always trying to be one step ahead of God. It was Jesus' ultimate responsibility to save the world, and yet we never read about how he charged around in panic mode. If anyone had reason to be worried and downcast, it was him, but he trusted completely in his heavenly Father. Instead of anxiety and insecurity, Jesus radiated peace, confidence and love.

Merciful Lord, you have made us who we are, and you are with us even when we cannot sense your presence. Help us to believe that we are of worth to you. We ask for the peace that passes understanding in our lives today. Amen

Read Luke 12:22–31.

PHILIPPIANS 3:8–9 (RSV)

Christ above all else

Indeed I count everything as loss because of the surpassing worth of knowing Christ Jesus my Lord.

Paul had plenty of reasons to be proud of his background. He was a good Jew, he had observed all the rituals required, and he had kept the law perfectly. Yet after he was temporarily blinded by the Lord on the Damascus road, he realized that he had got his whole life wrong. He was turned around 180 degrees, and he never looked back. The former persecutor of Christians became one of the most fearless of Christians.

Unlike Paul, I was brought up in a Christian family in a culture shaped by Christian ideals. I have never had to go completely against my upbringing, my family or my religion. Even so, it has sometimes been extremely difficult to follow the Christian way. At times I felt like a salmon swimming upstream, as I tried to be true to Christ as a teenager in a very individualistic, selfish and hedonistic culture.

When I came to England from America, I learned the hard way just how many crutches I had been using. One by one, familiar support systems gave way, and I felt alone, stripped of all I had previously relied on. I had to rediscover God, without any of the comfortable trappings I had taken for granted. A process which could have destroyed me gave me, instead, a whole new understanding of God and of myself. Nowadays, many things crowd in to claim my attention, but I suppose, because of my experiences, I am a bit better at spotting the imposters pretending to be the most important things in my life.

Whoever we are, and whatever our experiences, once we have met with the Lord it is impossible to remain unchanged. We may not have as dramatic an encounter as Paul had, but we will have started along the same path—trying to live as disciples of Christ, and learning that we are loved and forgiven.

Lord of power and surprises, thank you for disturbing us with your truth. Please help to keep us unsettled enough so that we will rely on you, trust in you and always put you first. Amen

Read John 15:1–5.

✣

PHILIPPIANS 3:14; 2 CORINTHIANS 5:11–21 (RSV)

What's your motivation?

I press on toward the goal for the prize of the upward call of God in Christ Jesus.

When I was newly married, getting invited to certain parties was important to me. If the invitations didn't come, I would be very hurt. My happiness depended on an unpredictable social life, made even more unpredictable by my husband's work, which required him to drop everything and vanish at short notice! In time, I stopped caring whether or not the invitations came. I still get excited when I am asked to go to various functions, but I no longer feel personally rejected if I'm not on someone's list for a special event.

Whether it's invitations or belongings, holidays or salaries, many of us have chased things that are not of lasting value. It's great to have goals and to be ambitious. It's also fine to have many different interests and passions but, for a Christian, there has to be an underlying motivation that puts all our pursuits into perspective.

When Paul was converted he gained a whole new vision: he saw life as Christ saw life. His one overriding aim became the desire to know Christ better and to tell others about the liberating love of Christ. So powerful was his desire that he spent the rest of his life in reckless obedience to Jesus Christ. His vision got him shipwrecked, whipped, imprisoned and finally killed.

By the time Paul wrote to the Philippians, he didn't care whether he lived or died, as long as he could be sure that he was doing what Christ would have him do. All that mattered to him was to receive 'the upward call of God in Christ Jesus'.

I believe every follower of Christ has to discover what 'the upward call' means, and then life will take on a new meaning, infused with all that our faith reveals, and fired with vision and purpose that put our other passions into their proper place.

Forbid it, Lord, that I should boast,
Save in the death of Christ my God;
All the vain things that charm me most
I sacrifice them to his blood.

ISAAC WATTS (1674–1748)

⁘

PHILIPPIANS 4:2 (RSV)

Putting Jesus first

I entreat Euodia and I entreat Syntyche to agree in the Lord.

It intrigues me that the great Paul who wrote such glorious passages as the chapter on love in 1 Corinthians 13 would take the time to mention a local dispute between two women in Philippi. It seems that these two Christians had worked closely with Paul when he was ministering in their city. Together with a small group of other Christians, they had helped to spread the good news of Jesus Christ.

We are not told any details about what happened, but clearly Euodia and Syntyche had fallen out. Paul does not simply ask these women to sort things out between themselves, he begs them to be reconciled with each other. What is more, he asks the other Christians to help them.

Whatever it was that went wrong, it seems it was bad enough to be causing problems in the young church in Philippi. Again and again in his letters, Paul's overriding passion for winning people to Christ comes across so clearly as he writes specific commands to specific people in specific circumstances. Nothing must be allowed to get in the way of the liberating message of God's love.

Paul's own life had been turned upside down by his encounter with the risen Jesus, and he was ruthless about anything that would hamper or hinder other people's opportunities to meet with his Lord. We might be surprised by the mention of these two women, but in Paul's eyes their inability to get along was marring the truth and glory that he was later prepared to die for.

Lord, help us to put our love for you above everything else in our lives. Please help us to be willing to swallow our pride, and to forgive those who have offended us. Help us also to accept your forgiveness and your never-ending love for us. Amen

Read Ephesians 4.

✣

PHILIPPIANS 4:4 (RSV)

Look up!

Rejoice in the Lord always; again I will say, rejoice.

Being joyous is a breeze when things are going well, but I believe that God wants us to keep a kernel of joy in our hearts even when things look bleak. I am not suggesting that we slap a stupid grin on our faces and pretend that our dear friend isn't gravely ill, or that our child isn't in trouble, or that whatever else is happening isn't really happening. We need to acknowledge those things that cause us pain and grief, and we need to let ourselves weep or be silent, or whatever it takes to work through the bad times. But what we must not do is to confuse our temporary darkness with a corresponding darkness on God's part. God is with us in our pain, and in ways I don't fully understand he aches with us, but his compassion for us does not diminish his eternal brightness.

Whenever I fly in an aeroplane, I get a thrill when we finally burst through the clouds, out into the clear bright sky. No matter what the weather conditions are on the ground, above the clouds the sun is always shining. When we praise God and express our joy in him, it is a way of showing God that we know he is always there for us. The very act of reaching through our own difficulties towards our loving Father lifts our spirits and gives us a new perspective.

Expressing joy, even when life is tough, can help us to align ourselves with God, who is beyond time and death, and who dances for ever in a never-ending dance of joy with all those who love him.

'Bless the Lord, O my soul; and all that is within me bless his holy name!' (Psalm 103:1).

Read Psalm 146.

✣

PHILIPPIANS 4:8 (NRSV)

Forming the mind of Christ

Finally, beloved, whatever is true, whatever is honourable, whatever is just, whatever is pure, whatever is pleasing, whatever is commendable, if there is any excellence and if there is anything worthy of praise, think about these things.

This was one of my Uncle John's favourite verses from the Bible. Like so many people, he often felt swamped with the daily deluge of news on the radio, television and in the papers. He liked to keep up with what was happening in the world, but he would not let himself dwell on the seamier side of life.

The way he looked at it, we had a choice: either we could fill our minds full of salacious and titivating stories, or we could try to concentrate on what God would have us think about.

Uncle John was not a prude, nor did he ignore information about injustice and cruelty, but he did not allow himself to wallow in lurid tales of debauchery. He also applied this principle to conversations with friends. He and my aunt were very generous and hospitable and loved to entertain, but when the talk turned to gossip, he would very gently remark that none of us was perfect and that the person being verbally dissected was probably just somewhat 'immature'.

I still think of my uncle when I catch myself squirming in disgust as I read the juicy titbits of some headline-grabbing scandal. I remember that I have a choice: I can saturate myself with pointless information about human weaknesses and wickedness that will play on my mind, or I can move on to learning about other people and events.

There is much pain and horror in this world that Christians can, and should, help to heal, but there is also the type of information that will eventually blunt our sensitivity and may well distract us from what God has called us to be and to do.

Lord of mercy and grace, help us to grow more like Christ in what we think and say and do. Help us also to see other people and situations as you see them. Amen

Read Colossians 3:1–17.

✣

PHILIPPIANS 4:19 (RSV)

God knows what we need

And my God will supply every need of yours according to his riches in glory in Christ Jesus.

The university I attended was three thousand miles from my home. Thankfully, some of my mother's relatives lived nearby, and would often invite me over for the weekend.

One Friday evening after all my classes were finished, I went wearily back to my room. I had not arranged to have dinner with anyone, and both my room-mates were out. My aunt who lived in the next town phoned, but only to ask me a quick question. After I put the phone down, I burst into tears.

I was feeling lonely. I ached to be with my aunt, laughing, talking, sharing some of her wonderful home cooking. I assumed she and my uncle were busy or had other guests. I knelt by my bed and all I could pray was, 'Lord, if possible, please let my aunt invite me over.'

Within seconds the phone rang. When I answered it I could hear my aunt's voice, apologetically saying, 'I don't know what's the matter with me, Christina, I wasn't thinking. Would you like to come over this weekend?'

I have never forgotten what happened that night. I was feeling so low, and the Lord answered my prayer before I had even finished praying.

If only all prayers could be answered as quickly and perfectly! I admit that there have been times when I have learned more about God and myself by not having my prayers answered, but I haven't detected any pattern or formula when it comes to praying. Prayer remains for me a way of keeping the lines of communication open between me and God, of putting into words some of the deep desires of my heart, of listening for what God might be saying to me, and, most of all, of being in the presence of Christ.

Dear Lord, please help our whole lives to become an open prayer between your heart and ours. Help us to be able to discern your will for us. Today we pray for all those who ache for a sign of your love. Amen

Read John 17.

CONFIDENCE IN GOD

EPHESIANS 3:7–13 (NIV)

Confidence and freedom

Although I am less than the least of all God's people, this grace was given me: to preach to the Gentiles the unsearchable riches of Christ... In him and through faith in him we may approach God with freedom and confidence.

In the film The Shawshank Redemption, there is a poignant episode when Brooks is released from prison after spending 50 years inside. After decades of having his every move dictated to him, he suddenly has freedom to make his own decisions. But after only a few weeks of liberty he climbs on to a chair and hangs himself. Before he dies he writes to his old friends in prison: 'I'm so tired of always feeling afraid.' Life outside was too strange for him. He was used to the world of prison and felt at home there. He couldn't make the adjustments necessary to live as a free man. He was utterly friendless and always looking over his shoulder in fear, wondering what new and strange experiences each day would bring.

Here is an example of someone who has freedom but no confidence to embrace what that freedom offers.

How many of us believers are like Brooks? We know we have been delivered from sin by Christ's sacrifice, and we are therefore free from condemnation and judgment. Colossians 1:13–14 tells us, 'For he has rescued us from the dominion of darkness and brought us into the kingdom of the Son he loves, in whom we have redemption, the forgiveness of sins.' We are out of the prison, but how confident are we to approach our holy God and stand before his great white throne? Our sins have been forgiven, but how many of us live with needless guilt? How many of us fear what God might ask us to do if we gave ourselves unreservedly to him and put him in the driving seat of every area of our lives—job, marriage, time, holidays, future, money?

Is there something that is robbing you of confidence in God's presence? Bring this fear to him and ask for his forgiveness.

✣

LUKE 18:9–14 (NIV)

Confident yet humble

To some who were confident of their own righteousness and looked down on everybody else, Jesus told this parable: '... I tell

you that this man, rather than the other, went home justified before God. For all those who exalt themselves will be humbled, and those who humble themselves will be exalted.'

There is nothing worse than a smug Christian—someone who smiles beatifically, saying, 'I'm going to heaven. God loves me.'

Jesus reserved his sternest comments for the Pharisees who were so proud of their scrupulous obedience to God's law that they'd forgotten they were sinners in need of forgiveness. They thought that obeying God made them better than other people. They became proud and complacent and looked down on others.

Christians can often be accused of being hypocrites. We affirm that we believe in a God of love and mercy, yet our lives often demonstrate the opposite. We are critical or judgmental about anyone who doesn't fit our chosen mould of Christianity, let alone those who have not yet embraced the gospel. Our confidence before God needs to be firmly anchored in Christ's death and resurrection, not our obedience or good deeds.

When I was a missionary in Africa I was sometimes, figuratively, put on a pedestal by other Christians. They thought a missionary must be a few steps nearer to God than ordinary mortals. It is easy to start believing that God is extra pleased with me because I've made significant sacrifices for him. This is complete and utter rubbish.

When we talk about being confident that God loves and accepts us, we need to express it with a humble, grateful attitude. It needs to be abundantly clear to everyone that we are not confident in our own righteousness but in his mercy and grace to a hopeless sinner.

Not the labours of my hands can fulfil thy law's demands;
Could my zeal no respite know, could my tears forever flow,
All for sin could not atone; Thou must save, and Thou alone.
Nothing in my hand I bring; simply to thy cross I cling.

AUGUSTUS MONTAGUE TOPLADY (1740–78)

✣

2 CHRONICLES 32:1–8 (NIV)

Inspire confidence

'Be strong and courageous. Do not be afraid or discouraged because of the king of Assyria and the vast army with him, for there is a greater power with us than with him. With him is only the arm of flesh, but with us is the Lord our God to help us and to fight our battles.' And the people gained confidence from what Hezekiah the king of Judah said.

Words can hurt, words can heal. In the changing-room at half-time in a football cup final, one can imagine the words the coach uses to inspire and encourage the team. If you are two goals down, you can feel tired and defeated before you even start the second half. But the right word from the coach galvanizes the team. They burst out on the attack and score a goal. Tiredness is forgotten as motivation surges through the team and they go from strength to strength.

Hezekiah chose inspiring words when the Israelites were facing a huge army. Humanly speaking, they were doomed. No doubt they were terrified and had perhaps given up and were preparing for surrender. You can't fight well if you are discouraged and already defeated in your mind.

They needed a pep talk from the king. But encouragement had to be based on fact, not on wishful thinking. Hezekiah hit the right note: God was far stronger than the enemy, and he was with them.

How about our words? At work, at home or with friends, do our words encourage or discourage? Are your encouragements based on good evidence? Do we turn people to God when they are in difficulty? How are you using this great gift of speech that God has given you? 'Watch the way you talk, let nothing foul or dirty come out of your mouth. Say only what helps, each word a gift' (Ephesians 4:29, THE MESSAGE).

Lord, I pray that today you would give me words to help people gain confidence in their particular situation and that each word I utter would be a helpful gift.

✣

PSALM 27:1, 3 (NIV)

Confidently facing fear

The Lord is my light and my salvation—whom shall I fear? The Lord is the stronghold of my life—of whom shall I be afraid? ... Though an army besiege me, my heart will not fear; though war break out against me, even then will I be confident.

What scares you? Cancer, financial problems, teenagers going off the rails, getting old? Probably few of us can relate to King David's situation. He feared invading armies and war, suffering the humiliation of defeat and being robbed of his possessions, deported, even killed.

We know that he did suffer defeat at the hands of his own son! That is a mighty humiliation. In the same way, some of the things we fear may happen to us. How could David be confident and not afraid? How can we walk confidently into an unknown and potentially difficult future?

David was not saying, 'The Lord is my light and my salvation, my stronghold, therefore my life will be stress-free with no problems and nothing bad will ever happen to me.' He seems to be saying, 'When war comes, my ultimate confidence is in God, and his good plans for me; therefore I will not fear because he is with me as my stronghold in whatever situation I face.'

A Christian friend announced to me that she was giving up her faith. When I asked 'Why?' she said, 'Because God didn't give me what I wanted.' In her case, what she wanted was a godly husband. How many of us are like my friend? We want God to make life nice and cosy for us. To judge from some of the adverts on telly, one would assume that life should be great fun and we should always have what we want, because we're worth it. Life is not like that for anyone, but with God as our stronghold we can face whatever comes with confidence, just as David did.

Lord Jesus, I bring to you my fears of .... Thank you that you are my light, my salvation and my stronghold, so I am safe with you.

JEREMIAH 17:5–8 (NIV)

Confidence in God = fruitfulness

Cursed are those who trust in mortals... They will be like a bush in the wastelands... But blessed are those who trust in the Lord, whose confidence is in him. They will be like a tree planted by the water that sends out its roots by the stream.

There is a stark contrast here between the one who puts confidence in human endeavours and the one who trusts God. One life will be barren and dried up, whereas the other will be always fruitful and life-giving.

Living in Wales, I don't often get the opportunity to see what happens to plants when they get insufficient water: we have abundant rain! But even here it is obvious that the banks of rivers are very fertile places—the trees are strong and green even in times of relative drought.

The analogy here is that just as the tree pushes its roots nearer and nearer the source of water, so we should strive to put our spiritual roots deep into God. The tree draws up nourishment from the stream and that produces leaves, blossom and fruit. As we tap into God's resources our lives will become fruitful, which means that we will produce the fruit of the Spirit as in Galatians 5:22–23 and also that we will bring other people to him.

So, how do we put spiritual roots down into God? We need to stay close. One way is to keep talking with him in prayer, bringing daily concerns, hopes and desires to him. We need to feed on his word, the Bible. What I've found helpful is to learn a verse and then think about it when I get a free moment during the day. Often God will show me ways of making that verse more real in my life so that it is not just buzzing around in my brain, but actually being demonstrated in my attitudes, actions and words throughout the day.

Trusting in my own wisdom and abilities will lead to a barren, parched life. Putting my confidence in God's wisdom and abilities will lead to a beautiful and fruitful life.

✣

PROVERBS 31:10–31 (NIV)

Do others have confidence in you?

A wife of noble character who can find? She is worth far more than rubies. Her husband has full confidence in her and lacks nothing of value. She brings him good, not harm, all the days of her life... Charm is deceptive, and beauty is fleeting; but a woman who fears the Lord is to be praised.

As a single person, I have in the past gleefully skipped over Proverbs 31, thinking that it didn't apply to me and I couldn't possibly be that superwoman par excellence anyway.

However, I have since learned that it is unwise and even dangerous to ignore portions of God's word, so I thought I'd better take a closer look. The principles in Proverbs 31 can be applied to any relationship—friend, parent, child, as well as spouse.

Do my friends have full confidence in me? Do I support them when others criticize or gossip about them? Can I be trusted with confidences? Do they lack anything of value that I can give them—loyalty, encouragement, prayer support, honesty? Am I willing to confront them when I see them going off track? Do I bring these people good and not harm all the days of my life?

As the years take their toll, it is helpful to be reminded that beauty is fleeting! No amount of creams, potions, pills or exercise programmes can delay the ageing process for ever. Thankfully there is much more to being a woman than just our appearance. Proverbs affirms that praise is to be given to the woman not for her beauty, but for her fear of the Lord. Even though this woman devotes herself to her husband and family, it seems that first place in her life is given to God. Her relationship with God is the source and wellspring of all these beautiful qualities that she brings to her relationships.

Lord, I pray that you would work in my life so that others would have confidence in me and that I would bring them good, not harm, all the days of my life.

✣

1 JOHN 2:28—3:3 (NIV)

Hello Jesus!

And now, dear children, continue in him, so that when he appears we may be confident and unashamed before him at his coming... We know that when he appears, we shall be like him, for we shall see him as he is.

Jesus is coming back. And he could come today! This time, instead of coming as a vulnerable baby in an insignificant town in Israel, he will come with the deafening trumpet call of God, with blazing fire and powerful angels (1 Thessalonians 4:16; 2 Thessalonians 1:7).

The question for all of us is, will we be confident and unashamed before him at his coming? We know that Jesus has paid the penalty for our sin so that those who trust in him and his work on the cross will be received into heaven (1 Peter 3:18). But when you look at Jesus face to face and see him as he is, will you hang your head or try to hide in a corner? Or will you look up into his glorious face confident and unashamed? Will there be things you will regret?

Choices you've made, priorities you've neglected, words you've said, relationship problems that you haven't sought to reconcile?

Two of my aunts had a row and didn't speak for about 25 years. The nearest they got to reconciliation was when one went to the other's funeral. Too late, far too late.

The condition that the apostle John puts on being confident and unashamed before him at his coming is to 'continue in him'. This is a daily walk of faith, seeking to know God better, and not letting anything hurt or hinder that relationship, asking forgiveness as soon as you're conscious of having sinned. This doesn't necessarily mean doing more—attending more meetings or exhausting yourself in Christian service. It is a matter of the heart. If your heart is open and tender to God's promptings, then you can be confident and unashamed before him when he returns.

'He who testifies to these things says, "Yes, I am coming soon." Amen. Come, Lord Jesus' (Revelation 22:20).

EPHESIANS 1—3

EPHESIANS 1:1–3 (NIV)

Get rich one day

Praise be to... God... who has blessed us in the heavenly realms with every spiritual blessing in Christ.

Our family is hopeless at finance. The language of pension plans and savings schemes—it is all gobbledegook. (I am the person who once referred to a 'Tessa' as a 'Teresa'.) So we acquired a financial adviser, who undoubtedly understands our financial position better than we do, and who gets really excited about the possibilities of saving-schemes for us.

Now our financial adviser has a little girl of about six, and over coffee he told us of his plans for her. 'Fortunately we can give her so much,' he began. I smiled, thinking of puppies, wonderful doll's houses, piano lessons, even ponies!

He went on, 'I started the week she was born, and now she has got...' and he reeled off a list of funny words. No puppies, no dolls, but—saving-schemes?! 'Yes,' he concluded, as my eyes glazed over, 'she is looked after for life. By the time she is 40, she'll have a substantial private income. She is one lucky little girl.'

When I read this verse in Ephesians now, I think of him and his daughter. We are blessed in the 'heavenly realms with every spiritual blessing'. I know how that little girl must feel when her daddy excitedly tells her he has treasures for her that she can't play with, can't cuddle, can't ride, can't even see!

I suspect the little girl would at present prefer the doll's house. But her father really loves her. He has provided an umbrella that will protect her all her life, and which will yield great riches one day.

The book of Ephesians glows with the warmth of God's love towards us. So I know that whatever these 'blessings in heavenly realms' may be, they will be well worth having. Even more so than all my current adult versions of doll's houses!

'My future is as bright as the promises of God.'
ADONIRAM JUDSON

✣

EPHESIANS 1:4–6 (NIV)

Better than Reader's Digest

For he chose us in him before the creation of the world.

Do you ever suspect that your name is on a list somewhere? We get companies we have never heard of writing to us by name, offering us summer homes, exotic cruises and huge loans. Since the coming of computer mail-merge wizardry, of course, companies have seized the chance to personalize an offer—making you think that they care about you as a particular person.. The Reader's Digest are geniuses at this—I know a lonely person who buys their books just because of the buzz he gets when they write to thank him effusively, and to beg him to enter their prize draw. I suspect he really thinks that the prize draw manager is sleepless at nights, desperate to give him personally the £250,000 prize.

The Reader's Digest man sends you a personalized chance of winning a big prize, but only one person among hundreds of thousands is lucky. And even the Reader's Digest man does not know ahead of time who will win.

God was in business long before the Reader's Digest. Since before the creation of the world, he has prepared for each one of us a personalized invitation to an immeasurably bigger winning—the prize of eternal life. And he does know ahead of time who will win—all those who respond to Jesus Christ.

Predestination versus free will is a vast topic that has kept male theologians busy for centuries. But I think every woman understands the situation perfectly. We have all held parties and drawn up guest lists based on whom we would ideally like to come, if only we could get them to agree. But even as we send out the invitations, we know who is going to say no and refuse us, and who will respond gladly, and come and enjoy themselves. So they are the ones for whom we really prepare.

'The future belongs to those who belong to God.'
W.T. PURKISER

✣

EPHESIANS 1:11–14 (NIV)

Vanilla slice guaranteed

Having believed, you were marked in him with a seal, the promised Holy Spirit, who is a deposit guaranteeing our inheritance until the redemption of those who are God's possession.

We are spoiled in Alderley Edge: we have a deluxe Continental pâtisserie shop. It is open only three days a week, but what business it does! From Thursday morning onwards, dozens of people converge on that shop, eager for their weekend supply of glistening fruit flans, curranty tea cakes, gateaux like snow fortresses, delicate florentines, vanilla slices, and various deliciously gooey pastries.

It's every man for himself when you are outside on the pavement. But if you can just reach the shop door, you are admitted and given a little ticket with a number on it. As soon as people get their sticky fingers on their ticket, you can see them relax, even though the crush inside the shop is something to be seen.

This verse reminds me of that weekly scrum. Those people have been given a deposit guaranteeing their inheritance... of a tea cake. Once they have got their ticket, they smile, and look around for people they know to chat to. It gets quite jolly.

They may not be able to see the counter, they may be jostled here and shoved there, but they feel secure that no matter how long the wait might be, they will not be forgotten. Their ticket is their deposit, guaranteeing them their pâtisserie delights, as soon as the ladies behind the counter are ready for them.

Of course, Paul here is recalling the whole history of salvation, from God's calling of Abraham to the inclusion of the Gentiles following the resurrection. And just as circumcision set the Israelites apart, so Christians have now been given a new seal, the promised Holy Spirit. His presence within us reassures and guarantees us our future, heavenly inheritance. We may have to wait a bit, but our place in heaven is secured.

'The Holy Spirit is the heavenly lover's engagement ring given to us.'
MICHAEL GREEN

✣

EPHESIANS 1:15–18 (NIV)

Seeing is believing

I pray also that the eyes of your heart may be enlightened in order that you may know the hope to which he has called you, the riches of his glorious inheritance in the saints.

Two weeks ago I was knee-deep in Americans. A childhood friend from New York brought over her three nieces, laconic teenagers in baggy jeans and fleeces who lived on Diet Coke and bagels (yes, for breakfast as well). This kind, I have discovered, is not easily impressed by middle-aged enthusiasm. On the way back from Manchester airport, I got a few 'uh huh', 'yeah, OK's when I tried to excite them with descriptions of the beautiful places I was going to show them.

It wasn't until I had them around my kitchen table (Diet Cokes in hand) and showed them the leaflets of all the beautiful places we would visit (from London to Chester to Dublin) that they began to 'see' the marvellous things in store for them. Then I got the highest accolade: 'Oh, cool...'

I expect that most of us, when we get to heaven one day, and see what God has got in store for us, will express ourselves along the lines of 'Oh, cool...' But it seems to me from this verse that just as I wanted my young Americans to enthuse with me ahead of time, so Paul wants the Ephesians to get excited about their spiritual riches now.

It is a question of being able to fully appreciate what they have been given. My husband reluctantly agreed to come to a Greek island with me one year. He had little curiosity or excitement—until he got off the plane and caught his breath at the stunning scenery.

We have all met Christians who seem to get little joy from their faith. Their eyes of faith seem clouded and cast earthward. If that is us, we can pray that God will enlighten the eyes of our hearts.

'Joy is the serious business of heaven.'
C.S. LEWIS

✣

EPHESIANS 1:19–23 (NIV)

The pecking order of life

Christ... far above all rule and authority, power and dominion... [and] head over everything for the church, which is his body.

Do you ever feel at the very bottom of the heap of life? Far below all rule, authority, power and dominion? It's easy to feel powerless when you have a big mortgage, a demanding job, exacting family members, and a tight schedule that seems to devour every minute of your time.

The passion for demanding that we 'be given a choice' strikes me as funny. Is this supposed to give us power? Just what are these choices? Choice over whether to work at all or not, or simply which job—if we can get it? Which house to own, or simply which mortgage company to pay? It's like rearranging the deckchairs on board Titanic. If you feel in control, it is because you don't understand the situation.

I have a friend who knows exactly where she comes in the pecking order of life: one above her collie, and one below her elk-hound. (The collie lets her have the squeaky toy; the elk-hound growls.)

So it can be easy to think of these verses: well, that is very nice for Christ, and I am sure he is enjoying it up there, but in the meantime I seem to be subject to just about everyone. But Paul is trying to give us some tremendous news. In effect, he is saying that earthly might does not make right, and that evil will not triumph for ever. Everyone will one day be judged by divine justice.

And the best news is that we have nothing to fear. Though in this life we may have to 'give unto Caesar that which is Caesar's', earthly powers can have no lasting effect on us: no one owns our souls—except the King of kings, who so loves and identifies with us that he considers the Church his very body.

'Christ is the still point of the turning world.'
T.S. ELIOT

⁘

EPHESIANS 2:1–3 (NIV)

Shop till you drop?

When you followed the ways of this world and of the ruler of the kingdom of the air...

Some say shopping is the new religion, and I for one believe it.

A Sunday newspaper reported that women who feel unloved often turn to shopping for solace. Certainly modern department stores are more appealing than most churches, offering you a warm welcome, unconditional acceptance, and a chance to make yourself over, to be born again in any form that you choose. We've all held up clothes in stores and cried, 'This is me! I'll look great.' And we feel affirmed, comforted, lovable. Redemption is... buying new clothes?!

Several years ago, I had a weird experience in one of Manchester's finest department stores. Everywhere, beautiful items were displayed, only the best, and plenty of it. Wonderful, but... suddenly I saw the place with different eyes. What was going on here? This place was not just set aside for selling, but dedicated to it. I was in a temple that worshipped materialism, pure and simple. As a Christian I could not accept this creed, and my spiritual hackles rose. As I mentally questioned the values that were being trumpeted all round me, the atmosphere of the store rose up and seemed to engulf me with hostility. It was uncanny and frightening.

I shrugged off the experience, thinking I'd gone crazy, until recently. Two girls in my prayer group were discussing their visit to a magnificent new shopping complex nearby. To my astonishment, both had also encountered this overwhelming feeling of alienation and hostility, the minute they had walked in. 'I felt I was in a truly pagan place,' said one. 'With its huge dome, and colonnades, it even looks like a pagan temple,' said the other. I don't know if anyone else has ever felt this while out shopping, because I suspect that 'the ruler of the kingdom of the air' has temples everywhere. Meanwhile, new clothes are fun, but they're just sticking-plasters when it comes to covering spiritual pain.

Read Galatians 5:16–26.

EPHESIANS 2:4–7 (NIV)

Two's company

Because of his great love for us, God, who is rich in mercy, made us alive with Christ even when we were dead in transgressions.

I like to get on with things on my own. At school I always preferred it when I was given a piece of classwork to take away and do... and then show to the teacher.

In the 1940s a great spiritual revival swept across Uganda. Tens of thousands of Baganda discovered that God loved them, and were born again in Jesus Christ. So far, wonderful. Then the problems began. Like me, the Baganda were eager to do well, and like me, the Baganda hankered to do it on their own. So they nearly killed themselves trying to lead a pure and holy life. Soon they were failing, and hating themselves, and scarcely daring to pray because they felt so ashamed.

Then some of them woke up: how had they come to God, how had they pleased him at the start? By simply responding to Jesus. Had he required that they be perfect first? No. So how should they continue to try to please God? By keeping Jesus on one side, and leading holy lives on their own? Not only was this impossible, it missed the whole point of their redemption. They must, as it says in John's Gospel, 'abide in me'.

This has been one of the hardest lessons for me, personally, to learn. I turn to God, hit a spiritual 'high', and then try to maintain it on my own, so as not to let God down. Of course, then I sin, and then I feel embarrassed about going back to him.

I've got to learn that leading a holy life is not a matter of just keeping all the rules but of, as Paul says, walking daily in the Spirit. It is not a case of doing good for God but of living in daily harmony with him.

You need never be alone again.

'I am the vine; you are the branches... apart from me you can do nothing' (John 15:5).

✣

EPHESIANS 2:8–9 (NIV)

Such perfection!

For it is by grace you have been saved, through faith—and this not from yourselves, it is the gift of God—not by works, so that no one can boast.

Years ago and far away, I joined a church with an extraordinary elderly woman in it. She was full of saintly good deeds. She had not worked for years, because unlike lesser mortals, Jesus answered all her prayers for things... because she was such a blessing to everyone. She could change a person's life on any morning convenient to her. You bring 'em, she'd bless 'em. She had seen it time and time again.

How did I know? Because she told me so. Dozens of times. Same as she told everyone. Same as she told everyone exactly what she was 'trusting God' for that day, how much it cost, how obvious it was that you were God's answer, and how she preferred cash...

When you first met her, it was overwhelming. Here must be a veritable swordmaiden of Christ. After all, she explained, everyone said so... Soon, however, you realized that actually she was the only one who ever used this description of herself. Other unassuming folk would just sigh when her name was mentioned.

Spiritual pride, of course, comes in many guises. Most of us are a bit more subtle than this poor deluded woman. Most of us agree with the Pharisee's observation, 'I thank thee, Lord, that I am not as other men', but keep the thought to ourselves!

Self-righteousness is one of the most nauseating of traits to find in another person. The trouble is, most of the time such people are very respectable, because their pride feeds on their good behaviour. It's sad that we could ever try to take credit for attaining our salvation—especially when you consider what it cost Jesus Christ.

I think this verse is Paul's way of warning us: 'Who do you think you're kidding? Where do you get off?!'

'The best way to see divine light is to put out thine own candle.'
FRANCIS QUARLES

✣

EPHESIANS 2:10 (NIV)

Haberdashery

For we are God's workmanship, created in Christ Jesus to do good works, which God prepared in advance for us to do.

Each winter, ladies at our church occasionally arrive with carrier bags. Inside are dozens of scraps of material, ripped clothes, and offcuts from sewing projects. Just odds and ends. No one wants them... except Edith.

Edith bundles the bags into the boot of her old car after church, whisks them off home, and that's it... until the parish fête in July. Edith arrives, unpacks her boot, and her stall fills up with the most fantastic, exquisite creations. Peg bags, carrier bag holders, pyjama bags, pin cushions, aprons, stuffed animals, rag dolls, doll blankets... Each of us visits the stall to see what became of the worthless scraps that we gave her. Sometimes they are hard to recognize—an old shirt of mine reappeared as part of a stunning patchwork sun-hat which I then paid £6 to have back!

God takes damaged, spoiled humanity and, through Jesus Christ, transforms us. 'Workmanship' implies a creative product—that's us. He deals with our torn bits, and by the time he has finished we are ready to start a new life.

Edith has never turned anything away. She can salvage anything. She cleans and irons it and then begins work. She plans a future for each little scrap and, in her hands, it turns into something new and lovely—and useful, from tea cosies to pin cushions.

Edith does not alter the given properties of any bit of material: the linen remains wrinkled luxury, the cotton practical, the velvet delicate, and the gold lamé exotic. She does not interfere with their individuality, but transforms each one into an object making the most of its unique capabilities. God does not change our families, social backgrounds or educational qualifications, but instead works with them to create something beautiful for him—and for others.

By the way, Edith likes cotton best—'You can do most with it!'

Prepare for your future. Read 1 Peter 1.

EPHESIANS 2:11–13 (NIV)

The outwitted hypnotist

...without hope and without God in the world... But now in Christ Jesus you who once were far away have been brought near.

When a non-Christian is desperate and scared, how does Jesus get their attention, to bring them near? Here's one imaginative way.

Someone I know has cancer. I've been praying for her, and we've had some chats about life and death. She is not a reader, so I borrowed some tapes of an excellent vicar friend of mine, who has a gift for evangelistic preaching. But how to give them to her without seeming pushy?

Yesterday the tapes arrived and, like everything else in this house, landed on the kitchen table to be dealt with 'later'. Two hours later, this person was suddenly knocking at the back door, hoping for a coffee. Her visit was out of the blue—I hadn't even seen her for nearly two weeks. She marched in. 'I've been feeling so down that I decided to visit a hypnotist,' she announced. My heart sank. 'We had one session, and he gave me a tape. He told me to buy a Walkman, so that I could listen to the tape each day with maximum concentration.' My heart sank even further.

'So I bought the Walkman, bought the tape, brought them home... and now Joanna [her daughter] has accidentally recorded Spice Girls over it! So now I've got a Walkman and no tapes!' She looked tired and frustrated.

I gulped, and stammered: 'Well, ah, that's OK, because as it happens, ah, I've got some great tapes right here, somewhere on this kitchen table... They arrived from a vicar friend of mine only two hours ago.'

'Oh, great! Can I borrow them? Vic's snoring drives me crazy—I was going to use my hypnosis tape in bed each night to give me peace to think. I'll use these instead.'

Hypnosis tape out, Christian tapes in! Great timing. Heavenly timing?

Lord, use me today to help someone find you.

✣

EPHESIANS 2:14–18 (NIV)

Bridge over troubled waters

For he himself is our peace... His purpose was... making peace... He came and preached peace.

'Peace' sounds so soothing—but is so costly to achieve!

Many years ago, a missionary was working in the wilds of Papua New Guinea. There was fighting between two local tribes that had gone on for several generations. It had begun with the murder of one of the tribesmen, and continued in tit-for-tat revenge attacks that meant the deaths of dozens of people.

The missionary worked with the tribes for years, and kept urging them to stop the killing. Gradually one tribe softened towards Christianity, until one day they told him that they were preparing to put aside their tribal gods and become Christians.

'And the killings?'

'Only one more,' they said.

He pleaded, but they were adamant: one more must die.

And so late that night a small party of the tribesmen set out for the bush, to a place where they knew some of the enemy tribesmen would be. Sure enough, as they crept along, they came upon a man on his own. They grabbed him and knifed him to death. In the morning they found out who it was. It was the missionary. Knowing where they would go, he had made sure they found him first, and not a victim from the other tribe. The tribesmen were so shocked that they laid down their arms and converted that day to Christianity. The fighting was over for good.

Jesus said, 'Blessed are the peacemakers.' Can you bring peace in your community? A friend had two neighbours bickering over one rabbit cage, of all things. So she spent hours chasing another rabbit cage, and drove miles to collect it. Then the neighbours—and presumably bunnies—were happy, and peace reigned!

It won't be easy: peacemaking can try your patience and take an inordinate amount of time—and being a bridge means you get walked on. But you will be 'blessed'.

'Make me a channel of thy peace.'
FRANCIS OF ASSISI

✣

EPHESIANS 2:20–22 (NIV)

Building site

Built on the foundations of the apostles... with Christ Jesus himself as the chief cornerstone. In him the whole building... rises to become a holy temple in the Lord.

Temples were widespread in the ancient world. People built them to honour various gods, and hopefully attract their favour.

But Paul is talking about something radically new. First, he said, we believers are not building anything. God is our gracious master builder. And we are not even abject servants, trying to win favour. Instead, we have been made members of God's household. This was unheard of! A god who called you a member of his household?! Lots of people today get into one of two muddles. Like the ancient pagans, they hope by good behaviour to attract God's approval. They feel like servants, not family. Or else they get busy building temples to their own personal gods—houses, careers, cars, whatever.

Secondly, of course, the temple Paul describes is not of stone. (Curiously, nowhere in the New Testament is there even a mention of building churches. Curious, because when you think of all the money, time and effort that have been spent on churches over the centuries, you'd be forgiven for thinking that building them was commandment number one!) No. We may love our church buildings, but when we go we take God with us—we don't meet him there—for God indwells us. We are called to be part of God's living temple. Our foundations are the apostles and prophets. I thought of that verse when I visited Liverpool Cathedral, one of the five largest cathedrals in the world. Its foundations are vast, stupendous. Beside them, you feel totally insignificant. But then I thought, even such gargantuan foundations are incomplete on their own. To be truly complete, a building needs other things as well—even humble doorknobs!

You are part of God's heavenly building. What role has he called you to fulfil? It will bring glory to God, and support to fellow Christians.

Read Revelation 21.

✣

EPHESIANS 3:1–13 (NIV)

Better by letter

This grace was given me: to preach to the Gentiles the unsearchable riches of Christ.

Read this entire passage and imagine the gruesome context in which it was written. Paul is glowing with the incredible honour of being used by God to bring Christ to the Gentiles. More than even most Bible characters, Paul has a profound sense of divine call about his life—as having a very specific job.

It's a sublime subject—and all the more staggering when you think that Paul wrote it in chains in a Roman prison (see Ephesians 6:20). Poor lighting, poor bedding, no sanitation, appalling food, fleas, rats… you name it.

The Roman soldiers thought they'd seen it all before. Prisons were full of lunatics with bizarre notions. 'Paul,' they'd say, 'you are the craziest we've heard yet! You think the great Almighty is using you to bring eternal salvation to the Gentiles—that's only everyone on earth who isn't Jewish. Forget it! You're in chains. You can't even get out of this prison cell!'

But Paul had eyes of faith that helped him see far beyond the confines of his cell. God had called him, and he would provide the way. You never see Paul in a lather about being confined—you never hear him saying, 'If only I could get out, I would fulfil my calling.' His whole being had said 'yes' to God, and he was conscious of fulfilling his calling every day—as in fact, of course, he was. He could not visit his young churches, so he wrote to them. Day after day, his scribe scratched away on a parchment. The soldiers would have shrugged. The little man was powerless. Over the centuries those letters from prison have reached hundreds of millions of Gentiles.

Perhaps there's a lesson here for us. We need not fret about circumstances beyond our control. All it takes for us to do God's will is our willingness to do it. He will provide a way.

Read Proverbs 3:5–6.

✣

EPHESIANS 3:14–21 (NIV)

What is the 'real you' really like?

I pray that out of his glorious riches he may strengthen you with power through his Spirit in your inner being.

You inner being is the real you. It is that 'private part of life where we know ourselves best of all: this is where self-esteem is forged, where basic decisions about motives, values and commitments are made, where we commune with our God'. Thus writes Gordon MacDonald in his excellent little book, Ordering Your Private World (Highland, p. 8).

We all have a private world, and its well-being is vital to the smooth running of the rest of our lives. MacDonald compares it to the bridge, or control deck of a submarine. Waves may crash all over us, but if, down deep below the surface in our very selves, we are in control of our destiny, then we can ride out the roughest storm.

People's inner lives sometimes cave in. We call the sad results burn-out or breakdown. Human beings disintegrate before our eyes because they lack the interior resources needed to support them in the face of pressure in the outer world.

One Gospel story tells of the disciples caught in a raging storm on the sea, and crying out to Jesus in despair. After he had calmed the storm, he put his finger on the main interior resource that we need: 'Where is your faith?'

We each of us have a choice: are we going to nurture and build up our inner selves? If we do, before God, our inner selves will then influence and direct our outer world. Or are we going to neglect our private world? If we do that, then inevitably we will allow the outer world around us to shape us.

It is a choice we need to make every day of our lives. Paul urged the Romans (12:2), 'Do not conform any longer to the pattern of this world, but be transformed by the renewing of your mind.'

'Watch over your heart with all diligence, for from it flow the springs of life' (Proverbs 4:23).

BLASTS FROM THE PAST

EPHESIANS 4:22–24 (NIV)

Blast from the past!

You were taught, with regard to your former way of life, to put off your old self, which is being corrupted by its deceitful desires; to be made new in the attitude of your minds; and to put on the new self, created to be like God in true righteousness and holiness.

A few months ago, pain, like someone stabbing me in the ribs, kept me awake for three nights. Thinking I'd trapped a nerve in my spine, I went to see a physiotherapist. Puzzled at first, because I could move without trouble, eventually she spotted two tiny marks on my back. 'Do you know, I think you've got shingles!' she said.

Next stop the doctor, who explained that once you've had chickenpox the virus lurks in your body until something—stress, trauma, illness or cause(s) unknown—triggers it to attack a nerve. The pain can last for months or even years. Charming!

I remember having chickenpox. I was six. How weird for the virus to resurface all these years later and bring my life to a complete standstill! Yet can't other things, long dormant and apparently forgotten, trigger violent pain or emotional paralysis? Why else can an innocuous remark make me feel utterly inadequate or rejected? Tongue-tied, I spill things and trip over... anything. No longer a reasonably together middle-aged woman, suddenly I'm a mixed-up teenager again, unsure of who I am or whether I have a right to exist! Other times I'll lose my temper over the silliest details, and only later realize that I've suppressed my anger about something else that disturbs me so much I won't even look at it.

A drug stopped my shingles getting worse, but the virus remains in my body and could resurface any time. The verses above, though, suggest that God wants our co-operation as he deals more effectively with some of the emotional 'blasts from the past' that strike us all sometimes. Let's look at this together over the next few days.

Read Colossians 3.

PROVERBS 17:22 (NIV)

A crushed spirit

A cheerful heart is good medicine, but a crushed spirit dries up the bones.

We all know people so crushed that they seem shrunken in body as well as spirit. Since childhood they've been told they're no good so often that they walk the opposite of tall. That's a terrible thing. Proverbs 18:14 says, 'A man's spirit sustains him in sickness, but a crushed spirit who can bear?'

None of us can go through life without being crushed a little, whether by teachers or peers at school, parents or bosses... or even people at church! Does this proverb imply that we can reverse the effects of crushing simply by cultivating a cheerful heart, looking on the bright side and smiling when we don't feel like it? Sometimes we can short-circuit negative spirals like that, but we don't want to live in unreality—we need some reason for a cheerful heart.

It's the truth that sets us free. Never mind for a minute what others say; what is God's truth about us? He values us so much that he bought us with the dearest price. Yes, he knows about the dark, sinful side of us, the side that deserves not only crushing but obliteration—but he sent Jesus to 'be crushed for our iniquities; the punishment that brought us peace was upon him' (Isaiah 53:5).

Encouragement from others works wonders too, building us up, literally giving us courage to do things. A friend was asked to sing a simple solo during communion at a conference and many people told her afterwards how it had moved them. We found out that this was the first time she had sung in public since a church leader had made a crushing remark about her voice, but the spontaneous encouragement enabled her to continue sharing her very real gift to worship God... and to encourage others.

Proverbs 15:30 says, 'A cheerful look brings joy to the heart, and good news gives health to the bones.' Read 2 Corinthians 4:6–8 and think about what the good news might be!

✣

PROVERBS 3:5–8 (NIV)

Out of control!

Trust in the Lord with all your heart and lean not on your own understanding; in all your ways acknowledge him, and he will make your paths straight. Do not be wise in your own eyes; fear the Lord and shun evil. This will bring health to your body and nourishment to your bones.

I had a secure childhood and a mother with eyes in the back of her head, as they say. Even so, as a toddler I turned round in a shop once… and she wasn't there. My safe world had collapsed; my panic-stricken yells brought concerned adults running. Are incidents like this at the root of our strong reactions today when we feel out of control?

When my baby wouldn't stop crying and I had no idea what was wrong, when my husband's kidney stone was causing him unbearable agony and I couldn't help, when I was supposed to collect someone else's child from school and couldn't find her, when my teenage son puts himself in situations I know are far from healthy, when I feel manipulated, when I've upset someone who won't say why—in all these situations my reaction to feeling out of control can be primitive and inappropriate in its strength. With anxious thoughts churning, my head starts to ache. I may yell at the kids, the shop assistant or the rabbit—whichever happens to be around!

The Bible passage above means a lot to me because I need its truth to penetrate through the layers to the half-understood, frightened child inside. When the news reveals that whole swathes of humanity could be wiped out by weapons of mass destruction, all of us must know that we aren't in control and never have been. We have to believe that, ultimately, God is in control. That feels scary too, but all (!) he asks is for us to fear him, shun evil and trust that he will make our paths straight.

Help us to trust you, Lord!

✣

HEBREWS 12:15; PROVERBS 14:30 (NIV)

Bitterness and envy

See to it that no one misses the grace of God and that no bitter root grows up to cause trouble and defile many.

A heart at peace gives life to the body, but envy rots the bones.

We describe a bitter person as having a 'sour face' or a 'chip on her shoulder'—very physical terms. Cultivating bitterness or envy damages not only our minds and spirits but also our bodies, as do so many of these 'blasts from the past', according to Proverbs. They damage other people too. They can wreck churches—and the credibility of the gospel itself.

Right now I look at some of the young people in our church who are sold out for God. I'm ashamed to say, I have to work really hard at rejoicing for them and blessing them. That's because my own son is thoroughly rebellious at the moment—and it hurts. Envy nudges me down the 'Why me, what did I do wrong?' road—to rail at God and resent others' rightness. If I take that road, it will be disastrous.

This morning, something reminded me of a couple who hurt me over 20 years ago and I had to think, 'For goodness' sake, I've forgiven them, haven't I? I need to let this go, these thoughts aren't helpful!'

It's so easy to let tiny, unguarded thoughts grow until, like bindweed in the garden, their tangled roots and shoots invade everywhere. But the scripture talks about not missing the grace of God and, thankfully, there are other roots. Revelation 5:5 says, 'The Root of David has triumphed.' God has put good roots in all of our lives—his powerful word and Spirit. People have prayed for us, planted good teaching, good example; they have loved us and sacrificed themselves for us. So which am I going to choose to think about and to cultivate today? Bitterness and envy, or love and grace?

I can so easily fall away from your grace, Lord. Enfold me again!

✣

2 CORINTHIANS 7:10 (NIV)

Regret

Godly sorrow brings repentance that leads to salvation and leaves no regret, but worldly sorrow brings death.

Regret for things that we have done wrong, or for good things that we have failed to do, can leave us feeling that 'there is no health in us'. But sin's not a problem to God. As Paul says, repentance, a true turning around, will bring salvation—and that's really good news. We don't need to wallow in guilt for past selfishness or wrongdoing if we allow God to remove our sin as far as the east is from the west and to show us how to bring good where once we brought wrong.

But there are other kinds of regret. Someone I knew felt she was being groomed to become head girl of her school, but somehow it never happened. It still affects her confidence even today—it stops her taking other opportunities. We can become paralysed with regret—regret that we've not married or had children; regret that we didn't have the education that we longed for; regret for opportunities missed, poor health, a lost childhood; regret that we had no opportunity to say goodbye to someone we loved. It can destroy us.

Fixing our sorrowful eyes on the past and indulging in 'poor me' syndrome helps no one, yet many things we regret do genuinely hurt us and they wouldn't have happened if the world had remained as good as God intended. What of him? Does he regret making humans, who wreak so much havoc? No—he makes new beginnings, new opportunities, new plans, new patterns.

'So I say, "My splendour is gone and all that I had hoped from the Lord." I remember my affliction and my wandering, the bitterness and the gall. I well remember them, and my soul is downcast within me. Yet this I call to mind and therefore I have hope: because of the Lord's great love we are not consumed, for his compassions never fail. They

are new every morning; great is your faithfulness' (Lamentations 3:18–23).

✣

PSALM 27:9–10 (NIV)

Rejection

Do not hide your face from me, do not turn your servant away in anger; you have been my helper. Do not reject me or forsake me, O God my Saviour. Though my father and mother forsake me, the Lord will receive me.

Rejection's another thing that, just when we think we've dealt with it, can sneak up and beat us to the ground. For those whose father, mother or spouse has forsaken them, their struggle is all the harder, but all of us know what it is to feel rejected to some degree. We were the last picked for a team, we weren't chosen at an interview, we've been left out of a group of friends, the person we poured out our hearts to suddenly has better things to do.

As our self-esteem takes a nose-dive, many of us go into hedgehog mode, rolling in on ourselves in self-protection, prickling at anyone who tries to come near. Though some daft misunderstanding triggered this, suddenly every rejection we've ever felt thumps us between the eyes. It's obvious that nobody likes us, everybody hates us—we might as well eat worms!

And why should God be the exception? Well, because scripture makes it very clear that he is! Jesus understands rejection and betrayal. He suffered it so that, instead of being cut off from him, we can stay in close relationship. Doesn't that restore our self-esteem? He's always loved us. He always will. We can turn our backs on him but he will never turn his back on us. And the challenging thing is, he even loves the people who have rejected us—and wants us to love them too.

These 'blasts from the past' can make me so childish, Lord, so touchy and insecure, so far from your kind of love which believes all things, hopes all things, endures all things. Instead of my selfish desire for affirmation, help me to choose to be filled with more of your love and compassion. Amen

✣

HEBREWS 12:1–2 (NIV)

Taking off and putting on

Let us throw off everything that hinders and the sin that so easily entangles, and let us run with perseverance the race marked out for us. Let us fix our eyes on Jesus, the author and perfecter of our faith.

'Everything that hinders' or weighs us down can include blasts from the past. If we're supposed to be athletes running the race with our eyes fixed on Jesus, the last thing we need is to be carrying baggage from the past—hidden emotional 'viruses' that can suddenly trigger to bring us down.

Depending on our own area of weakness, blasts from the past can heighten anger, lust, gluttony—all the seven deadly sins and more! You may have looked at Colossians 3 a few days ago. In verses 8, 12 and 13, Paul writes of taking off one set of clothes and putting on another: 'Rid yourselves of all such things as these: anger, rage, malice, slander and filthy language from your lips... As God's chosen people, holy and dearly loved, clothe yourselves with compassion, kindness, humility, gentleness and patience. Bear with each other, and forgive.'

As we get dressed every day it might be helpful to think quite consciously about what things (other than clothes) we are putting on and, in the heat of the day, what things we need to take off!

Coming before God as his 'chosen person, holy and dearly loved', you might like to ask him about things from the past that you know bring you down from time to time, whether they are sins or weights. Ask him for the courage to face them—and for his way forward. Remember that although medical science can't remove the physical virus from our bodies once we've had chickenpox, God can turn around some of the damage done in our past. Jesus is the 'author and perfecter of our faith'. He started us on this adventure and, as we co-operate with him, he will see that we finish!

BELIEF AND VALUES

PSALM 119:27–40 (NIV)

Beyond belief

Let me understand the teaching of your precepts; then I will meditate on your wonders... I have chosen the way of truth; I have set my heart on your laws... I run in the path of your commands, for you have set my heart free... Turn my heart towards your statutes and not towards selfish gain. Turn my eyes away from worthless things; preserve my life according to your word.

Almost all people believe in a God of some shape or form—but few allow that belief to influence how they feel, think, make decisions and act. Once we put our trust in Jesus, we start to discover what lies beyond belief—that living faith can radically change our whole existence. We find out what matters to God; how he plans to work uniquely in each of us—and through us—to redeem this suffering, sinful world. Our goal is to be like Jesus Christ who spent his whole life for others, even to the point of dying for our sins, always completely obeying his Father.

These verses (do read the whole passage in your Bible) make it clear that spiritual growth is not automatic or easy—it is the believer's choice to pursue the new life God has bestowed. He has given his word, revealed creation's wonders and set our hearts free, but it is up to us to 'work out our salvation with fear and trembling' with the Holy Spirit there to help us.

For the next week we will explore how what we believe can transform the way we are, how our faith can change the values by which we live and be reflected in our relationships. However long we have known the Lord, whether it is days or decades, we can ask him to move us forward.

Father, let the vibrancy of your life course through every part of my life. May belief develop into faith and faith produce perseverance to change us from one degree into another into the likeness of our Lord Jesus Christ. Amen

✣

HEBREWS 11:1, 6 (NIV)

From belief to faith

Now faith is being sure of what we hope for and certain of what we do not see... And without faith it is impossible to please God, because anyone who comes to him must believe that he exists and that he rewards those who earnestly seek him.

Just before my conversion I described my misgivings about becoming a Christian like this: 'I look at Christians and imagine they are sitting around a table laden with delicious food. "Come and join us!" they cry. "All you need to do is take a seat beside us to become one of the family." But although it is fine for them, I fear that if I try to sit, the chair will collapse under me, so I hesitate to accept Christ.'

Someone once defined faith as 'a decision to trust God'. Finally somebody took time with me to explain the gospel clearly and at an evangelistic service I was faced with the choice of either believing or rejecting his promise of forgiveness and new life. I had to take the proverbial 'leap of faith', hoping he would catch me. He did then, and has ever since, whenever my faith has been tested.

That evening I walked to the front of the church, prayed the sinner's prayer with the pastor, listened to his counsel but left disappointed—I felt no different. Had it worked or was there no 'chair' for me? It was later, sitting with my Christian friends at supper, that I knew something monumental had happened and I had been brought across from a place of non-belonging to sit at the table, part of his family. Allowing shaky belief to progress to this saving faith—even my mustard-seed speck of it—meant the yawning gap that had always separated me from God was bridged, by a wooden cross.

'Glory be to you, Jesus, who made his cross a bridge over death, that souls may pass over it from the dwelling of the dead to the dwelling of life!'

EPHREM THE SYRIAN (EARLY FOURTH CENTURY)

2 TIMOTHY 3:15–16 (NIV)

Illuminated manuscripts

You have known the holy Scriptures, which are able to make you wise for salvation through faith in Christ Jesus. All Scripture is God-breathed and is useful for teaching, rebuking, correcting and training in righteousness, so that God's servant may be thoroughly equipped for every good work.

A thousand years ago Bibles were only found in monasteries. Monks spent years painstakingly manufacturing elaborately decorated Bibles and Gospel books. Although today these treasures, no longer of any practical help, are displayed in museums and cathedrals, then they were used for the everyday worship and study of Christian believers, revered and valued as the living word of God. One Celtic psalm book was the 'Cathach of St Columba'. Cathach means 'fighter' and the book was carried into battle as a talisman—an interesting instance of using the 'sword of the Spirit which is the word of God' in spiritual warfare!

It is amazing how God's word has come safely down the generations to us. Through the oral traditions of the Jews, scrolls unearthed by archaeologists, handwritten copies by medieval monks, translated into English only in 1526, revised by succeeding generations... until today's scores of versions in thousands of languages, available on paper, cassette and even the Internet. The Bible possesses the same potency and truth today as when its 66 books were first written by the Holy Spirit's inspiration.

The Bible shows us what God is like. It reveals his dealings with us, his perfect will for the human race. Only God's word has power to change individual lives, put flesh on the bones of belief and breathe life and action into our faith.

The well-worn Bibles you and I read every day can never compare with the beautiful medieval gold-leafed vellum pages produced by those venerable monks—but when it comes to enlightening our minds they are equally 'illuminated manuscripts'.

Lord, thank you for the Bible, brought to us through the centuries, as vital now as it has always been. Amen

HEBREWS 4:12 (AMPLIFIED BIBLE)

Sword of truth

For the Word that God speaks is alive and full of power—making it active, operative, energizing and effective; it is sharper than any two-edged sword, penetrating to the dividing line of the breath of

life (soul) and the immortal spirit, and of joints and marrow, of the deepest parts of our nature, exposing and sifting and analysing and judging the very thoughts and purposes of the heart.

Anyone who ever watches hospital drama on TV is familiar with the image of the surgeon in theatre, gowned and masked in that green crinkly cotton, wearing rubber gloves and strange-looking spectacles. Surrounded by colleagues, he or she periodically issues terse instructions and carries out frighteningly complex procedures upon the flesh of the patient. At some point they always say 'Scalpel!' and the cameras home in on the heavily mascaraed eyes of the attractive nurse passing over this lethal-looking, life-saving knife.

Today's passage describes how the Master Physician uses the incisive words of scripture to penetrate the deepest, most hidden parts of our being. A human surgeon's skill is amazing—the ability to transplant organs, sever and reattach arteries and cut away diseased tissue saves lives. But Jesus operates on the invisible parts of us, our souls and spirits, exposing and sifting the thoughts and attitudes we hide from others and even ourselves.

Our understanding of the human brain is still minimal. Psychologists still tussle with conflicting theories about personality and how the mind words. But God understands entirely who we are and, with his word, cuts through the confusion to the nub of the situation, usually with mind-blowing simplicity. The Bible may be regarded by many as an irrelevant anachronism but those who allow it to dissect their inner life will discover its power to expose the good and the bad, the spiritual and the earthbound.

'Surely you desire truth in the inner parts; you teach me wisdom in the inmost place. Create in me a pure heart, O God, and renew a steadfast spirit within me' (Psalm 51:6, 10, NIV).

·:·

JOB 28 (NLT)

True wisdom

Do people know where to find wisdom? Where can they find understanding? For it is hidden from the eyes of all humanity... God surely knows where it can be found... he saw wisdom and measured it. He established it and examined it thoroughly. And this is what he says to all humanity: 'The fear of the Lord is true wisdom: to forsake evil is real understanding.'

This poetic passage describes how cleverly people subdue the earth, exploring beneath it and finding all manner of precious metals and stones. But despite all their efforts, the discovery of knowledge and wisdom—infinitely more valuable and so well hidden that no living creature can find them unaided—eludes them because of their refusal to come to God. Unbelief leads to foolishness and empty living.

Wisdom is knowing the best way to achieve desired results and is essential in every walk of life. The Bible talks about two kinds of wisdom—worldly wisdom, which rejects God's truth, sets itself up and is doomed to fail, and the wisdom rooted in reverence and faith in the Lord.

Psalm 19 says, 'God's laws... protect us, make us wise, and give us joy and light. They are pure, eternal, just... more desirable than gold... sweeter than honey. They warn us away from harm and give success to those who obey them' (LB). Putting aside our own opinions and learning to honour and obey God's directions will help us become wise, and this takes humility and faith.

The high point of God's wisdom is Jesus lifted up on the cross. Here worldly values are contradicted completely and his sacrificial love overcomes the power of sin, death and the devil. People may laugh at our Christian faith, calling it foolish, but wisdom founded on gospel truth will never fail us.

Heavenly Father, in whom is the fullness of light and wisdom, enlighten our minds by your Holy Spirit, and give us grace to receive your word with reverence and humility, without which no one can understand your truth. For Christ's sake. Amen

JOHN CALVIN (1509–64)

✣

EPHESIANS 5:1–21 (NIV)

Living as children of light

Live as children of light (for the fruit of the light consists in all goodness, righteousness and truth) and find out what pleases the Lord. Have nothing to do with the fruitless deeds of darkness, but rather expose them... It is light that makes everything visible... Be very careful, then, how you live—not as unwise but as wise, making the most of every opportunity.

There are many kinds of light—the diffused glow of moonlight reflected in water, the soft flicker of candles, the blandness of fluorescent tubes, coloured spots on a stage, the beaming lighthouse signals, probing lasers bringing healing, the glory of the sun, flashes of lightning... Each has its own characteristics and functions; there is infinite variety and nuance in the quality of light.

Light was created before anything else; God saw it was good and separated it from the darkness. Light always dispels darkness; the old proverb reminds us that not even the blackest night can extinguish one feeble flame. It always reveals what lies in the shadows.

So what does it mean for us, 'living as children of the light'? It comes back to where we began at the beginning of this week—how we can progress 'beyond belief' to develop a real relationship with Christ. As we allow the word of God to direct us and change us, we grow in wisdom, and day by day we can ask the Holy Spirit to dispel the darkness in our lives and shine through us. Sometimes it will be fitting to be a soothing candle, while in another situation a powerful searchlight will be more appropriate. As we become increasingly convinced of the truth, may we be compassionate and courageous to reach into the darkness to rescue those trapped within it. As we come humbly before the Lord, ready to hear and obey his voice, he will guide and direct us.

O Great Chief, light a candle within my heart, that I may see what is therein and sweep the rubbish from your dwelling place. Amen
PRAYER OF AN AFRICAN GIRL

✣

PSALM 111:3, 7–9 (NIV)

What a God we serve!

Glorious and majestic are his deeds, and his righteousness endures for ever... The works of his hands are faithful and just; all his precepts are trustworthy. They are steadfast for ever and ever, done in faithfulness and uprightness. He provided redemption for his people; he ordained his covenant for ever—holy and awesome is his name.

What we believe shapes our values and shows us how God wants us to live, and this psalm reminds us what God is like. Everyone has pictures of God lodged in their imagination; some have been there since childhood and are consequently rather quaint, others reflect personal experience—particularly of earthly fatherhood—or how we were taught about Jesus at school or in church. Let's face it, most of these images are incomplete and perhaps even misleading.

Another obstacle blocking us from a true vision of our heavenly Father is that the devil strives night and day to discredit him to the human race. Satan is God's implacable enemy and takes every opportunity to lie, insinuate and accuse, portraying our creator as an indifferent despot and the Lord Jesus Christ as a failure and a sham. How easily he seduces men and women to reject God and submit to false religion and empty philosophies instead of the Holy Spirit of truth and love.

To be frank, probably all of us have vestiges of this monstrous deception spoiling our vision of God. Perhaps this is a good opportunity to ask him to release us and forgive us for wrong thoughts. The words of today's psalm will correct our misconceptions. Just look at these descriptions! Faithful, just, trustworthy, steadfast, holy and awesome; our king, comforter, advocate and redeemer.

But to discover what God is really like, look at Jesus.

Loving Lord, as I meditate on your word, please reveal to me more of the wonderful truth of who you are and how you act. Then I will freely and joyfully praise and worship you, Father, Son and Holy Spirit. Amen

COLOSSIANS 1—2

COLOSSIANS 1:1–8 (NRSV)

Thankful prayers make thankful people

In our prayers for you we always thank God, the Father of our Lord Jesus Christ, for we have heard of your faith in Christ Jesus and of the love that you have for all the saints, because of the hope laid up for you in heaven.

When we first begin to pray, many of us fill most of our prayer time with 'asking prayers'. This is not necessarily a bad thing. It is good to bring these needs to God for his help. However, this is by no means all there is to prayer, as Paul shows here.

He says that when he prayed for the Colossian Christians he always thanked God for their good qualities. I find that word 'always' very challenging. It is all too easy to rush into asking God to do something about problems and difficulties, without thanking him for what he has done.

So why do it? Most importantly, because it is right and therefore pleases God. And it gives God some of the honour due to him.

Genuinely thanking God for someone's good qualities can also benefit them, as it means that, even if we see their faults, we value them. People are likely to sense that and be encouraged by it, especially if, like Paul, we can tell them about it. I wonder how the ordinary members of the Colossian church felt, on hearing that the great Paul always thanked God for them in his prayers.

Thanksgiving blesses us too, because it strengthens our faith. Acknowledging what God has actually done in people's lives nurtures our trust in him, like Abraham who 'grew strong in his faith as he gave glory to God' (Romans 4:20). And it helps to make us into more thankful people. Thankful people are more like Jesus and more of a credit to God. We shall probably also be more contented.

Lord, help me always to notice and thank you for the good in others, and please make me into a thankful person.

✣

COLOSSIANS 1:9–14 (NRSV)

Praying when there isn't a problem

We have not ceased praying for you and asking that you may be filled with the knowledge of God's will… lead lives worthy of the Lord, fully pleasing to him… bear fruit in every good work… grow in the knowledge of God… be made strong… be prepared to endure everything with patience… joyfully giving thanks to the Father.

Some people are almost impossible to buy presents for, aren't they? What do you buy for the man or woman who has everything? I have a similar question: 'What do you pray for the Christian who hasn't got a problem (as far as you know)?'

When people have a particular need or difficulty that you know of, it's relatively easy to know how to pray for them: you bring them and their need to God and ask him to help them and meet their need. It is good to ask the Spirit to help you pray too, and you may have a sense of some specific things to ask him for. But what do you pray for Christians when they haven't any special need, or when you don't know what their needs are? 'God bless So-and-so' will do, but sometimes we want to pray something fuller.

Well, if you look at today's passage it should give you plenty of ideas! What a list of things to pray for fellow Christians! The thrust of these requests is more than wanting to make life easier, or sort out people's immediate difficulties. It's about their growth into spiritual maturity and holiness. It's about them bringing honour and pleasure to God, fulfilling his will and purpose for them. It's about God's kingdom coming in their lives.

And how do you feel about the possibility of others praying these things for you? Are they things that you want too? If so, how about praying them for yourself, if you don't already?

Lord, help me to catch your big vision and teach me to pray accordingly.

COLOSSIANS 1:15–20 (NRSV)

Bright lights

He [Jesus] is the image of the invisible God... He himself is before all things, and in him all things hold together... he is the beginning, the firstborn from the dead, so that he might come to have first place in everything. For in him all the fullness of God was pleased to dwell, and through him God was pleased to reconcile to himself all things... making peace through the blood of his cross.

In 1999 we were in Devon during the solar eclipse. There were many warnings of the danger of looking directly at the sun and publicity about various ways of minimizing the risks. There were special sunglasses for sale and instructions for making a pinhole camera. We depend on the sun for our life and continuing existence, yet we cannot look at it without protection. We are weak and vulnerable to the power of its radiation. We cannot bear its full strength and glory. And if we tried to come close to it, we would burn up.

We cannot by ourselves come near God in his holiness and glory either, because we are sinful and cannot bear the full light of his presence. But Jesus is God, come to us in a way that we can bear to look at. He is 'the image of the invisible God'—God made visible to us. Through him God made it possible for us to come close so that we can relate to him directly without being shrivelled up by his glory.

Paul tries here to show us something of Jesus' own cosmic and eternal glory. Jesus is glorious both because of who he is and because of what he has done from creation onwards, but especially through the cross. Eventually in heaven he will have first place in everything, his glory seen fully and clearly. So let's keep looking at him, accustoming our eyes to his brightness.

Lord, as we recognize your glory increasingly, help us to give you the honour due to you.

✣

COLOSSIANS 1:21–24 (NRSV)

How can suffering ever be joyful?

I am now rejoicing in my sufferings for your sake, and in my flesh I am completing what is lacking in Christ's afflictions for the sake of his body, that is, the church.

This is a difficult verse! Paul is not saying that Jesus' suffering and death were in any way inadequate to deal with our sins. Nor is he saying that he has been seeking suffering, as if it were desirable for its own sake. That has cleared two potential theological difficulties out of the way!

But is it possible for anyone apart from a masochist to rejoice in sufferings? I suspect that anyone who has suffered injury through rescuing a person they loved from danger would give you a positive answer to that question. Or someone who has borne a burden for a friend. I like the story of the young African boy who was carrying another boy along the road. When asked if he minded carrying such a heavy burden, he replied, 'This is not a burden, it's my brother.'

Rejoicing in suffering doesn't mean no pain: suffering is by definition painful. It is about the inner attitude that delights to give, even until it hurts, for someone else's benefit. Paul says, 'I am rejoicing in my sufferings for your sake.' Bringing the gospel to people was costly for Paul, but the gain was worth the pain.

Paul was also suffering for Christ's sake. He counted it a privilege because he had a sense of suffering with Jesus, for the sake of his church, as well as for him. Jesus had warned his disciples that following him would be liable to bring suffering. There is a 'sharing in his sufferings' (Philippians 3:10) which, far from lessening our joy, may even increase it.

Lord Jesus, give me such love that I am able to give gladly even when it hurts. Thank you for the knowledge that when we are hurting, you are hurting too.

COLOSSIANS 1:25–29 (NRSV)

Christian maturity

This mystery, which is Christ in you, the hope of glory. It is he whom we proclaim, warning everyone and teaching everyone in all wisdom, so that we may present everyone mature in Christ. For this I toil and struggle with all the energy that he powerfully inspires within me.

I suppose none of us wants to remain immature in any area of life. So when we read the phrase 'mature in Christ', we see that as a desirable aim. And Paul, as a pastor, wants it for all those in his care. So he channels his energies in that direction.

Whom do you know who is a mature Christian? Take a moment to think about it. It is not necessarily the people who have been Christians the longest. What, then, is Christian maturity and how do people grow into it? I think there are two main aspects to this growth.

The first aspect is growing into a deeper knowledge and appreciation of God himself, which involves developing our relationship with him. This appreciation of God will show itself in gratitude and praise. It will also be seen in a steadiness of trust in God even in times of frustration, disappointment or suffering. For this we need to spend time with him in prayer. We also need teaching about God and, sometimes, help to discern what he is doing and saying in our lives, especially in times of difficulty. Paul spent a lot of time and energy doing this, teaching and proclaiming Christ.

The second aspect is becoming more like Christ. We need to learn what it means to be like Jesus and how to cooperate with the Holy Spirit in his work of making us like that. Here again, we need teaching, such as Paul gives, and plenty of practice!

If you know people who are already mature in Christ, why not ask them for tips? And try to encourage others in their growth too.

Lord, please help us all to grow up to be mature in Christ.

COLOSSIANS 2:8–15 (NRSV)

Turning point

When you were dead in trespasses... God made you alive together with him, when he forgave us all our trespasses, erasing the record... He set this aside, nailing it to the cross. He disarmed

the rulers and authorities and made a public example of them, triumphing over them in it.

There are moments in life that seem to change things decisively. For an individual with a serious illness, there can be a time, maybe a day, or even an hour, of such significance that we say they have turned the corner. They are not fully recovered, but we now have the confidence that they will do so. The illness has loosened its grip; they are beginning to win the battle.

Or in war time there can be a particular battle, or event, like the Normandy landings in World War II, that seems to change the whole course of the war. Such moments are turning points.

Christ's death on the cross was a turning point—in fact, the greatest turning point in the world's history, yet it is possible even for Christians to lose sight of it. Paul here addresses Christians who have been taken captive by clever ideas and merely human traditions. He calls them back to freedom. He reminds them of how God turned their own lives around through Christ: they were 'dead in trespasses' and he made them spiritually alive together with Christ, forgiving their sins. He reminds them, too, that on the cross Jesus won a decisive victory for the whole world over all the forces of evil—something that human traditions and philosophies can never do.

Paul exhorts them (and us) not to be deceived by any traditions, or groups, or so-called spiritualities that play down the unique significance of Christ and what he did on the cross. These will lead us away from the freedom God wants for us.

Father God, thank you for turning things round for me and for the whole world through Christ and his cross. Please keep me focused on him and walking in your way of freedom.

✣

COLOSSIANS 2:16–23 (NRSV)

No condemnation

Therefore do not let anyone condemn you in matters of food and drink… festivals… sabbaths… All these regulations refer to things that perish with use; they are simply human commands and teachings. These have indeed an appearance of wisdom in promoting self-imposed piety, humility, and severe treatment of the body, but they are of no value in checking self-indulgence.

Some years ago, the leader of my fellowship group suggested that on the day of our next meeting we should all fast before coming together to pray. I didn't dare to question this, for fear of sounding unspiritual. That was my mistake. When the day came, the fasting idea felt like a rule to be obeyed, rather than merely a suggestion (my second mistake). I did fast, but I felt resentful and angry. I also had such severe hunger pains that I couldn't really concentrate on the prayers! Later experiences of fasting, when I felt that God was calling me to do it, were much better.

Unfortunately, we all too easily distort good ideas, or even God's call, into rigid rules. He calls us to pray, to receive Communion and to meet for fellowship and encouragement. He hasn't said, 'You must have a quiet time every day'; 'You must go to Communion every week'; or 'You must go to a home group'—though these may be helpful guidelines.

We each need to hear what God's call is to us in our individual circumstances, but we also need to listen to the church's wisdom. Helpful guidelines come from people's experience down the years of trying to live as God wants. We can learn from them, but they aren't God's rules. A danger of living by rules is that those who manage to keep them become proud and condemning and the rest feel condemned as guilty failures.

Lord, help us all not to make rules where you have none, and not to be condemning of ourselves or other people.

COMMENDED BY JESUS

LUKE 21:1–4 (RSV)

Well done, giver

And he saw a poor widow put in two copper coins. And he said, 'Truly I tell you, this poor widow has put in more than all of them.'

Whatever else we want to hear when we come face to face with Jesus in heaven, I'm sure we all long to hear the words, 'Well done, good and faithful servant; you have been faithful over a little, I will set you over much; enter into the joy of your master' (Matthew 25:21).

In aspiring towards being included in the 'Jesus awards', it might help to have a look at the lives of those whom Jesus commended while he was on earth. Take, for instance, one poor old woman. By giving her widow's mite, small and seemingly insignificant as it was, she gave all that she had. God does not measure generosity by monetary value but by the degree of spiritual sacrifice and love entailed.

I once witnessed a small five-year-old letting go of her mum's hand in the street and running to a beggar lying on the ground. The child opened her tiny purse and upturned it. As the few coins fell into the man's begging-bowl, she shook the purse heartily to make sure none were lodged in the lining.

Her mum's irritated comment was, 'That's all you had. You needn't think you'll get any more pocket money this month!' The child pointed down to the old man and replied, 'That's all right, Mummy, God loves him.'

The child and the widow had something in common. When we learn to believe that God knows our every need and how to supply it, then we will trust him enough to empty our purses and our hearts into the lives of those who need his love.

Dear Lord, teach me to give—not just my finance but my time, energy and love, until the container that held it all is shaken empty. Then help me to trust your generosity to fill it according to my need. Amen

✣

MATTHEW 9:20–22 (RSV)

Well done, outcast believer

And behold, a woman who had suffered from a haemorrhage for twelve years came up behind him and touched the fringe of his garment; for she said to herself, 'If I only touch his garment, I shall be made well.' Jesus turned, and seeing her he said, 'Take heart, daughter; your faith has made you well.'

Against the law, this sick woman ventured outside her house when the religious people considered her 'unclean'. Against the law, she approached a holy teacher, a man, not merely to speak but to risk a touch. Believing that God cared enough for a woman (in that time and culture, a second-class citizen), 'unclean' according to religious tradition with the scourge of blood illness, she claimed a tactile healing from a sinless master.

In her audacity she risked more than not being healed: she risked the penalty of the Pharisees, the scorn of her family and friends, and, if God himself was insulted, perhaps his wrath also. But Jesus, himself an outsider, willingly allowed some of his power to flow from him. Jesus had enemies in the highest earthly places, not because he was a troublemaker but because his love and compassion superseded all other barriers. Can we stand 'outside' the popular camp for him?

First he calmed her fears: 'Take heart.' Then he said, 'Your faith has made you whole.' And in the case of another outsider, a Canaanite woman considered by some to be heathen and descended from the ancient enemies of Israel, Jesus once again commends her faith (Matthew 15:21–28) regardless of all other historical, cultural or traditional qualifications. Faith is rewarded.

Dear Master, help me never to be afraid to come close to your holy presence, despite my failings. Thank you for always making yourself accessible when I am afraid. Increase my faith. Please accept it as it stands—battered, stained or fractured—and please build it strong and ready for the task. One day, I pray, may it be enough for you to take pride even in me. Amen

✣

MARK 14:3–9 (RSV)

Well done for unconditional love

But Jesus said, 'Let her alone; why do you trouble her? She has done a beautiful thing to me.'

Jesus, who had already shown his concern for the poor by many words and deeds throughout his ministry, was not advocating irresponsible extravagance. His commendation of this girl was for her sincere devotion in doing all she could for him at a time when no one else on earth could help. One place where we should never hold back is in our exuberant, sacrificial and all-consuming love of the Master. To ration or restrict our devotion to him would make us mean and ungenerous towards a world which desperately needs God's love.

Mark places this incident just two days prior to the last Passover that Jesus would celebrate before his death. The chief priests and the scribes were already planning Jesus' downfall, and Judas finally made up his mind to betray him. At this crucial time, when Jesus himself sensed the negative influences closing in around him, what joy and encouragement it must have brought him to experience in such a tangible manner how God had inspired this girl to minister to him in love.

Our heavenly Father will not leave us without comfort. I can testify to this through times of pain, suffering and, worst of all, persecution from those I trusted. It was often on the worst of days that the postman brought a card of appreciation from someone to whom I'd ministered; or when a phone call came, thanking me for my work; or when God allowed me to know of a life brought to Jesus, perhaps as much as a decade or more ago. God's timing is perfect.

We no longer have Jesus' physical presence with us but thousands of our fellow sufferers on earth desperately need his love. Jesus said, 'Truly, I say to you, as you did it to one of the least of these my brethren, you did it to me' (Matthew 25:40).

Dear Jesus, can I help you? Open my eyes and my hands to those whom I can love in your name. Amen

LUKE 7:1–10 (RSV)

Well done, humble leader

'Lord, do not trouble yourself, for I am not worthy to have you come under my roof...' When Jesus heard this he marvelled at him, and turned and said to the multitude that followed him, 'I tell you, not even in Israel have I found such faith.'

Jesus finds true humility and marvels at it. Who is he commending here? Yes, ladies—it's a man, and a man of authority, a centurion who admits himself that he can 'boss' many who are under his command (v. 8). He is an enemy of the Jews, an officer of the occupying army that has invaded and is dominating the land. Yet he has already shown great kindness to those under his authority (v. 5). He even treated his slaves decently (v. 2). This leader possessed all the prestige and authority necessary to march up to Jesus and order him to obey his wishes. Yet he did not. Instead he placed himself lower than an itinerant teacher, a mere carpenter's son from Galilee (an area despised by the Roman rulers for its troublemakers and rebels against the state).

We cannot imagine the degree of jeopardy into which this high soldier placed his army commission, his family, perhaps even his life, to seek help from Jesus—and for what? A cherished wife, a beloved child, his own mother? No, a slave, officially a non-person whose life was legally the centurion's property, to save or to take at a whim. No wonder Jesus said he had not found such faith in Israel. Such humility in faith was quickly rewarded and the servant was made well. I wonder how many times, in how many ways, our pride becomes the greatest barrier to our healing?

Master, have I truly made you Lord, or am I still claiming 'authority' over my life? Take your rightful place as Lord of my world. May I repent without fear or pride. Help me learn true humility in thought, word and action. Help me to stoop to conquer in your name. Amen.

✣

JOHN 20:24–29 (RSV)

Well done to the 21st century

Jesus said to him, 'Have you believed because you have seen me? Blessed are those who have not seen and yet believe.'

We began the week with aspirations to be on the Lord's shortlist for commendation one day. As followers of Jesus, we know that the journey through life is a constant battle and the struggle to know and obey God's will is a daily, continuous task of faith and effort. Isn't it encouraging, then, to know that the disciples (in this case Thomas), although they had physical proof of the miracles of Jesus and his resurrection, were sometimes no better off when it came to 'marks out of ten' for belief than a 21st-century inhabitant of this planet?

They too suffered doubts and fear, weakness and testing, failures and success of spirit and faith. Jesus understood the doubts of Thomas as he understands our inadequacies today. When Thomas repented, Jesus forgave him, not only because the road to discipleship is not a competitive game where marks out of ten should be sought, but because God knows that, in this regard, human beings could never get 'full marks' no matter how hard we try. That's why Jesus came.

Without his sacrifice on the cross and without his strength offered to us now in our weakness, we would not stand a chance. But it's great to have that little advance reference to encourage us, because when Jesus commends those who believe without having seen, he is speaking of the future generations, including those of us today who believe and follow where he leads.

Dear Lord, thank you for encouraging me. When the marks are handed out at Judgment Day, who knows where I'll be in the queue? But I know I should not be looking for accolades, only love—your unconditional love offered freely to a sinner like me. Help me to build on the clues from those whom you commended in scripture, to grow more like the person you wish me to be by the power of your grace. Amen

THE COMMUNITY OF THE CHURCH

GENESIS 2:7, 18, 21–25 (NRSV)

Not alone

The Lord God said, 'It is not good that the man should be alone.'

Samuel, a former elder of our church, has recently returned to his home country of Tanzania to make contact with a group of five hundred Tanzanian Christians who have come together in the village where Samuel's family originated, with the desire of starting a church. Samuel hopes to minister to this community of believers.

For the next few days, we are going to look at the local church as a community—a concept that perhaps many Christians and many churches have lost sight of in our day and age, and possibly more particularly in our Western culture. We tend to be so very individualistic. Many people choose to live alone. Others have no choice in the matter and are just plain lonely.

However, that is not how God intended it to be. Having created man in his own image, God said it was not 'good' that he should be alone, so he created another human being—woman—to come to his rescue, to be one with him. This is the beginning of community, of togetherness, which reflects the oneness clearly existing already from all time within the three persons of the Trinity. 'Community is deeply grounded in the nature of God... Therefore the making of community may not be regarded as an optional decision for Christians' (Gilbert Bilezikian, Community 101).

We shall learn, through the passages of scripture we shall be studying together, God's purpose for the local church and how we can live out more fully in practice this fundamental teaching about community, explained and illustrated in a variety of ways in the Bible.

Lord, open our eyes as we look into your word. Help us to grasp and understand your teaching about the church. Show us the importance of being part of a body of believers, and reveal to us the part you want us to play within the church where you have placed us.

1 CORINTHIANS 1:4–9 (NRSV)

Amazing grace

I give thanks to my God always for you because of the grace of God that has been given you in Christ Jesus.

In October 2000 our church embarked upon a study of 1 Corinthians. Twice a year, we are accustomed to do what we call an 'integrated Bible study'. During however many weeks the study lasts, personal study, group study and Sunday sermons all centre on the same topic or passage of scripture. Our fellowship Bible study groups are good ways to encourage the sense of community, as people get to know one another more easily in a small group and generally feel comfortable sharing.

1 Corinthians was rather a daunting study to begin, because of the many problems reflected in the church in Corinth, which the apostle Paul deals with in this letter. It struck me, in the light of all these difficulties, that the opening words of the apostle Paul are most encouraging. In spite of their imperfections, these Christians formed the body of Christ; they had been set apart for God; they were beneficiaries of his grace, and lacked no spiritual gift. And what's more, they would be 'blameless on the day of our Lord Jesus Christ' (v. 8). We wonder how that could be when we read of divisions within the church, of immorality, of lawsuits among the members, and many other problems. It is certainly not through their own efforts that they would become blameless. It is due to God's grace and faithfulness. 'God is faithful; by him you were called into the fellowship of his Son, Jesus Christ our Lord' (v. 9). God called them, and he will not abandon them. He will see them through to the end of time and for all eternity. When we look at our own churches, we see imperfections and problems; we see divisions and sin. But God is still faithful.

Lord, we praise you for your faithfulness, and for the work you are doing within us to make us like Jesus so that we might be blameless on that day.

1 CORINTHIANS 12:12–27 (NRSV)

Great is your faithfulness

You are the body of Christ and individually members of it.

'We are the body of Christ.' So sang a small group of members of our church in Geneva on the occasion of its 30th anniversary. For the 30 years of its existence, this church has grouped members of many different nationalities and cultures. Being an English-language congregation in a French-speaking city, the turnover tends to be fairly rapid, as people are relocated to jobs in Geneva for a relatively short time before moving on elsewhere. So it was particularly heart-warming to see the number of former members who came back for our special weekend of celebration and thanksgiving. They came from Korea, South Africa, Lebanon, USA, Holland, UK and other parts of Switzerland to celebrate God's faithfulness.

Jim and Charlene had not been back to Geneva since returning to the USA in the 1970s. Converted soon after their arrival at the church, through the quiet, consistent testimony of a fellow American, they have gone on to serve God in their own country. 'We can't even begin to tell you what this trip has meant to us,' they exclaimed, as they once again found themselves in Geneva, gathered with their brothers and sisters in Christ from around the world.

Florence too was back. Now 80 years old, she testified to the fact that 'in 1968 I was a jaded, worn-out person with a life that was a disaster, but because of people who became the nucleus of this church, and their loving-kindness and their caring' she and her children all became Christians.

As we concluded our service that Sunday by singing 'Great is thy faithfulness', I looked around the greatly increased congregation. As all these people from different periods of the church's history stood together to sing God's praises, once again I thought, 'What a foretaste of heaven!'

'The steadfast love of the Lord never ceases, his mercies never come to an end; they are new every morning; great is your faithfulness' (Lamentations 3:22–23).

✣

ROMANS 12:1–8 (NRSV)

Belonging

We, who are many, are one body in Christ, and individually we are members one of another.

Our church in Geneva tends to be a rather transient 'body', as members come and go. So, in order to encourage people to get involved in the church and to help them discern their gifts, a list of church activities and areas of service has been drawn up. Once a year, we are encouraged 'not to think of [ourselves] more highly than [we] ought to think, but to think with sober judgment, each according to the measure of faith that God has assigned' (v. 3) and to see where we can most effectively use our gifts in service through the church. The list is not exhaustive, leaving open the possibilities for new ministries to develop according to the gifts represented in the church at the time. 'Each of you should use whatever gift you have received to serve others' (1 Peter 4:10, NIV).

Here in our passage today, Paul uses the human body as an illustration of the church. This is true community—working together, serving together, suffering together, rejoicing together. 'Togetherness' was a characteristic of the early church right from the beginning. In Acts 2 we read, 'When the day of Pentecost came, they were all together in one place... All the believers were together and had everything in common... Every day they continued to meet together in the temple courts. They broke bread in their homes and ate together with glad and sincere hearts' (Acts 2:1, 44, 46, NIV).

God did not intend us to live in isolation. We are meant to be in relationship with one another. We are brothers and sisters in Christ, members of the same family, parts of the same body. We need to function as such.

'We must grow up in every way into him who is the head, into Christ, from whom the whole body, joined and knit together by every ligament

with which it is equipped, as each part is working properly, promotes the body's growth in building itself up in love' (Ephesians 4:15–16).

✣

ROMANS 12:9–15 (NRSV)

Rejoicing and weeping

Rejoice with those who rejoice, weep with those who weep.

Three of the phone calls I had today from members of our church stood out to me as significant for a number of reasons, and not least in relation to the theme of these notes, the church as community.

Nana, a Ghanaian member, phoned this morning, rejoicing and praising the Lord because she has successfully defended her thesis and is now 'by the grace of God, a qualified social worker'. Her thesis was exceptionally well received by the examiners, who praised her for her excellent work. Nana, who knew that the church had been praying, felt supported and upheld throughout the ordeal and phoned to share the good news and to thank us for our prayers. She remarked how precious it was to be part of the body of Christ.

In the evening, another member phoned to say that she has just been diagnosed with cancer, already in an advanced stage, which has metastasized into the brain. With no family of her own, she counts on the love and care and support of the church family.

The final phone call of the day was from Apollo, a Chinese Christian, to announce that his wife has just given birth to their second child. Their joy was increased by the fact that their baby boy was delivered by Annie, a Scottish midwife, also a member of our church, thus keeping it all in the family!

Yes, we are to 'rejoice with those who rejoice, and weep with those who weep' (v. 15). This is true 'body life'. 'If one member suffers, all suffer together with it; if one member is honoured, all rejoice together with it' (1 Corinthians 12:26). We rejoice with Nana and with Apollo and his family at their good news. We 'suffer' with

Esther and will continue to uphold her in prayer in the days to come, and seek to be a comfort and an encouragement to her.

'Bear one another's burdens, and in this way you will fulfil the law of Christ' (Galatians 6:2).

✣

ROMANS 12:16–21 (NRSV)

Harmony

Live in harmony with one another.

If the apostle Paul thought it necessary to exhort the members of the church in Rome to 'live in harmony with one another', it was obviously for a reason. Human nature being what it is, harmonious relationships have to be worked at; they don't just happen. The remainder of this verse suggests that some of the people in that church considered themselves superior to others: they were too 'haughty' to associate with the more 'lowly' members. To the Philippian believers Paul writes, 'In humility regard others as better than yourselves' (Philippians 2:3) and he encourages them to be like Jesus, 'who, though he was in the form of God… emptied himself, taking the form of a slave, being born in human likeness. And… he humbled himself and became obedient to the point of death—even death on a cross' (Philippians 2:6–8). Paul mentions by name two women in that church who were having trouble agreeing. 'I urge Euodia and Syntyche,' he writes, 'to be of the same mind in the Lord' (Philippians 4:2).

It is very easy to focus on causes of irritation and annoyance rather than on the Lord. A church such as ours, with members from all over the world, representing widely varying cultures and customs, is asking for trouble! In practice, however, what could have been divisive has in fact been tremendously enriching—which is not to say that we never have any problems and misunderstandings.

Sushila, a former member, now back in India, wrote at the time of our 30th anniversary that it was here she had 'understood the real meaning of unity in diversity. People from all the four corners of the world and from all walks of life saw eye to eye because their gaze was fixed on Jesus, the author and finisher of our faith'. If only we could always keep our eyes fixed on him!

Lord, forgive our arrogance and pride. Help us truly to consider others as better than ourselves and to keep our eyes fixed on Jesus.

✣

MATTHEW 18:21–35 (NRSV)

Forgiveness

Then Peter came and said to him, 'Lord, if another member of the church sins against me, how often should I forgive? As many as seven times?' Jesus said to him, 'Not seven times, but, I tell you, seventy-seven times.'

How often do we hear on the news, or even in the street, and all around us, of conflict, hatred and a desire for revenge? If evil is done to you, then retaliate by giving as good as you get. Stand up for your rights. Your honour is at stake. We seem to have an acute sense of justice—especially when we are personally wronged—and we are quick to retaliate and condemn.

Nowhere, I think, is the Christian message so radically opposed to the way of 'the world' than in the area of forgiveness. 'See that none of you repays evil for evil, but always seek to do good to one another and to all,' writes the apostle Paul (1 Thessalonians 5:15). 'Love your enemies,' says Jesus (Matthew 5:44), and Paul adds, 'If your enemies are hungry, feed them; if they are thirsty, give them something to drink' (Romans 12:20).

In his reply to Peter, the Lord makes it clear that we must forgive not once, or twice, or even seven times, but repeatedly. It is only as we realize how much God has forgiven us that we in turn will be able to forgive others. It is a well-known fact that those who harbour a spirit of hatred and revenge in their heart are the ones who will suffer most as these negative emotions begin to fester. So, for our own good, as well as for harmony within the body, forgiveness is to be characteristic of the Christian.

Jesus teaches that the forgiveness we receive from God is conditional on the forgiveness we offer to others: 'For if you forgive others their trespasses, your heavenly Father will also forgive you; but if you do not forgive others, neither will your Father forgive your trespasses' (Matthew 6:14–15).

✣

1 PETER 2:4–8 (NRSV)

Living stones

Like living stones, let yourselves be built into a spiritual house.

Soon after the 30th anniversary celebrations of our church, my husband and I left for the USA to visit other former members in Minnesota, North and South Carolina, and Maryland, some of the 'living stones' who had gone to make up the building whose 'foundation is Jesus Christ' (1 Corinthians 3:11). We had been intrigued to learn, some months earlier, that business had drawn together Scott from North Carolina, and Charlie from South Carolina, and caused them to discover, with surprised delight, that they had both been a part of our church family in Geneva at different times of its history, about 20 years apart!

In Maryland, we enjoyed another happy time of reunion when our hosts invited other past members of our church family from the surrounding area, mainly Americans, but one British couple and a girl from Sierra Leone. Some of them already knew each other, as their time in Geneva had overlapped, but others met for the first time on that joyful occasion. Members of different churches now, we remain united by our common faith in Jesus Christ; all children of the same Father, with the same lifeblood coursing through our veins; all bound together with love; all committed to following Jesus.

The picture of the building is only one illustration used by Paul in chapter 3 of his first letter to the Corinthians, along with that of the field and that of the temple. Addressing this church, where there are divisions, immorality, and many other problems, he makes the following amazing statement: 'Do you not know that you are God's temple and that God's Spirit dwells in you?' (1 Corinthians 3:16). Imperfect as our churches may be, that is where God has chosen to dwell by his Spirit and that is where he is going to be manifest today.

'God's temple is holy, and you are that temple,' continues Paul at the end of 1 Corinthians 3:17. What, then, are the implications for us in terms of holy living?

✣

1 PETER 2:9–10 (NRSV)

God's people

You are a chosen race, a royal priesthood, a holy nation, God's own people.

Here we have four expressions illustrating the church as community: 'a chosen race, a royal priesthood, a holy nation, God's own people'. Modern usage of the word 'church' can often lead to misunderstanding. In many cases, it has come to refer to the building where Christians meet for worship, rather than to the people worshipping there. Hence we talk about 'going to church', when in actual fact, together as believers in Jesus Christ, we are the church. As 'priests' we are to 'offer spiritual sacrifices acceptable to God through Jesus Christ' (1 Peter 2:5) as we worship him and minister to one another. As God's people, we are to be holy in all our conduct (see 1 Peter 1:15–16).

Nancy, from Lebanon, writing after our anniversary weekend,

remarked that ours 'is a church that shouldn't work—with a changing congregation and people from different cultures, denominations, economic situations. How is it that they do so well at getting along?' She concluded that it is due to 'the honour given to the Lord'.

Douglas, another of our former members, stressed how important it is that people be made to feel welcome when they first come along to a service. This initial contact can often turn into an invitation to a meal and then perhaps to a Bible study group. This kind of sharing is unfortunately not characteristic of all the churches he has visited since leaving Switzerland. He pointed out that in many churches people are 'just attenders'. Writing to the Christians in Ephesus, Paul says, 'You are no longer strangers and aliens, but you are citizens with the saints and also members of the household of God' (Ephesians 2:19).

Let us determine, in so far as it depends on us, to be welcoming to newcomers to our church, so that they will quickly feel themselves to be 'members of the household of God' and no longer 'strangers and aliens'.

1 PETER 4:7–11 (NRSV)

Entertaining angels?

Be hospitable to one another without complaining.

Being in a multi-cultural church implies very often eating multi-cultural meals—Chinese, Indian, French, Ghanaian, Eritrean, Italian, and so on... even English!—an activity that most of us thoroughly enjoy. On a Sunday, after the service, when everyone is invited to partake, or in smaller groups in homes, or on the occasion of 'international evenings', there are many opportunities for extending hospitality. Church members often open their homes to offer accommodation to those passing through the Geneva area. Arising from this, some years ago we ran a column in our magazine entitled 'Feasting in fellowship', where members contributed recipes from their home country. These recipes were later compiled into our own church cookbook! The editor wrote in the foreword, 'The overall purpose of this book is to encourage you to show hospitality to one another.'

Having frequently benefited, particularly during my student days, from the hospitality of others (in fact, it was in the home of missionaries in France that I first met my husband), I realize what a good way this is to get alongside people and show love to them. At one stage of our ministry, our home was filled each week with unchurched, hungry French teenagers, who shared our meal before we opened up the word of God to them. Peter tells us to do this 'without complaining'. True, it can be hard work, but it is well worth it, so let us do it ungrudgingly. Surely part of living out the reality of the body of Christ is to invite members into our homes. Hospitality is a great way of deepening fellowship and contributing to the body life of the church. And, through offering hospitality to strangers, who knows but that you may have 'entertained angels without knowing it' (Hebrews 13:2)!

Thank you, Lord, for all those who have offered hospitality to us. Thank you too for the homes you have given us. Show us how best to use them for you.

JOHN 13:1–17 (NRSV)

Servants

'If I, your Lord and Teacher, have washed your feet, you also ought to wash one another's feet.'

Bill, a top executive and successful businessman, became part of our church. After a fellowship meal or other activity, whom would we see sweeping the hall or cleaning up? Yes, you've guessed—Bill. Because of his humility and consistency and because, as one person who was converted through Bill's testimony put it, 'he lived out Monday through Saturday what he was on Sunday', people were drawn to Jesus.

In our passage today, we have a supreme example of service and servanthood shown to the early disciples and to us by our 'Lord and Teacher', the Son of God himself. This humble act of service leaves no room for pride or hierarchy. Why didn't one of the disciples perform the traditional foot-washing? Probably because they all expected a servant to do it—which would have been customary. But no servant appeared. Even if it didn't occur to them to wash each other's feet, couldn't one of them at least have washed the feet of their Master? But no, it is the Master himself who gets up, takes off his outer garment, puts a towel round himself, fills a bowl with water and begins to wash and dry the feet of men who thought themselves above such a menial task. What an impact this visual aid must have had upon them! What an acted-out lesson in humility and servanthood! And, as if that weren't clear enough, just in case they haven't yet got the message, Jesus states explicitly, 'You ought to wash one another's feet. For I have set you an example, that you also should do as I have done to you' (vv. 14b–15).

Lord, forgive our selfishness and pride. Help us to follow your example to 'serve one another in love' (Galatians 5:13, NIV).

JOHN 15:9–17 (NRSV)

Love

'This is my commandment, that you love one another as I have loved you.'

Many years ago, in the early 1970s, the years during which our children were being born, we lived in an apartment block in France, near the Swiss border. People from the church would come across with meals, offers of help and gifts for the children. One of our neighbours had obviously noticed what was going on and, amazed, remarked to me on the love that was being shown by our Christian friends. Probably many of us have benefited from the love of our brothers and sisters in Christ in many practical ways—a meal in times of illness, transportation, baby-sitting... There are many ways of expressing love in action. Laura, one of our church members, some years ago had to go to the hospital every day for radiotherapy. We took it in turns to drive her there. One day the nurse remarked on all these different people who accompanied her. 'Oh, they are all my brothers and sisters!' said Laura.

'Love one another deeply from the heart,' writes the apostle Peter (1 Peter 1:22). Love should be such a striking characteristic of the church that Paul writes about it repeatedly in his letters; James exhorts his readers to show love in very practical ways; Peter picks up on the theme, and it is a recurring subject in John's letters. Add to that the very specific teaching by Jesus about love and we are obliged to acknowledge the importance of it.

In fact, our love for one another is proof of our love for the Lord. 'Just as I have loved you,' says Jesus, 'you also should love one another. By this everyone will know that you are my disciples, if you have love for one another' (John 13:34b–35). Writing to the Thessalonians, Paul acknowledges the fact that they love 'all the brothers and sisters throughout Macedonia', but he urges them 'to do so more and more'.

Let us love one another, more and more!

✣

ACTS 12:1–17 (NRSV)

The church at prayer

While Peter was kept in prison, the church prayed fervently to God for him.

We often think of prayer as a private, personal occupation. And so it must be, of course, but not exclusively so, and not always. We certainly need to spend time alone with God in prayer. However, as we have mentioned more than once already in these notes, the Christian life is not meant to be lived out in isolation, but in the fellowship of other believers. We have a special promise from Jesus concerning our meeting together to pray: 'If two of you agree on earth about anything you ask, it will be done for you by my Father in heaven. For where two or three are gathered in my name, I am there among them' (Matthew 18:19–20).

In our passage today we see a church at prayer. 'While Peter was kept in prison, the church prayed fervently for him' (v. 5). These prayers were effective, and God answered. 'The Lord has sent his angel and rescued me,' realized Peter, when he eventually 'came to himself' (v. 11). Immediately he went 'to the house of Mary, the mother of John whose other name was Mark, where many had gathered and were praying' (v. 12). They were 'overjoyed' (v. 14) and 'amazed' (v. 16), and Peter 'described for them how the Lord had brought him out of the prison' (v. 17). What a tremendous answer to prayer!

I wonder how many gather for prayer meetings in your church? What an immense privilege to be able to meet together in the Lord's name, knowing that he is present in our midst, and to bring before him people who need his touch upon their lives, and situations which he is powerful to transform.

The apostle Paul encourages the church at Ephesus to 'always keep on praying for all the saints' (Ephesians 6:18, NIV), and James writes in his letter, 'Pray for one another' (James 5:16). Let us do just that! And, praise God when he answers!

✣

1 THESSALONIANS 4:13—5:22 (NRSV)

One another

Encourage one another and build up each other... Always seek to do good to one another.

It is amazing how often the little phrase 'one another' appears in the scripture passages that these notes are based upon. 'Love one another'; 'live in harmony with one another'; 'be hospitable to one another'; 'wash one another's feet'; 'bear one another's burdens'; 'forgive one another'; 'pray for one another'; 'encourage one another'; 'do good to one another'. If there were any evidence needed that an isolated Christian is an anomaly, and that we are meant to be in relationship, I think we have it in these two words repeated over and over again in the New Testament.

What wonderful churches we would have if we all lived out to the full these various exhortations! Maybe we should start taking them seriously, and put them into practice. Love, service, hospitality, prayer, forgiveness, burden-bearing, doing good, encouragement, will result in harmonious relationships and a healthy body with all the members working well together and functioning as God intended.

The world can be a hard place to live in, and we are easily subject to many kinds of fears. In the light of this, and in contrast to it, the church is to be a place where believers are to encourage one another, build each other up and do good to one another. We can do this in a variety of ways, through drawing alongside in sympathy, through offering practical help, through our prayers. Paul's focus in this passage, however, is on the glorious truth that Christ is coming back and 'we will be with the Lord for ever' (4:17). We can build each other up and encourage one another most of all by reminding one another of this great truth.

Lord, thank you for my brothers and sisters in Christ. Help us to put into practice the exhortations in your word, so that your body will function as you intended. May we always seek to do good to one another.

PART THREE

Learning from others

Isn't it encouraging to know that we are not alone on our journey of faith? As well as giving us his Holy Spirit, Jesus has also made us part of his body, the Church, so that we can help each other live God's way. Our fellow believers—and those who lived before us—have much to teach us. Aim to find at least one godly friend to share what you are learning through these notes. Encourage one another as you notice the changes God is making in your lives.

The Bible outlines the lives of hundreds of men and women who have something to teach us, as this next set of studies will show. Some of the characters we will be looking at were virtually unknown; others have become part of the fabric of our faith; but all can teach us about God who loves to interact with the people he has created. Many of these characters were flawed, stubborn, sick, suffering rejection, even angry with God—just as we are at times—but God had a part for them to play in history.

Use your imagination to get to know some of the characters and the way they interacted with God. The first 14 readings, by Fiona Barnard, are an imaginative look at some Bible characters. Each of these notes is written as if the person themselves was writing. If you find this style helpful in developing your relationship with God, try to imagine what it would be like to be some of the other characters in later notes. Use all of your senses to get into the stories. What can you learn from the sounds, tastes, smells and sights? What would it feel like to be that person? Are there new aspects to their story that you haven't noticed before?

As you read about these characters, write down the aspects of their stories that you find most striking. Were they like you in any way? How did God respond to them? What is God teaching you about yourself? How can their stories help you as you seek to be more like Jesus? During the day, let the words of Scripture take root in your heart and mind as you think over what you last read. What can you learn about the way God responds to the people he loves?

Share what you are learning with a friend or small group as you encourage each other to become more like Jesus.

GO... MAKE DISCIPLES

JOHN 3:16 (NRSV)

Go... and make disciples

God so loved the world that he gave his only Son.

'When I was a young boy in Taiwan, I lived beside a church,' Hua told me. 'I even went to Sunday school, because they offered sweets. There were extra if we learnt words from the Bible.' Having met Hua about six times at an international students' enquirers' Bible study, this was the first time he'd admitted any connection with Christianity. I was curious. 'So, Hua, can you recall any Bible words?' I asked. 'No, not really. It was a long time ago. All I can remember is something like, "God loved the world so much that he gave his only Son that whoever believes in him won't die, but live for ever." Have you heard that one?' He grinned, proud of his good memory.

It's at times like these that I marvel at God's guiding hand in and behind my encounters with people. Years ago and miles away, he'd already been reaching out in love to Hua through Christians. Who knows if his attendance in our Bible study group was the result of their prayers for a sweet-loving boy?

From the beginning of creation, God has longed for a relationship with humanity. In Old Testament times, he said, 'Come', choosing one nation to be like a magnet to draw surrounding peoples to himself. As part of his plan, God sent his Son as a missionary to woo a sinful world. This shifted the focus from a magnetic 'Come' to the ballistic 'Go... and make disciples of all nations' (Matthew 28:19). As Christ's body on earth, we have the privilege of continuing his work.

It is not an optional extra for 'keenies'. We are all 'sent'—some to leave home and live abroad, others to witness locally—but everyone to pray and give and support mission throughout the world.

For the next two weeks we enter imaginatively into the worlds of various Bible characters who communicated something of God to people from different cultures. May we learn from them and be encouraged to love the world like Jesus does.

Lord, give us your heart for the nations!

✣

GENESIS 12:1–7 (NRSV)

Saying 'Yes'

Now the Lord said to Abram, 'Go...' So Abram went, as the Lord had told him.

Perhaps there is a certain love of adventure in my blood, but by the age of 75, I figured my days of risk-taking were over. I guess I had a bit of my father in me: when he was a grandfather, he had taken us away from our home in Ur and set off for Canaan. In the end, we settled en route, and grew quite comfortable in our adopted land. We accumulated wealth and servants, so that the future looked secure and trouble-free. However, I must admit that in my quieter moments I felt a certain wistfulness, a questioning: 'Is this it? Is this what life is all about?'

Then, out of the blue, the Lord spoke a startling, uncomfortable word: 'Leave your country, your people and your father's household and go to the land I will show you.' So much for retirement! No beating about the bush: it was 'Leave' and 'Go'. Stark, clear words, but ones pregnant with promise because they spoke of blessing: 'I will make you into a great nation.'

So I left and went.

Some people might call me radical, even mad for giving up

everything that I had for something I might never possess—but I trusted this God (most of the time). I believed that he was big enough to do what he had promised. And eventually he did give Sarah and me our long-awaited miracle son (how we laughed!) and he did give me land—land to bury Sarah (how I cried!). I don't see it yet, but both of these are just the beginning of unimaginable things to come—that through me, somehow, all the peoples on the earth will be blessed.

Thank you, Lord, for giving each of us a particular background and character which you can use in your call to us. Help us to leave those things that stop us from going and doing and being the people you want us to be. Amen

✣

LEVITICUS 19:34 (NIV)

Loving strangers

The aliens living with you must be treated as your native-born. Love them as yourself, for you were aliens in Egypt. I am the Lord your God.

When you have been the victim of racial abuse, you develop a strong sense of identity and an inherent mistrust of others. I grew up knowing that I was scum. Even as a child, I felt the hostile stares long before my tearful mother had to explain that I was hated not for anything I had done, but simply for who I was. Over the years, I saw how suspicion could turn to loathing and violence. Our people were viewed as a threat to the natives, so we were forced to work as slaves. We thought our suffering would never end. There was no one to speak for us, no one to fight for us. No one cared.

But God heard our cry and sent Moses to lead us out of slavery to freedom. Freedom—the word is like a beautiful song I want to sing and sing for ever. Never again will anyone treat us cruelly; never again will we be told what to do. God has promised us our own land where we will all be equal and where we can hold our heads high as Israelites.

Here in the wilderness, as we wait to enter the Promised Land, we have been receiving God's law through Moses. It tells us how we are to live as the Lord's people. Some non-Hebrews have joined us, and I admit that we are suspicious of them. They are different; they don't share our history or our customs. Now it is someone else's turn to be 'them'.

They are the vulnerable ones now. So God tells us not to mistreat them, but to love them. It is hard, because the memory is there for us—but perhaps that is also why it is not so difficult.

Lord, help us to show your love to the international communities in which we live—visitors, immigrants, restaurant workers and students.

✣

RUTH 1:15–22 (GNB)

Being vulnerable

Your God will be my God.

No one could ever call me a good advert for the faith. Sometimes life deals you so many blows that it is easy to become bitter and blame God for it all. First there was the famine that forced my family to leave the land God gave us, and to live as foreigners in Moab. Next I was widowed. The last straw was when both my dear sons, who were my providers, my social security, also died. I felt totally and utterly bereft.

When I returned to my own land, I winced when people called out, 'Naomi, is it really you?' You see, suffering had changed me from the inside out, and whereas once my name, meaning 'pleasant', fitted my personality, now I told them to call me 'Mara', signifying 'bitter'.

'Why should anyone want to be part of God's people?' I asked myself many times. 'He certainly doesn't seem to have shown much favour to me.' Imagine my astonishment when Ruth, my foreign daughter-in-law, who had her own religion and her own gods, insisted on embracing the

God of Israel. That moment on the long, sad journey home was a turning-point in my life, though I didn't realize it at the time. 'Wherever you go I will go,' she said, her eyes looking straight into mine. 'Your people will be my people and your God will be my God.'

Now, I hold Obed in my arms, the son of Ruth and her new husband Boaz. I marvel that despite my emptiness and anger against God, somehow Ruth saw something about Yahweh that drew her to him and his people. She exchanged the religion of her upbringing for a foreign God, our God. I am full of praise that this God, under whose wings she took refuge, did not leave us on the margins. He has indeed provided for both of us. I am greatly loved.

Thank you, Lord, that in our weaknesses as well as our strengths, you are able to use us to draw others to yourself.

✣

1 KINGS 10:1–9 (NRSV)

Working for God

When the queen of Sheba heard of the fame of Solomon (fame due to the name of the Lord), she came to test him with hard questions.

You know, it is so easy to get distracted when you are king. There are so many demands on your time—establishing trade links and foreign alliances; maintaining a powerful army and fleet even if you rely more on peaceful diplomacy rather than war; encouraging all types of learning, science and the arts; constructing and furnishing the temple for the Lord, along with many other buildings—the list just goes on and on.

And then there are all the trappings of sovereignty. You can imagine, they go with the job—pomp and palaces and parties, wine and wealth and wives. I find that all too soon I can get caught up in the demands and the delights of my position and forget how I got here in the first place and the reason I am here.

So I am thankful for the Queen of Sheba who made a costly, arduous

2,000km journey to pay me a visit. She came bearing many beautiful gifts, but also with many searching questions and concerns. By the end of her inspection, she overcame her speechlessness to tell me how impressed she was with what she had seen: it had surpassed all her expectations. Then, from the lips of this pagan, materialistic woman came words that reminded me of the One to whom I owe everything: 'Blessed be the Lord your God, who has delighted in you and set you on the throne of Israel! Because the Lord loved Israel for ever, he has made you king to execute justice and righteousness.'

I thank the Lord, who, by enabling me to do my job well, has glorified himself among those who do not know him. I do my best for his sake.

Thank you, Lord, for work and the everyday tasks you have given me to do. Help me to be faithful in them, so that people will be drawn to you.

✣

2 KINGS 5:1–15 (NRSV)

A group effort

Now I know that there is no God in all the earth except in Israel.

It was just a casual remark. I had no idea that it would bring healing—and more, the conversion of one of the most important people in this foreign country.

I never asked to live here. I was brutally snatched from my own land and family in Israel. 'Here's a pretty young girl,' those cruel Arameans seemed to be saying. 'She'll do nicely as a rich lady's slave.' So I ended up serving the wife of the army's commander. Ironically, I even grew to like her, perhaps because I saw the desperate unhappiness she and her husband suffered. You see, he had a horrible skin disease which caused him terrible pain and discomfort. No money or medicine could buy him relief.

'If only my lord were with the prophet who is in Samaria!' I remarked casually one day as I tried to comfort my distraught mistress. 'He would cure him of his leprosy.' I certainly never envisaged that having pumped me for an account of the wonderful works of this man of God, she would bother to raise the hopes of her despairing husband.

Yet she did, and Naaman, her husband, made the journey to my country. Eventually he humbled himself and obeyed the prophet Elisha's instructions to wash in the Jordan river seven times. He was made clean. He returned a different man—completely healed, but also declaring that there is no God in the whole earth except Yahweh and he would worship only him.

His wife thanks me over and over again—but I did nothing. I just indicated the direction where they could find true help, from the Lord's prophet, who pointed them to the one living God.

Thank you, Lord, that you do not ask us to do the whole job of evangelism alone. Thank you that you prepare a chain of people to link those who do not yet know you to your loving, healing heart.

JONAH 4:2–4 (NRSV)

Compassion and grace

You are a gracious God and merciful, slow to anger, and abounding in steadfast love, and ready to relent from punishing.

I had such terrible problems with the Lord's message. I tried everything to get out of having to give it—ignored God for a while, got busy doing something (anything) else, suddenly 'remembered' I had a very important trip to make in the opposite direction from the one in which I was being sent, and so on.

But you can't really fob God off, and for some reason he did not give up on me as his messenger. He went to tremendous lengths—

yes, a storm at sea and extraordinarily big fish in that water—to persuade me that obedience is better.

And so I travelled to that hateful city and delivered the message to its disgusting, wicked inhabitants. In fact, it gave me great pleasure to cry out, 'Forty days more and Ninevah shall be overthrown!' Well, blow me down if those pagan, idolatrous, vile people didn't actually listen and believe God. Before I knew it, they had taken to fasting, prayer and repentance.

When God relented (I just knew he would), I was furious. Trust him to show compassion and mercy to our foes (and, by extension, his enemies). He just can't help himself, pouring grace and love on those who deserve punishment. All it seems to take is repentance.

If you really take it seriously, God's message is always so very uncomfortable.

Dear Lord, give me your compassion, tact and strength to explain about sin and salvation with integrity, so that those who hear may turn their backs on their old ways and give themselves to you.

Read the whole story of Jonah today.

✣

ESTHER 4:13–16 (NRSV)

Dependence on God

If you keep silence at such a time as this, relief and deliverance will rise for the Jews from another quarter, but you and your father's family will perish. Who knows? Perhaps you have come to royal dignity for just such a time as this.

I remember so vividly, as though it were yesterday, the day I grew up. Just when our people were chugging along happily, as fairly free subjects in the Persian empire, we suddenly found ourselves in fear of our lives. Haman, King Xerxes' right hand man, was plotting the death of all Jews. The situation seemed hopeless, and it was then that I recognized God calling me—me?—to intercede and to act so that his people might be saved. I was terrified.

Yet it seemed that my whole life had been leading up to that moment of crisis. Until then, it had been a mixture of mundane (regular Jewish upbringing by my guardian cousin Mordecai) and extraordinary (being picked in an imperial beauty contest to be the wife of the Persian King Xerxes). It was at that point that I realized I could no longer be passive and allow others to make decisions for me. I had to decide whether I would use my position and go out on a limb to save God's vulnerable people, or whether I would bury my head in the sand and continue to keep my Jewish identity a secret. Mordecai laid down the gauntlet: 'Who knows but that you have come to royal position for such a time as this?'

First we prayed and fasted with a passion, because we were powerless. All we could do was trust in God and await his leading. We believed he would deliver his people somehow. And he did. 'The rest,' as they say, 'is history.' Amazingly.

Lord, we pray for your people in vulnerable places, especially in Muslim and communist countries, many of whom have to be secret believers. Lord, please provide Esthers at the right time and place to save and strengthen and encourage them.

✣

LUKE 2:25–35 (NRSV)

Focusing on Jesus

My eyes have seen your salvation, which you have prepared in the presence of all peoples, a light for revelation to the Gentiles and for glory to your people Israel.

The Spirit said, 'Go', so I went to the temple to meet the man for whom I had been waiting all my life—only he wasn't a man, he was a baby.

Yet as I stood with this child in my arms, I knew he was the fulfilment of promises—a promise made to me that I would not die until I had seen the Lord's Messiah, but also the promise made to Israel that a Saviour would come.

We hoped for a victorious political Messiah to free us from the Gentile yoke. The Spirit whispered, 'No' and showed me a suffering servant who would save us another way. Our people imagined that his coming would usher in national happiness. The Spirit reminded me that Emmanuel would be 'a rock one stumbles over' (Isaiah 8:14). Many assumed, with insular arrogance, that the Anointed One was only for them. The Spirit signalled, 'No' and reminded me of Isaiah's words to his Chosen One, 'It is too light a thing that you should be a servant to raise up the tribe of Jacob... I will give you as a light to the nations, that my salvation may reach the end of the earth' (Isaiah 49:6).

So as I, the Lord's servant, held the Servant of the Lord, this child of pain and promise, I saw the unexpected. There in that bastion of exclusive religion, that most holy of places, which kept outsiders at a distance, I had a vision of its doors flung open so that unclean Gentiles too could experience God's glory. I saw the revelation of God not confined to our people, but calling forth a response in the hearts and minds of many, reaching to the ends of the earth. All thanks to this child.

I praise you, Lord, that in Jesus your light and salvation are open to everyone, even me.

✣

JOHN 4:39–42 (NRSV)

'Gossiping' about Jesus

They said to the woman, 'It is no longer because of what you said that we believe, for we have heard for ourselves, and we know that this is truly the Saviour of the world.'

'Don't tell me she's after another man,' I hear you whispering amongst yourselves. You look intrigued and scandalized all at once. This is not my way, I know. Usually, I keep my distance from groups and gossip, because although a scarlet woman like myself may be the object of great private interest, outwardly the stance is one of hostility and blame.

Now you really are curious, because I am announcing this new man. He is different from my five husbands. This man treats me with respect: he has taken the time to discuss religious issues with me, something no other man would deign to do. Not that I was thinking about spiritual stuff—I was just concentrating on drawing my water from the well and escaping the noonday sun as soon as possible. In fact, the conversation started when he asked for a drink. Have you ever heard of a Jew asking a Samaritan for anything? Yet he has shown such gentleness and courtesy. Most of all, he knows everything I have ever done, and while you treat me, 'an immoral outcast', with contempt, he displays concern for my dignity. He is obviously a prophet from God—and more: he has just told me he is the long-awaited Messiah who will explain how to worship God properly. What do you make of that? Do you think it could be true?

You can't help but notice, can you, that my encounter with this man has changed me? Can't you see it? For once, I can't wait to tell you what is happening in my life.

Come, please come and see for yourselves!

Jesus, we worship you as Saviour of the whole world. Thank you that we do not have to be part of any 'socially respectable' class or sex to know you and to make you known. Use us, we pray.

✣

LUKE 24:44–53 (NRSV)

Spirit-empowered

Thus it is written, that the Messiah is to suffer and to rise from the dead on the third day, and that repentance and forgiveness of sins

is to be proclaimed in his name to all nations, beginning from Jerusalem. You are witnesses of these things. And see, I am sending upon you what my Father promised.

We've been given what seems an impossible task: tell all the nations about Christ! Even worse, Jesus has left us to it without him. We've spent a lot of time puzzling over his command. How could we ever sum up the life and teaching of this amazing man? How could we make sense of what happened when he died a cursed man's death, and then, as we were reeling with shock and grief, burst back to life?

What's more, the world is a big place. How can we travel to distant lands? How will we be understood amid languages and religions and customs different from our own?

And anyway, who are we? We're just simple folk—not academic nor theologically trained, but cowardly and afraid. Whoever will even listen to us?

Yet we love Jesus. As his disciples, we have witnessed breathtaking events. Even his death was part of God's plan to bring us forgiveness. Everyone needs to know the good news about Jesus!

OK, we are nervous, but also excited—and all because of Pentecost. That's when Jesus sent the promised power in the person of the Holy Spirit. God is with us; he is in us. We've been transformed! The Spirit has given us everything we need—the words, the message, the language, the opportunities, the boldness—to obey Jesus. We have been thrilled to see the Spirit at work!

If we yearn for his power, we need to be where he is, working with him to reach the nations. His presence really is promised to all Christians everywhere who go in his name.

Thank you, God, for your Holy Spirit who teaches us and empowers us with your message to reach the nations.

✣

ACTS 8:26–39 (NIV)

Led by the Spirit

Now an angel of the Lord said to Philip, 'Go south to the road—the desert road—that goes down from Jerusalem to Gaza.' So he started out, and on his way he met an Ethiopian eunuch, an important official.

'How did you feel when God seemed to banish you to the desert?' people have asked me many times. 'Did you begin to doubt him or your ability to hear his voice? After all, it meant leaving an exciting, thriving situation for an extremely unpleasant, uncertain one.' It's true. We were in the middle of wonderful blessing. Huge crowds of Samaritans, keen to hear the good news about Jesus, were becoming Christians. Demons were leaving with great shrieks of defeat, and paralytics and cripples were being healed.

Then came the strange command to leave it all behind, and to go to a desert road. However, I have learnt that when God speaks, you obey, even when you don't understand—especially when you don't understand.

You see, this was a divine appointment. After several hot, weary, dusty miles of walking and prayer, I met a high-ranking government official from Ethiopia. It so 'happened' that he was desperately trying to make sense of an Old Testament passage which actually spoke of Christ. God had prepared his heart, so he responded eagerly to the gospel. When we came to some water, he requested baptism as a sign of his newfound faith in Jesus. I realized, as we parted, that this was a man from 'the ends of the earth' who would continue the work of taking the gospel to another far-flung corner of the world.

God has amazing surprises in store, even in lonely, barren deserts.

Lord, make me attentive to your Spirit. Help me to be willing to go to the margins of society and to take the initiative with those who may be far from home. May I keep the appointments you have made for me. Use me that the good news may be spread to the ends of the earth.

✣

ACTS 17:16–34 (NRSV)

Eyes and ears

As I went through the city and looked carefully at the objects of your worship, I found among them an altar with the inscription, 'To an unknown god'. What therefore you worship as unknown, this I proclaim to you.

As I walk around, I see people everywhere who are spiritually starving. They are looking for God, though some are more aware of it than others.

I notice this searching in poetry, in traditional stories and the arts which ache with longing for meaning, for some structure that will give shape and intelligibility to chaotic and senseless lives. I hear philosophers and intellectuals reading and discussing, pouncing on new ideas like underfed dogs and wagging their tails when it seems they have won an argument. I'm aware of those who resort to eating and drinking and making merry, who sing, 'This is life: it's all about enjoying ourselves, so party on', and will do anything to block out the pain.

All these, in their different ways and replicated in every nation on earth, are calling out for one who seems illusive, far away. That inner God-shaped vacuum is littered with poetry or philosophy or parties. In the cold light of day, it leaves an ever-deeper sense of emptiness.

This ignorance makes me angry, and yet the climate of spirituality gives me the opportunity to tell the good news. My burning passion is to preach Christ where he is not known, because Jesus is food for the hungry and water to the thirsty.

So, having looked and listened and understood these Athenians, I will proclaim that this their 'unknown God' is their creator and judge. He has come close to them in the person of his Son, and calls for a radical change of direction in their lives. May the Lord grant me gracious authority as I speak.

Lord, help us to listen and learn from the culture around us, so that we will be able to speak of Jesus in a way that is relevant and clear to people who may not know him.

✣

REVELATION 7:9–10 (NRSV)

From every nation

I looked, and there was a great multitude that no one could count, from every nation, from all tribes and peoples and languages, standing before the throne and before the Lamb, robed in white, with palm branches in their hands. They cried out in a loud voice, saying, 'Salvation belongs to our God who is seated on the throne, and to the Lamb!'

'Lord, how long?' we shout when the cost of living for Christ is too much, when people mock us and have no interest in hearing the good news. 'How long, Lord?' cry Christians living with the uncertainty and fear of physical harm and even death. 'How long?' I too have asked—until God showed me the ultimate reality of things.

One Sunday in worship, God gave me a vision of heaven and my whole earthly perspective changed. All my anguished 'Why bothers?' were answered a thousand times over as I saw countless worshippers from every tribe and tongue, people group and nation before God's throne. What a wonderful array of shapes and sizes, colours and ages! Did I see Abraham, Ruth and Naaman, folk from Nineveh, Samaria, Ethiopia and Athens? Yes, I think I did, along with—oh, I don't know—Iranians and Italians, Chinese and Canadian, Jamaicans and Japanese, asylum seekers, restaurant workers and eminent professors, shopkeepers and business people, and millions more. Each sang of how they had been far from God, and yet he had sought and found them.

So despite the heartache, victory is assured. When we are discouraged by hostility or apathy, there is more than meets the human eye. God is at work in the world. Hallelujah!

Lord Jesus, as we gaze on you, we are reminded that you are king, not any human ruler. As we praise you, the Lamb sacrificed for our sins, we understand that we owe our forgiveness and our very lives to you. Thank you for using scared, flawed Christians like us to call worshippers from every land to your awesome presence. We worship you!

WOMEN IN THE EARLY CHURCH

ACTS 12:12 (NIV)

Mary, John Mark's mother

[Peter] went to the house of Mary the mother of John, also called Mark, where many people had gathered and were praying.

The doors were locked. The atmosphere was tense. One of their closest friends had been murdered and another thrown in prison over the Passover. The household was under severe spiritual stress, yet it is to this home that Mary invites people to gather for prayer.

All the ingredients are here for a gripping fly-on-the-wall docusoap. Luke calls it Mary's house, so presumably she is a widow. Maybe she had left her native Cyprus when her husband died, and travelled with her son, John Mark, to be in Jerusalem near her brother Barnabas. This would have given John Mark the opportunity of being in the garden of Gethsemane to watch the terrible drama of betrayal unfold (Mark 14:51).

Mary was certainly one of Jesus' close followers, and if, as is widely held, her son was the author of Mark's Gospel, her home was a unique haven for all those who had experienced the despair of the crucifixion, the miracle of the resurrection and now, the anxieties of persecution.

In fact, Mary's home was so well known that it was the first place that came to Peter's mind on his escape from prison. In her own right, Mary was a highly respected lady. The sister of a Levite, Barnabas, she was able to give her son the advantage of education, and kept a servant to care for the household. The little servant girl, Rhoda, instantly recognized Peter's voice, so he too must have been a regular visitor.

What a strong woman Mary must have been! For new believers and disciples alike, her table was prepared and shelter given. Years later in Rome, we can imagine John Mark's thoughts nostalgically returning to his mother's house as he wrote his 'Good News about Jesus Christ the Son of God'.

Lord, I pray for Christians who are persecuted today.

Further reading: Mark 14:32–51.

ROMANS 16:1 (NRSV)

Phoebe

I commend to you our sister Phoebe, a deacon of the Church in Cenchreae.

Paul wrote his letter to the Romans from Corinth. Paul tends to get such mega publicity that it's easy to overlook the fact that a Christian congregation had been founded in Rome by other disciples. Paul longed to visit this group of Christians and his list of greeting to them sheds much light on the travelling co-workers spreading the gospel.

His letter also highlights the pastoral ministry already in place in the new churches, and specifically names Phoebe as a deacon. Reading between the lines, Phoebe may have been a wealthy businesswoman and her inclusion by name provides evidence that women had important roles to play from the very beginning. Paul wrote that she had been a benefactor to many, including himself. The actual Greek work means 'one who stands by in case of need' so we can speculate that Phoebe may have been one to offer support to Paul over his 'thorn in the flesh'.

Paul held this woman in highest regard and in his letter to Rome he made it clear that they should give Phoebe any assistance she required. Because of this commendation, many believe that Phoebe was the courier for Paul's letter. If so, she was undertaking a long and hazardous journey from Cenchreae, the town which was really the port for Corinth, all the way over to Rome.

In every church there are so many 'jobs' to be done and we do need our frameworks for pastoral care, for administration, hospitality and so on. I find it encouraging to feel that I am a link in a 2000-year-old chain with women like Phoebe, but I wonder what Phoebe would make of our all-too-often lacklustre commitment and our apathy in sharing the good news for which she risked her life.

Dear Lord, thank you for those who have been alongside me when I have been in need.

Further reading: Romans 16:1–27.

2 TIMOTHY 1:5 (NIV)

Lois and Eunice

I have been reminded of your sincere faith, which first lived in your grandmother Lois and in your mother Eunice and... now lives in you also.

Because my mother went out to work, I was brought up by a very special Christian woman. Instead of teaching me nursery ryhmes, she told me stories from the Bible. I loved them, and I owe more to her gentle faith than I shall ever know. She enabled me, as a child, to realize and accept the presence of Jesus.

In Paul's letter to the young Timothy, we see the immense influence of a mother and grandmother. The family home at Lystra was the place where Paul had healed the crippled man, and the crowds thought he and Barnabas were gods! Paul's teaching obviously had an enormous effect on the Lystra population but it could be that Lois had already heard of Jesus. She may even have been in Jerusalem when Jesus was crucified. Precise facts we cannot prove, but the irrefutable fact stands that Lois had accepted Jesus as her Saviour and Lord and her vibrant faith passed to Eunice, her daughter. It's interesting that Luke bothers to mention that Timothy's father was 'a Greek', implying that he took no part in the family Christian worship.

Lois and Eunice are examples of all that is best in the home environment. Whatever the standard of material possessions or the excellence of available education, nothing can compare with the teaching of right and wrong and the sharing of God's love learnt at a mother's knee. All children need 'contact time'. Timothy had enjoyed this contact and Paul spotted his potential to be a co-missionary.

Another missionary, Augustine, spoke movingly of the great debt he owed to his own mother, Monica. So, are you a mother or grandmother? Or godmother, auntie or child minder? You are in a unique relationship, with an opportunity to share your faith in a natural and loving way.

Pray for the children you know.

✣

ACTS 21:7–9 (NIV)

Philip's four daughters

The next day we reached Caesarea and stayed at the house of Philip the evangelist... he had four unmarried daughters.

Many names flit across the pages of scripture never to be heard of again. In Acts 21 we meet four women who didn't even manage to be names, but whose lives made a deep and lasting impression upon all who received their hospitality. Their father, Philip, is mentioned in Acts 6:5, and may be the same Philip who met the Ethiopian official on the road from Jerusalem to Gaza. Tantalizingly, we cannot tell if it was the same Philip called by Jesus in John 1:43 and the disciple who was mentioned at the feeding of the five thousand.

These four young women appear to be running the house for their father, so we presume that their mother had died. From Acts we trace the incredible spread of the gospel message as it was taken along the trade routes and through the villages. Luke also shows us how new Christians were nurtured in strategic house-churches. One such house-church was in the Mediterranean port of Caesarea, and was run by Philip's four daughters.

Luke seems to have openly respected these unmarried sisters who chose to follow the teaching of the risen Jesus Christ above the expectations and peer pressure for family life. Through the centuries women have given themselves to a life of prayer and service in the name of their Saviour and have been a priceless blessing to the poor and needy in their community. We easily remember Mother Julian or Mother Teresa, but countless women even today are caring for others and setting aside their own dreams.

These four daughters of Philip ran a home where prayer, preaching and vision went hand in glove with warm hospitality. They had not withdrawn from the world but were in the very centre of missionary activity, a real force within the spread of Christianity.

Thank you, Lord, for the role models of service and serenity.

✣

ACTS 10:24 (NIV)

Mrs Cornelius

Cornelius was expecting them and had called together his relatives and close friends.

Peter's visit to Cornelius' house in Ceasarea marked a momentous new phase in the spread of the gospel. In a dream, God had shown Peter that he had no right to be prejudiced against Gentiles, and Peter, by the act of baptizing the Gentile household, had taken a revolutionary step to affirm equality in God's sight.

So much for Peter and Cornelius—what about Mrs Cornelius? For any army wife, life abroad is a mixture of adventure and homesickness. Mrs Cornelius was probably counting the weeks before she and the family could return to Rome, but as a loyal wife she recognized the importance of her husband's career.

We read that Cornelius was not the usual Roman officer. He revered the God of Israel, along with all his household, which definitely meant his wife as well. He was acknowledged to be a fair and even generous man and, most surprising of all, he prayed.

As centurions would have passed on their stories, so too would their wives! Stories of Jesus would have been rife and Cornelius felt a deep longing to know more. I like to think of him and his wife discussing these stories and praying together. However, she must have been daunted by the thought of Peter the Galilean disciple coming into her home. Not just that, but Cornelius had invited his relatives and close friends to come over and hear Peter. What preparations—shopping, cooking, extra sleeping arrangements—and then, all the household received the Holy Spirit and were baptized! God must smile at all our human preparations.

If Cornelius' tour of duty had lasted long, there is the distinct possibility that some of his household would have been in contact with Philip's household, also in Caesarea. And so, from household to household, the Christians encouraged and built each other up.

Dear Lord, today I pray for an open mind and a generous heart.

Further reading: Luke 23:44–49.

✣

ACTS 16:11–15 (NIV)

Lydia

One of those listening was a woman named Lydia, a dealer in purple cloth... who was a worshipper of God.

In Lydia we meet a woman who could happily step from the pages of this week's Sunday supplement. A shrewd, successful, articulate and upwardly mobile businesswoman, just enough is said about her by Luke for us to be able to build a thumbnail sketch of her lifestyle.

She was born in the city of Thyatira (in present-day Turkey), which was renowned for its specialized fabric dyeing. Having aquired her skill, Lydia left for Philippi to consolidate her business in selling the expensive purple cloth. You could say her fabrics had 'designer label' status, for she was immediately recognizable.

So we gather from these scanty verses that Lydia was already a believer in God: it does not say she was a Jewess, but she gathered with the Jews each Sabbath for prayer. There, by the riverbank, in an echo of the exiles in Babylon centuries before, the Lord God was worshipped by the faithful.

Busy and successful she may have been, but Lydia still made time for her own devotional life. Surely, this is a real lesson that she has to teach us today. Paul, the Pharisee, seemed quite at ease within that female group and did not hesitate to sit with them to speak to them of Jesus.

I've been privileged to witness adult baptism in the river Jordan and I can quite imagine the radiant expression on Lydia's face as she emerged from her baptism. The action that followed her baptism only goes to underline her wealth and position. Attended by members of her household, she invited Paul and Luke to be her guests. Lydia had room and means to spare and she offered them both for God's work. Lydia became one of the founder members of the church in Philippi, and may have been one of the deacons referred to in Paul's greeting in Philippians 1:1.

Lord, may I never be too busy to hear your word.

ACTS 18:2 (NIV)

Priscilla

[In Corinth Paul] met a Jew named Aquila, who had recently come from Italy with his wife Priscilla.

The persecution of Jews in Rome had made Priscilla and Aquila refugees. We meet them in the cosmopolitan trading city of Corinth where they are working as tent makers. Tent makers in those times would also have been skilled in working leather and were always in demand. It was natural, then, that Paul, also a tent maker, should lodge with them.

It's amazing how, in just a few sentences, the Bible writers paint vivid pictures of ordinary people being used in extraordinary ways to be channels of God's grace. Priscilla had shown courage and resilience in the face of persecution and, in new surroundings, was rebuilding her life. From Acts 18, it looks as though Paul was their guest for some 18 months, but such was his impact upon the pair that when he moved on to Ephesus, they travelled with him. It was in Ephesus that Luke records the episode of Priscilla the tactful, patient teacher. She didn't publicly argue with the enthusiastic Apollos, but invited him home, where deep discussions and spiritual insight from her own experience recharged Apollos' ministry (Acts 18:24–26).

From Paul's letter to Rome, chapter 16, we realize that Priscilla and Aquila travelled back to Rome with a whole group of believers. Not only that, but Priscilla had bravely risked death on Paul's behalf and for the sake of the gospel. Here was a couple highly respected and much loved in the early Church.

I am fascinated and humbled by Priscilla's life. I marvel at her hospitality and the way in which she and Aquila worked side by side, both in tent making and in their witness for Jesus Christ. There is no mention of their own children, but I'm sure that Priscilla was seen as a loving 'mother' for all the new converts.

Dear Lord, help me to create a home of warmth and welcome where all may find the blessing of your peace.

Further reading: the rest of Acts 18.

WOMEN IN THE BIBLE

LUKE 1:26–38 (NEB)

Obedience

'Here I am,' said Mary; 'I am the Lord's servant; as you have spoken, so be it.'

I recently attended a meditation—by accident! The talk was advertised as 'cloth scripture', The speaker talked as she artistically turned odd bits of cloth and cardboard, with liberal splodges of glue, into a beautiful figure of Mary, mother of our Lord.

She encouraged us, gently and sensitively, to get close to the woman who had been chosen to bear God's Son. We were invited to put ourselves in her place. What must it have been like to be pregnant and unmarried at that time? Then there was the exhausting journey to Bethlehem. Scenes of the nativity make giving birth in a stable look a lot more attractive than the reality! To cap it all, there were the visitors—strangers, not even family and friends. This was but the beginning for Mary. She had to learn to 'let go' of Jesus very early on in his life. To come was the agony and grief of seeing him die a cruel and unjust death.

Our meditation took us through the Gospel accounts from the visitation of the angel Gabriel to the crucifixion of Jesus. We listened and reflected; we became aware of the courage, determination, devotion and great faith of Mary. Above all, she was obedient to God, willing to carry through his plan for her, no matter what sorrow, suffering, anxiety and pain it would bring her. She never shrank from complete obedience to God.

Hers was a special responsibility as the mother of Jesus, but she had about her qualities that are to be found in all good mothers. She gave service, experienced anxiety and sorrow, she had common sense. Above all, she recognized her need of a Saviour.

Mary saw her responsiblities as a mother through to the end. Much in the Christian life is not a matter of faith. It is a matter of obedience.

How obedient and faithful are we to what God is calling us to be and to do for him in our lives?

JOHN 8:2–11 (NEB)

Judgment

Jesus said, 'Nor do I condemn you. You may go: do not sin again.'

The Bible is full of things we come across in our everyday lives—pleasure, grief, loneliness, jealousy, frustration, goodness, evil, highs and lows. The list is endless. Humour also has a place.

I smile when I read of the endless attempts the enemies of Jesus made to trap him. More often than not, they ended up being 'netted' themselves. The enemies of Jesus must have been really confident of success this time. After all, the woman was caught in the act of adultery. They were sure Jesus couldn't win the argument this time. If he commanded that she be stoned, he would surely lose popularity. If he let her go, they could accuse him of rejecting the law of Moses. But Jesus turned everything upside down, challenging those who considered themselves beyond reproach to cast the first stone. Not surprisingly, the crowd drifted away. Jesus, who was without sin, refused to condemn the woman in spite of her real and obvious guilt.

I was reminded of this story when I heard about Jane. A prostitute, an alcoholic, she was to the secular world 'beyond the pale', yet she has been transformed by the love and care of a Christian family. She has been given what no court, probation officer or psychiatrist could possibly provide—the consciousness of sins forgiven. Jane heard the good news by experiencing it first-hand. That's the real challenge of Christian discipleship because it was set by Jesus himself. He renounced all right to rank and privilege, serving reverently where needed.

Those in need in our communities are not always the most attractive or pleasant people to deal with. Even though we may not always like their actions, we are commanded to love them as Jesus loves us—unconditionally. Whatever their shortcomings, or our own, Jesus says, 'Go and sin no more.'

Jesus did not come into the world to condemn it. He came that through him the world might be saved. We should never then stand in judgment on others, for none of us is without sin.

✣

JOHN 4:1–30 (NEB)

Jesus has the answers

Jesus said, 'I am he, I who am speaking to you now.'

Some years ago I visited an African village that proudly showed off its new well. The excitement, pride and sheer gratitude were obvious. I was taken to try it out and, with the women, marvelled at the clean water that came up in the bucket. You could be forgiven for wondering what the fuss was about, unless like them you had previously walked miles each day to collect this essential commodity.

The well was, and still is, a place where the women gather; they chat and exchange news. This woman, however, was alone at the well. She did not have a good reputation, was sexually promiscuous and an outcast in her own village.

Jesus knew who she was and what she was, and yet he chose to spend time with her and lead her to faith. He ignored the centuries-old hostility between Jew and Samaritan and asked her for a drink of water. He spoke to her of life-giving water. She did not understand who he was but when he revealed that he knew her innermost secrets she wanted to know if he was indeed the long-promised Messiah.

These verses point out that we can hide nothing from Jesus. He knows us through and through. The woman at the well knew she was a sinner. Jesus knew it too, yet he still sought her as a worshipper. Would she face up to the truth about herself and come to him as she was? Are we prepared to meet him as we are, with all our shortcomings? The woman at the well went hot-foot back to the town, urging the people 'to come and see a man who has told me everything I ever did'.

The woman at the well knew God had promised to send a Saviour who would have all the answers to help us live each day in him. He kept his promise. Really that is all we need to know too.

✣

JOHN 20:1–18 (NEB)

Living the life

Mary of Magdala went to the disciples with her news: 'I have seen the Lord,' she said, and gave them his message.

I am puzzled that some find it difficult to understand why those who base their lives on Christ's teaching deliberately reach out to those who clearly live lives that fly in the face of that teaching. Throughout his earthly life that is what Jesus did. Time and again he commands us to get alongside those who need his love and saving grace, just as he did and does.

Mary of Magdala was far from perfect and Jesus in no way condoned her sins. However, she was penitent and he forgave her. The tears with which she washed his feet were tears of sheer joy. She had been forgiven, had the opportunity of a fresh start and had found faith. Jesus had accepted her love and devotion. She kept watch at the foot of the cross and was the first to meet and speak with the risen Lord. At the tomb she had first come face to face with a living angel and not with the expected dead body! She was trusted to take the message of the resurrection to the waiting disciples.

Mary Magdalene saw and experienced the evidence of the resurrection first-hand. We believe in the evidence found in the Gospels, but our greatest evidence comes from personal experience. We know Jesus lives because he has entered our hearts and we experience his presence through faith. Mary experienced forgiveness and came to faith.

Mary was penitent and her love and devotion brought her a place in the kingdom. If we truly love God, then we can do what we like, for we shall only wish to do that which pleases him.

Each day we remember that our lives are to be presented to the world as evidence that Jesus lives and saves.

WOMEN IN ACTS

ACTS 1:12–14 (NIV)

Unexpected outcome

They all joined together constantly in prayer, along with the women and Mary the mother of Jesus, and with his brothers.

Just a few verses into the book of Acts, we meet the women who were followers of Jesus. They too had obeyed Jesus' instruction to return to Jerusalem and wait for 'the gift my Father promised' (Acts 1:4), the Holy Spirit. They were probably fearful, bewildered and had very little idea what to expect. We should not be surprised to meet the women here as they appeared in Luke's earlier work, his Gospel, as followers of Jesus during his life on earth (Luke 8:2; 23:49).

However, they might have been surprised to find themselves there, and none more so than Mary, the mother of Jesus. When Jesus was only eight days old, his mother was told that 'a sword (would) pierce (her) own soul' (Luke 2:35). When he was twelve, he worried her by staying behind in the temple and astonished her with his statement that he 'had to be in his Father's house' (Luke 2:49). She did not understand then, but 'treasured all these things and pondered them in her heart' (Luke 2:51). She brought him up, cared for him and had to let go of him. She witnessed the beginning of his ministry, his miracles, his being admired and rejected, loved and hated; and, in the end, she witnessed his crucifixion. Did she have any idea then what was to come? Now Mary was in this room upstairs, praying with his friends. Everything was different now. This was not what she had expected. She had seen her son risen from the dead, she knew he was alive! That made all the difference. She, like the rest of Jesus' disciples, had the courage to wait, to be obedient, to face whatever was to come. And she did the most vital thing a Christian can do—she prayed.

Thank God for the gift of his Holy Spirit and pray today that you will have the courage to face whatever lies ahead.

ACTS 5:1–10 (NIV)

Who we really are

'Tell me, is this the price you and Ananias got for the land?'

This story may seem difficult, shocking, outrageous. Ananias and Sapphira lie, get found out and die immediately. They are not sent away to think about what they have done and repent; they do not get a second chance. How does this square up with Jesus' compassion and his willingness to forgive sinners?

This story is not about what Ananias and Sapphira do with their property but about their deceit. They want to appear better than they are. They want to be well thought of. Sapphira does have a chance to change her mind and distance herself from her husband's lie, but she responds with the same lie to Peter's question. She thought no one would know, no one would be able to find out. God would know, of course, but would that matter?

My landlord has a book on his bookshelf entitled Who You Are (When No One Is Looking) (Bill Hybels, IVP). This title made me think. Who am I when no one is looking? I like to think I live according to Christian values, but do I always? Do you? Of course we all slip up occasionally. Attaining perfection is not given to any of us this side of heaven. God will forgive us but we need to admit that we are not perfect, to ourselves and to others.

A few years ago I was the only Christian in the office I worked in at the time. My boss thought nothing of telling a 'little white lie' to our customers and expected me to do the same. I would not. I have to admit that I was tempted at times, but I knew I had to stick to my principles.

Sapphira pretended to be perfect. God had chosen to reveal to Peter what went on in her heart. Let us aim to be honest with God and with one another in the knowledge that he accepts us as we are.

Read Psalm 32.

✣

ACTS 9:36–42 (NIV)

How would you like to be remembered?

All the widows stood around (Peter), crying and showing him the robes and other clothing that Dorcas had made while she was still with them.

Dorcas (her name in Greek) or Tabitha (her name in Aramaic) had died. The widows showed Peter the robes she had made, as these robes symbolized how they remembered Tabitha—as someone 'who was always doing good and helping the poor' (v. 36). Caring for the poor was seen as a religious duty among Jews and was also practised by Christians. For Tabitha, it was more than just a duty. She was always doing good, so much so that this was what her friends remembered most about her. She made robes and clothes for others, thus using God-given gifts to help those in need.

When I went on a time-management course last year, it was suggested to us as an exercise to write our own obituary. How would we be remembered? What would people say about us if we died right now and our friends, colleagues or family had to write our obituary? Would we be happy with how they would remember us? This can be a sobering exercise. 'She spent most of her time in the office and had little time for her friends.' 'She was always at church meetings and never there when her family needed her.' Don't get me wrong: I am not suggesting that the Christian life is about good works, nor that it is about impressing other people. However, our actions say something about our priorities in life. If we make God our priority, we will be aware of the needs of others—just like Tabitha. Peter prayed, she rose to life again and many came to faith through this event (vv. 40–42).

How would you like to be remembered? What are your priorities in life? Spend some time today thinking about what is most important to you, then give these things (or people) to God in prayer.

✣

ACTS 12:13–16 (NIV)

An answer to prayer

'You're out of your mind,' they told her.

'You're out of your mind,' said one of the followers of the Way. 'It can't be true,' said another. 'Why should we believe her?' said a third. 'She's only a servant girl.' They had been praying, of course, praying for Peter's safety, praying for Peter's release (Acts 12:5). This was the right thing to do and the only thing they could do. They could not hire a lawyer for Peter, they could not go through the proper legal channels. So they prayed. But when they were told by the servant girl, Rhoda, that their prayer had been answered, they did not believe her. It seemed so unlikely, so improbable and they certainly could not believe a servant girl.

A friend of mine prayed for her boyfriend to come to know Jesus. Her boyfriend became her husband and went along to her church occasionally, but he still did not want to know about Jesus. My friend talked to him, tried to show him by example but most of all, she prayed. It was the right thing to do. After a few years, she had almost given up believing her prayer would ever get the answer she longed for, but she had not given up praying. God had not given up either. Today, both my friend and her husband are committed Christians and active members of their church. A miracle had happened. A prayer had been answered.

I heard the youth leader of a large church once say that she was still surprised by how much she could learn from the children of her church and how much they ministered to her. God does answer prayer and he uses those we often least expect to be his messengers—like Rhoda, the servant girl.

Think of someone you need to pray for today and commit yourself to praying for that person for a number of days, or weeks, or even months on a regular basis.

ACTS 16:1 (NIV)

Early influence

... where a disciple named Timothy lived, whose mother was a Jewess and a believer, but whose father was a Greek.

A big, dark, cold, scary building; boring services; slow, old-fashioned music. This is how I would have described my church when I was a child. The ancient building, the hymns, the service complete with liturgy and long sermons had nothing a child could relate to. There was no Sunday school, but there were midweek activities for children. I grew older and was confirmed at the age of 15. We had to attend confirmation classes beforehand. The class consisted of teenagers who could not wait for the classes to finish, who wanted to be confirmed to please their parents and receive lots of presents. The pastor tried his best to bring across the message of the gospel, but he struggled. I was confirmed because I wanted to declare publicly that I had chosen to follow Christ.

So where did my conviction that God existed and mattered come from? Church and RE lessons in school might have had some positive influence, but mostly it came from my parents. They were Christians, and although they were not perfect examples of followers of Christ, they were examples. They read Bible stories to me and sowed the seeds of faith. God used my parents, almost despite themselves.

How did Timothy become a believer? His father was Greek but his mother was a believer. 2 Timothy 1:5 suggests that Timothy's grandmother and mother were converted before Timothy was. What influence did their faith have on Timothy? What influence can you have in the lives of your children, your grandchildren, your god-children, the children of your neighbours and your friends?

Pray for a child with whom you are in regular contact. Pray that God will use you to be a good example of a follower of Christ. Remember that you do not have to be a perfect example.

ACTS 16:16–19 (NIV)

Used and valued by God

'These men are servants of the Most High God, who are telling you the way to be saved.'

She was only a slave. She had no rights, no freedom and no influence. She was gifted or afflicted (depending on whose viewpoint you want to take) with clairvoyance. She had little choice in the matter; in fact, she had little choice about anything. Her owners did not care about her. The slave girl was not a person to them, but only a source of income.

She was compelled to speak the truth. She knew that Paul and the others were 'servants of the Most High God, who are telling you the way to be saved'. This simple, truthful statement triggered a chain of events and changed the lives of several people (vv. 18–19). The owners of the girl lost their source of income and accused Paul and

Silas, who were beaten and put into prison. To cut a long and extraordinary story short, their jailer and all his family were saved as a result. All that because a slave girl had spoken the truth.

Look at Jesus' disciples. They were an uneducated, inarticulate group of men. They were not exactly the perfect team to convert the world.

Look around your church. Are your fellow members of the body a motley bunch of people? Who will arrange the flowers now that Sarah has left, and who will replace Mary as a homegroup leader? Why doesn't God send more gifted people to your church? Are you wondering why God has not equipped you with more gifts?

Look at Jesus' disciples. Look at the slave girl. God can take the seemingly small and insignificant and use them. God can use the new person next to you in the pew. God can use you.

Read the whole of this story (Acts 16:16–38) to see how the events unfold. Then ask God to show you how he wants to use you.

MOTHER HEN MINISTRY

---

1 CHRONICLES 4:9–10 (NKJV)

Branded by his mother

His mother called his name Jabez, saying, 'Because I bore him in pain.' And Jabez called on the God of Israel saying, 'Oh, that you would bless me indeed, and enlarge my territory, that your hand would be with me, and that you would keep me from evil, that I may not cause pain!' So God granted him what he requested.

We don't know this mother's name but we do know that she had such a frightful labour that she called her son 'Pain-giver'. Poor child! Every time anyone asked why he had such an odd name, he'd have to say, 'Because I gave my mum so much pain.' The feeling that he was destined to cause trouble and misery to those he loved obviously bothered him. Many of us grow up 'branded' by the attitudes and remarks of parents and teachers. They may not actually christen us 'Unwanted', 'Should-have-been-a-boy', 'Thick', or 'Not-good-enough', but the way they feel about us influences the way we see ourselves in later life.

That panics me! Did I permanently damage my children? Probably; but Jabez gives us all hope. God can heal the emotional scars we leave on others. No one has to be stuck with a bad self-image because of their childhood: like Jabez, we can ask God to change us.

For the last three months I've been praying Jabez's prayer every day. When my husband left me, I felt 'branded' as a failure. After a major grief it is easy to shrivel up inside and withdraw from other people to protect ourselves from further pain. So, like Jabez, I've been asking God to enlarge me (expand my love towards others) and to protect the relationships I still have. I want to catch this man's huge desire for God and the faith that God can undo the damage that others do to us—or that we have done to them.

Why not stick the 'Jabez prayer' on your fridge door to remind you to ask God every day to heal your scars and expand your life?

✣

MARK 6:16–28 (NIV)

Control

Herodias nursed a grudge against John and wanted to kill him... Finally the opportune time came... Herod gave a banquet... When the daughter of Herodias came in and danced, she pleased

Herod... He promised her with an oath, 'Whatever you ask I will give you...' She went out and said to her mother, 'What shall I ask for?' 'The head of John the Baptist,' she answered... (The executioner) went, beheaded John in the prison, and brought back his head on a platter. He presented it to the girl, and she gave it to her mother.

Ouch! The Bible contains some awful mothers but Herodias beats the lot! This was her daughter's big moment: she should have asked for something that would have benefited her future life. Instead, her controlling mother used her to fulfil her own goal—revenge. But when we point an accusing finger at someone, three of our fingers point back at us!

Do we ever try to live out our lives through other people? We've all heard of the mothers who never became ballerinas, tennis stars or musicians but who force their children to do it for them. A surprising number of adults feel bound by other people's expectations or feel failures because they fail to live up to them. Recently I met a nursing sister who efficiently runs a ward in a London hospital but suffers from bouts of depression because she feels she let her mother down. 'She wanted me to be a doctor,' she explained, 'but I never made the grades.' Another friend, whose husband died when her children were teenagers, told me that ten years on, she realized she was still using them as emotional props. 'I had to made a definite decision to let them go; then to fill the void with God himself.'

It is not only mothers who use and control other people; 'mother hens' can too. I've seen women 'take on' a new Christian or a young mum and instead of carrying out a normal discipling role they have totally dominated the other person's life in order to meet their own desire for control.

Think about your various relationships and ask yourself, 'Who controls me and whom do I control?

✣

GENESIS 21:5–21 (NIV)

Nightmare!

Abraham... sent (Hagar) off with the boy. She went on her way and wandered in the desert of Beersheba. When the water in the skin was gone... she thought, 'I cannot watch the boy die.' And as she sat there nearby, she began to sob... God opened her eyes and she saw a well of water.

Have you ever been stuck in a ghastly situation that you can't control or understand, and you can't find a way out? Every time you solve one problem, you create ten more, while the 'why' questions buzz in your head like wasps! When the nightmare concerns a child you love, the sense of powerlessness is overwhelming, and often the worst part is the feeling that God just doesn't care. Hagar must have felt all this as she sobbed in despair (v. 16). Theologians have always argued about why she was alone out there in the wilderness, and who was to blame—Abraham, Sarah, Ishmael, Hagar herself or God. Whoever it was, Hagar must have felt terribly hurt and rejected. The sense of 'this isn't fair' often adds to the pain of these situations, and our resentment can cut us off from God's comfort.

The first time Hagar had been lost in this desert was when she ran away from her mistress (Genesis 16), but God met her and told her what to do. Amazed that he knew her name and cared so intimately for a mere runaway slave-girl, she had called the place 'The God who sees me'. I've heard preachers say, 'Why did she forget about God's care?' but in these agonizing situations we don't always think straight. When my fourth baby was seriously ill, I felt I didn't have enough faith to pray, but 2 Timothy 2:13 helped: 'If we are faithless, he will remain faithful'. I realized that it is not our faith that counts but God's faithfulness! He could still see Hagar, even though she had temporarily lost sight of him—and he showed her the solution (v. 19).

The next time you feel trapped in one of these nightmares, stop struggling with the 'whys' and the 'hows'. Try asking God into the middle of the mess and leave him to sort it out in his own time.

✣

ISAIAH 49:15; 66:13 (NIV)

God the mother

Can a mother forget the baby at her breast and have no compassion on the child she has borne? Though she may forget, I will not forget you! ... As a mother comforts her child, so will I comfort you; and you will be comforted.

My fourth baby screamed incessantly. The only way I coped was by carrying him all day on my back, papoose style, where he invariably slept 'resting between my shoulders' (Deuteronomy 33:12).

The debate about whether God is male or female always irritates me because he can be everything we need him to be at different stages of our lives. He uses familiar human relationships to model the infinite variety of his love: he tells us he wants to be our Father, friend, husband, lover, brother, boss and king. Today's verses show that he can also mother us. Sometimes, when we have lost our mothers, or were never adequately mothered by them, we have an empty, lost feeling inside, and I am convinced that God can fill the emptiness with the gentle, tender side of his love. But we have to choose to let him.

Over the last few years I've lost several of the most important people in my life. While I want to allow God to fill the gaps they have left, sometimes I think, 'He isn't enough! I can't see, feel or hear him!' It is easy, then, to search for new human relationships to fill the vacuum, often with disastrous consequences. So I quickly pray, 'Lord you promised to comfort those who mourn, so I choose to run to you for that comfort.' Then I find that he either floods me with peace or sends someone to cherish me on his behalf.

Lord, I want to be like a baby kangaroo, hidden in your pocket.

Now read Psalm 131.

MATTHEW 12:46–50 (NIV)

A mother to Jesus

'For whoever does the will of my Father in heaven is my brother and sister and mother.'

When I think of the high value psychologists and theologians put on the role of a mother in a human's development, I often wonder what was so very special about Mary that she should be chosen, above all other women, to care for Jesus. He stayed at home with her until he was thirty, so the bond between them must have been very close indeed. She even stood at the foot of the cross, in case he needed her, in spite of the agony that it must have caused her.

Today's passage is hard to understand unless we realize that the brothers of Jesus did not, at first, believe he was God. When he became massively popular, they said, 'He's out of his mind' and set off, with Mary, to 'take him away' (Mark 3:21). They could not get to Jesus because of the crowds and he did not go out to them because he knew exactly why they had come! Instead he said something that many of us find strange. We are all happy to be his servant, friend, sister or child, but we are mystified when he calls us his mother. How can we 'mother' Jesus?

Even though my three sons have left home, they still seem to need me. When they lose a girlfriend, lose a job or face some big decision, home they come to offload on Mum, because they know that I'll listen and mind for them. But do we 'mind' about the grief Jesus faces every day? Prayer, on one level, is asking him to do things for us or others; a deep layer of prayer simply keeps him company, as a mother might sit with her son. Going even further, we can actually share the pain he feels as he looks at a suffering world and then weep with him.

Could Jesus come to you to be mothered sometimes, and sit with you, allowing you to share his load of grief and comfort him with your love?

UNSUNG HEROINES

READ EXODUS 2:8–21

Unsung heroines

All the women who were gifted artisans... whose heart stirred with wisdom spun yarn of goats' hair (Exodus 35:25–26, RAV).

The Bible is full of famous women whose saintly characters are dangled before the rest of us as visual aids in countless sermons. Yet the Bible also mentions many women who are dismissed in a few words because, in the male-dominated society in which they lived, they were considered totally unimportant. To God, however, they were so special that he wanted them included in the Bible, so that what they did could be remembered for ever.

Those 'skilled' and 'wise' women who spun goats' hair never became priests, dressed in glorious robes, performing grand ceremonies, but the hangings they created were part of the tabernacle where God was worshipped. He appreciated and enjoyed their careful work, colours and designs, just as much as he valued the work of the priests.

Isn't today's passage about the midwives fascinating? They did their job for God, too, so he honoured them.

The other morning I was watching a powerful evangelist on the Christian Channel. She was speaking to thousands of women in a packed auditorium, and countless more throughout the world. At the time I was crawling on the floor, ridden like a horse by the two small children I mind each Monday. I caught myself comparing the achievements of this glittering spiritual superstar and my own day, changing nappies and wiping noses! But surely, through today's 'unsung heroines' God is showing us that he values whatever we do for him. Each day our lives consist of a series of small jobs and activities, whether we are conference speakers or child minders. If we decide, each morning, to do every one of them out of love for him, his pleasure in our work will be equal, whether we communicate with thousands or wash dishes at the kitchen sink.

Lord, please take everything I do today as my gift to you. I pour out before you all the minutes that lie ahead, all the insignificant little activities and the vitally important jobs too. May every one give you pleasure. Amen

READ 1 KINGS 1:1–4

Carers matter!

'I tell you the truth, whatever you did for one of the least of these brothers and sisters of mine, you did for me' (Matthew 25:40, NIV).

What a special thing Abishag did! Nursing geriatrics could never be described as a glamorous job and when she agreed to care for this frail, bedridden old man, she forfeited her right to marry a young man and raise his children (1 Kings 2:21–23). Yet God valued her, and what she did for his friend David, she was doing for him.

People who look after an elderly or disabled relative are all too often forgotten by the rest of us, simply because they find it so hard to get out to social or church activities. Because carers can feel undervalued in the eyes of our busy world, they begin to feel under-valued in their own eyes, too.

I discovered another carer in 2 Samuel 4:4. When the news of King Saul's defeat and death arrived at the palace, she was nursing his five-year-old grandson—Jonathan's boy. In those days, when royal families toppled, every member of the dynasty was automatically butchered. So she picked up Mephibosheth and ran.

If you've ever tried carrying a squirming small boy, you'll easily guess what happened. Can't you hear him protesting, 'I'm not a baby' as he slithered out of her arms? We don't know what happened, but without medical help the poor child's injuries crippled him for life.

Disabled people in those days were disregarded, excluded from society and from places of worship. For years this nameless carer looked after Mephibosheth, loved him and kept him hidden. Then one day King David discovered where he was. She must have been convinced that Mephibosheth was about to die but David treated him like his own son, inviting him to live in the palace and eat at the royal table.

Lord, thank you for the way you value people who care for those challenged by disability, illness and old age. Please give them a special blessing today, particularly those who feel tired, isolated or discouraged. Amen

✣

READ JUDGES 1:12–15

The bride who asked for more

You do not have, because you do not ask God (James 4:2, NIV).

'Ask and it will be given to you... For everyone who asks receives' (Matthew 7:7–8, NIV).

Today's passage has a fairytale quality but actually Caleb forgot to give his daughter a wedding present so she had to 'urge' her new husband to ask him for a field (Judges 1:14). It was not a nice green meadow but a strip of dry, rocky wilderness. While on holiday in the mountains of southern Spain, I realized how much difference even a trickle of water can make to the farmers who struggle to make a living there. If Acsah wanted her field to be fruitful, she needed springs. So she plucked up her courage and visited her father. The field was the dowry she could have expected, but she dared to ask him 'for a blessing' (v. 15, AV) as well.

So many of us are content with our Christian lives just as they are. We get stuck in a spiritual rut and feel as dry and barren as Acsah's field. I often hear people say, 'I don't feel comfortable about praying for myself, when there are so many in need.' Of course we need to pray for others but God is a wonderfully lavish Father and, as Jesus said, he 'loves to give good gifts to those who ask him' (Matthew 7:11). It's sad when people say, 'I can't stand Christians who are always asking for some new blessing.' Would the daughter of a multi-millionaire who adores his children wear rags from a charity shop and sleep rough, simply because she 'didn't like to ask him for help'?

Is there some blessing you long for? The ability to pray, a gift of healing, some new ministry or a closer relationship with the Lord? Well, like Acsah, get off your donkey and ask your Father for it right now.

'Let anyone who is thirsty come to me and drink. Whoever believes in me... will have streams of living water will flowing from within' (John 7:37–38).

✣

READ 2 KINGS 11:1–3

The remarkable auntie

Arise, cry out in the night... pour out your heart like water in the presence of the Lord... for the lives of your children (Lamentations 2:19, NIV).

How brave of Auntie Johosheba to smuggle the baby prince out of the clutches of the murderous Athaliah. Seven years later, Joash became the king who loved God, and ruled his people successfully for nearly half a century. But where would he have been without his aunt?

Many of us have to watch our nephews, nieces or grandchildren growing up in homes where they never hear about God. Sometimes we feel like despairing, but Johosheba gives us hope. She rescued her nephew and hid him in God's house, and we can do the same by our prayers.

My brother took a group of Christian farmers to the Ukraine to stage an agricultural conference, to share both farming technology and Christianity. That week, many of the Ukrainians became Christians and said they could remember an ancient granny who believed in God and prayer. Those women must have died thinking that their families would all be hopelessly brainwashed by communism, but the seeds their prayers had sown germinated many years later.

Timothy had a mother and grandmother who prayed for him; Lois and Eunice are two more of the Bible's 'unsung heroines' (2 Timothy 1:5). Suppose they had not bothered to pray for such a timid, physically frail little boy? Would he have become one of God's giants?

When my own grandmother died, we found a card in her Bible on which she had written today's verse. She had seven children and many grand and great-grands too. How she prayed for us! As soon as she knew a baby was on the way, she would say, 'I must start paying money into its spiritual bank account.' A remarkable number of her descendants are now active Christians.

Write down on a card the names of children who are special to you, and stick it up prominently to remind you to pray for them frequently.

✣

READ HOSEA 1:6; 2:23

'Unloved'

You will be called by a new name that the mouth of the Lord will bestow... No longer will they call you Deserted... Desolate. But you will be called Hephzibah... and Beulah; for the Lord will take delight in you (Isaiah 62:2–4, NIV).

Fancy Hosea christening his daughter Unloved! Yet many people grow up blighted by the labels their parents gave them: 'Stupid... Ugly... Naughty... Troublemaker... Should-have-been-a-boy...'

Outwardly they may be called Jill or Sharon, but these hidden names haunt them, because the way we are treated as children influences the way we think of ourselves as adults.

Unloved's mother was man-crazy. Hosea knew he was not Unloved's father and, when he went to God with the pain and disappointment his family caused him, God said, 'I feel like that about the way my people reject and two-time me.' Identifying with God's suffering probably comforted Hosea, but where did that leave his poor daughter?

Her mother finally left to become a full-time prostitute, but she ended up in the slave market. God told Hosea to go and show her love again (3:1), so he bought her for a few silver coins and a bag of flour. In those days he had every right to stone her to death, but instead God told him to take her home and love her as an honoured wife. God wanted to use this family to demonstrate his faithful, forgiving love for his people. Unloved would also have been welcomed home and God must have told Hosea to rename her (2:23). So her story has a happy ending.

God can change the identities with which others have branded us. In Christ we are 'a new creation' (2 Corinthians 5:17), no longer chained to the past. Free of the attitudes or goals of others, we can start a new life with a fresh identity.

Stop and ask the Lord to show you the secret label branded by others on your heart. Then ask him to show you the new name he wants to give you.

✣

READ MARK 15:20–32

Adopted mother

Salute Rufus chosen in the Lord, and his mother and mine (Romans 16:13, NIV).

Who was this nameless woman who 'mothered' Paul? And why did Mark mention the two sons of Simon, the man from north Africa who carried the cross for Jesus? (Mark 15:21).

I love digging around between the lines of scripture. If Mark bothers to mention Rufus, maybe he had grown to know him later? Perhaps seeing Jesus die so impressed Simon that he became a member of that first church in Jerusalem. When persecution dispersed them throughout the Roman world, Cyrenian Christians went to Antioch (Acts 11:19–23) and founded a church, which Mark and Paul later joined (Acts 13:1–5).

Could Simon have been one of those church founders? Did Paul and Mark stay in his home, cared for and 'mothered' by his wife, who would have been the mother of Rufus? When Paul wrote Romans, he had never been to Rome so he must have met Rufus and his mother somewhere else.

Of course, I'm only speculating. What matters is that Paul remembered her kindness. He spent his life travelling from one church to the next and, in a small way, so do I. Recently I stayed in nine different homes in two weeks as I spoke at churches all over England. When you're exhausted after a long day of ministry and you arrive, late at night, to face a strange family, you never know how you will be received. Sometimes you're 'mothered', and you are so grateful for that love, but sometimes you feel nothing but a nuisance and you can't wait to leave!

Opening our homes and hearts to others is a vital ministry. Recently I met a new Christian, a single parent, who told me how her elderly neighbour had 'adopted' her family. 'She is like the mum I never had and a "granny" to my girls,' she told me. 'It seemed natural to go to her church and that's where we found Jesus.'

Is there someone in your church or neighbourhood who needs a 'mother'? It was practical human love in action that people saw in Jesus—and which drew them to God's love.

✣

READ ACTS 9:36–41

Tabitha or Scrooge?

Let us rejoice and be glad and give him glory! For the wedding of the Lamb has come, and his bride has made herself ready. Fine linen, bright and clean, was given her to wear. (Fine linen stands for the righteous acts of the saints.) (Revelation 19:7–8, NIV)

When my children were small, there was a woman in our church who reminded me of Tabitha. One day she arrived when I was staggering around with a migraine. She put me to bed, minded my children and demolished a mountain of ironing. Next morning I received an anonymous present of a new steam iron. Only 'Tabitha' could have known that my iron was dangerously old!

After my fourth baby, when I felt fat and depressed, she arrived with a lovely dress she said she no longer liked. It fitted perfectly and boosted my morale so much that I felt better at once. One day I ran out of housekeeping money and she arrived with three pounds of sausages. Her acts of kindness seemed endless, but it was not until after her death, when many of us pooled our memories, that we discovered just how many people she had helped, nurtured and encouraged. Her loving kindness lives on in our memories.

But how will we be remembered? Scrooge, in Dickens' A

Christmas Carol, was allowed to see into the future and he was so horrified by the way people felt about him on the day he died that he became a changed man!

The little secret acts of kindness we do for other people last for ever, not only in their memories. Revelation 19 tells us that they become part of the wedding dress we will wear when we marry our bridegroom, Jesus. Heaven will be wonderful for all Christians, but Jesus makes it clear that how we act during our earthly lives affects our eternal reward (Matthew 16:27). The Tabithas of this world are not thinking about that—they're far too busy loving people—but their wedding dresses will dazzle the rest of us one day!

Please, Lord, give me a Tabitha heart. Amen

✣

READ LUKE 8:1–3

A high-society lady

For the love of money is a root of all kinds of evil. Some people, eager for money, have wandered from the faith and pierced themselves with many griefs (1 Timothy 6:10, NIV).

We've all heard of the poor widow who put her last two coins into the temple treasury and was praised by Jesus for giving more than all the rich men who tossed in their bags of gold (Luke 21:1–4). Yet I've never heard a sermon about Joanna, the rich, high-society lady from King Herod's court. Because Jesus cared so intensely for the poor and hungry, it's easy to think he had no time for the rich, yet people like Joanna, Nicodemus and Joseph of Arimathea prove that was not so. We don't know if Jesus healed Joanna physically or released her spirit from Satan's oppression (Luke 8:2) but we do know that he changed her life. She may have travelled around the country with him, cooking and doing the disciples' washing, or she may simply have provided money to buy their food and accommodation. She was definitely one of the women who went to the tomb that first Easter Sunday morning, and perhaps it was her money that paid for the expensive embalming spices.

Today's verse makes it clear that it is the love of money that causes trouble. Making money can be a God-given ministry just as much as preaching or missionary work. God needs money makers to provide for his servants and build his Church. Yet, because money equals power and status in our world, we often give far more honour and attention to the 'Joannas' in our congregations who are rich in personality, gifts and material things than we give to people who have little to offer the church.

Jesus longs for us to give him everything we have—our time, gifts, skills, possessions and financial resources. He praised the widow because she held nothing back for herself, but Joanna did the same. By following Jesus she risked everything her world valued.

How much of what you are and what you own are you prepared to give to Jesus?

HANNAH

---

1 SAMUEL 1:1–2 (GNB)

Kith and kin

There was a man named Elkanah, from the tribe of Ephraim, who lived in the town of Ramah in the hill country of Ephraim. He was the son of Jeroham and grandson of Elihu, and belonged to the family of Tohu, a part of the clan of Zuph.

Normally I skip the long intros of who descended from whom. Not today.

Parking my car in our local cattle market, because it is the nearest traffic warden-free zone to the bank, I noticed something very odd. In the middle of the vast expanse of large, uneven cobblestones crouched a tiny woman, her head almost touching the ground, her wispy anorak tugged round her frighteningly thin form. It took half an hour of my sitting on the ground next to her to get her to look up and at least another quarter of an hour to persuade her to stand and, hanging on to me, walk shakily to the little market café. The bellowing from the cattle pens outside and from the farm workers at the other tables was strangely echoed in the cud-chewing eating style of this once-lovely girl as she tried to swallow her toast and tea. So alone, so ill, so afraid. The arrival of a representative from social services took the matter from my hands but I am left with an indelible image of her empty eyes, her silence and her isolation. Separated only by a formica-topped table and a mug of tea, I could have been a million miles from where she was.

In an age when it is fashionable to have a dysfunctional family from which one is escaping, probably with the help of a trained counsellor, pride in one's family history is decidedly outmoded. Perhaps today we could give thanks for our kith and our kin.

Dear Father, thank you for the family and friendship ties we have, however tangled they may be. We pray for those who have become untied at their moorings and are adrift. Help them to find you.

✣

1 SAMUEL 1:2–3 (GNB)

No choice for Hannah

Elkanah had two wives, Hannah and Peninnah. Peninnah had children, but Hannah had none.

The succinct style of the scriptures can sometimes be annoyingly lacking in detail, but here there is no need for more words, is there? Peninnah had children. Hannah had none.

Freedom of choice is the biggy these days. Choice to decide when it is convenient to have children. Choice to have or not to have children. Choice to work as a mother or not. Even choice to terminate the tiny life within us because it might cause problems. But sometimes we have no choice. At one point or another most of us experience loss of choice. Some of us have been bereaved, some of us overlooked for promotion or the job we desperately wanted. Some of us are forced through circumstances to experience separation from community and friends. Some of us find that the person we chose to marry chooses to leave. Some of us never find someone to marry even though we want to. Some of us are unhappy with our sexuality. Some of us want but can't have children—like Hannah.

It is so easy to know what to do in other people's circumstances. So easy to hold opinions about the knotty problems that advancing science is posing us as Christians—in vitro treatment, freezing embryos, surrogacy—or the moral freedoms our society aspires to. It is, of course, right to question and to try to make godly decisions, but before we voice our criticisms today at the decisions others are making, let us dwell for a moment on the area in our lives over which we have no choice and which is tearing us apart. Let us allow our tears to fall for those who are struggling to find a way out of their despair.

Dear Father, we know that you have always been wise and compassionate. We bring to you all those who are as unhappy in their circumstances as Hannah was. That might include me! Some of us are bruised with grief. Help us.

✣

1 SAMUEL 1:3–8 (GNB)

The bully

Peninnah, her rival, would torment and humiliate her because the Lord had kept her childless. This went on for year after year.

Do you remember those monster vegetables in old-fashioned horror films? Killer tomatoes which, having consumed their first victim, grew fatter and greedier for more. As the monster's power increases, there is always someone regretting that they didn't put weedkiller down while it was still only a bud on its mother's stalk.

This is the problem with bullying, isn't it? The bully grows fat with power and outrageously greedy for more. I imagine Peninnah looked forward to the annual trip to Shiloh in direct proportion to the extent that Hannah must have dreaded it, especially the moment when Elkanah shared out the portions of the sacrificial meat—a terrible visual aid serving to illustrate the difference between herself and her rival. And she powerless to stop it. What could she do, or say? Of course, the allocation of portions made sense. To ask for the same would have looked petty. She must just endure the taunts until someone put a stop to them. Unfortunately Elkanah couldn't see a problem and therefore did nothing. Does this make him blameless? Or is there, as has been argued in many a courtroom, a passive contribution made to evil by those who do nothing to break into the increasingly threatening pattern of monster behaviour?

Do you know someone who is being bullied? I don't just mean in the classic playground sense but, as with most abuse, in the family? Is someone being made to feel silly, inadequate and desperately unhappy on a regular basis? Is it you? Do you know someone who is a bully, someone who has grown accustomed to and greedy for power over someone else? Today let us search our hearts and, whether we are in the position of Hannah, Peninnah or Elkanah, let us take our situation to the Lord.

Today, Father, help us to face the truth, however difficult the task ahead may be for us.

✣

1 SAMUEL 1:7–9 (GNB)

Hannah's despair

Peninnah would upset Hannah so much that she would cry and refuse to eat anything. Her husband Elkanah would ask her, 'Hannah, why are you crying? Why won't you eat? Why are you always so sad? Don't I mean more to you than ten sons?'

Sometimes being loved isn't enough, is it? How I have longed for my love for my husband and children to be sufficient to suck out the poison from the wounds of life. How well I remember my mother's attempts to love out the pain in me when my first serious boyfriend decided to dump me. All too often, though, love is all we have to offer, and sometimes it can hurt us, as it clearly does Elkanah, that it is not enough to make life feel worth living for those we passionately care about. The worst day of my life was when my husband was emotionally ill and told me that 'either there is a God, in which case he will sort the whole mess out, or there isn't, in which case I want to kill myself'.

I was terrified but also profoundly hurt. Was not my love and the love of his three little boys enough to make him want to get well, to fight on? Later, I grew able to trust that God could never abandon someone who cared that much about his existence, but at the time it was as though the one phial of medicine that I had in my possession had been smashed on the floor. He was very ill and at that point only God's love was powerful enough to help.

Dear Father, we bring to you those who are in despair. Using Paul's words, we ask that their 'minds may be opened to see his light, so that [they] will know what is the hope to which he has called [them], how rich are the wonderful blessings he promises his people, and how very great is his power at work in us who believe' (Ephesians 1:18–19, NIV). Give us the faith to hang on to believing.

✣

1 SAMUEL 1:9–11 (GNB)

Out of control

Hannah got up. She was deeply distressed and she cried bitterly as she prayed to the Lord.

For years Hannah has suffered her humiliation in silence and with dignity, holding back surging waters of bitterness and grief, but the cruelty of Peninnah has broken through the last defences. The visible sign that the walls are crumbling is that she can no longer keep up the pretence that she is in control. We are told that she cannot eat, that she cannot stay in the room, that she is crying in public. All those years of swallowing the unpalatable combination of her solitary portion and Peninnah's insults—and now even her dignity is taken from her. Poor Hannah.

It's so awful to be out of control, isn't it? When we burst into tears in the supermarket because we've forgotten our purse. Or we scream at our children because they've spilt their drink in the car, or shout at the driver behind us, or slam the phone down. It's rare that we rationally discuss problems with the relevant person at a time or place we would have chosen because it is impossible to predict when our wall will finally succumb to the beating. Yet it is only when the pain does explode into a visible form that we can be helped.

What an explosion this is! Hannah is utterly fed up with God, who doesn't seem either to have noticed her or cared about her. The Jerusalem Bible has this wonderful translation: 'Should you condescend to notice the humiliation of your servant?' It may be Peninnah who has made her life a misery but it is God who has let her down. He must know what she wanted. Why has he not helped? The only possible explanation for her on this awful day is that he just doesn't care.

Dear Father, some of us just can't understand why you don't appear to care about the trouble we're in. We desperately need to know you care. Please help us to tell you how we feel, trusting that you really want to know.

✣

1 SAMUEL 1:11 (GNB)

Unwrapped

'If you give me a son, I promise that I will dedicate him to you for his whole life and that he will never have his hair cut.'

Brought to the end of her resources, Hannah's honesty is raw. The unsentimental nature of her bargain is perhaps a little hard for us to digest. We so like things to be wrapped up in pretty paper.

This is the reason we find very depressed or angry people a problem in our cosy churches. They are disturbingly direct, sometimes critically negative.

Hannah wants a baby boy primarily in order to put a stop to the humiliation. The baby is to be her 'show and tell' to the world of her value in God's eyes.

The more secure we are, the less we need visible symbols. I have often heard the criticisms hurled at teenage single mums over the extravagance of their infants' equipment. Having worked with so many young people who have been devalued in childhood, I can perhaps understand. Of course it's silly. Of course it would be more sensible, on their income, to buy a second-hand pram, but they also need to 'show and tell'. I remember one young friend who had grown up in care, expressing volubly her puzzlement over the delapidated buggy that, having served my sons faithfully, now carried our little daughter. Her firstborn of similar age was swanning around in a luxury Pierre Cardin creation bought from a catalogue, along with his clothes, his cot and a galaxy of soft toys and mobiles. The world was going to know that she, despite her single status and all her past failures, was a good mum. What is interesting is that we may disapprove of the way Hannah is talking to God but he doesn't seem to have a problem!

Dear Father, help us to stop waffling about and to be just as honest with you.

✣

1 SAMUEL 1:12–18 (GNB)

Finding her voice

Eli thought she was drunk, and said to her... 'Stop your drinking and sober up!' ... 'I am desperate, and I have been praying, pouring out my troubles to the Lord.' ... 'Go in peace,' Eli said. Then she went away, ate some food, and was no longer sad.

Between the point when she was unable to eat and 'began eating again', something amazing has happened to Hannah. She has cleared the emotional blockage in her throat and is at last listening, probably in astonishment, to her voice coming out loud and clear. Not only has she poured out what she describes here as 'grief and resentment' to God, but she has also defended herself against the horrific insult of Eli in a way she had clearly never done to Peninnah.

One of the things that can nearly destroy us is the belief that our problems are slight and silly and that if only we were stronger, braver, cleverer, we would be able to cope. We struggle to gain control over what we see as our failure to cope, often with disastrous results, withdrawal from relationships and eating disorders being two of the most common.

Hannah had thought that her best defence was to block her emotions and she had become unreachable by her loving husband, unable to find a value in herself and unable to eat. By unleashing her anger and despair at God, she has unstopped the bottle. The fizz has bubbled messily everywhere but is now gone. At last she can acknowledge with a new dignity that she is not a worthless woman but someone with a problem who needs help.

Her circumstances at this point haven't changed. She is still childless. She has just made a fool of herself in front of her family. She has given a good impression of being drunk to her priest. But she has changed. She is at peace with herself. Interestingly, Eli clearly responds to the new assertive Hannah and gives his blessing. No wonder she can eat now.

Dear Father, give us the voice you want us to have for your sake and ours.

⁘

1 SAMUEL 1:19–24 (GNB)

Celebration of motherhood

So it was that she became pregnant and gave birth to a son... She told her husband, 'As soon as the child is weaned, I will take him to the house of the Lord, where he will stay all his life.'

My son Matt and I stand, staring upwards, eyes straining in the swirling orange dust of the mountains of Gobystan, an area 60 kilometres south of Baku, Azerbaijan, where he has been working for the past year. We are transfixed by the numerous ancient engravings on the rocks that cover the mountains. Stick-like buffalo, deer, camels, snakes, fish, birds, hunters, dancers and women. The many carvings of women intrigue us—no arms but large rounded breasts, hips and thighs, representing a celebration of the mother-continuers of the kin.

Today's fashion denies this role strongly, its unformed shapes symbolizing freedom from a male-dominated world. Even maternity clothes are designed to minimize the signs of impending motherhood.

Returning to one's former shape as soon as possible is the goal of most new mothers. Women who choose to stay at home to look after their children are sometimes looked down on.

Here Hannah seems to span the centuries. Calmly and in absolute control, she announces to Elkanah her intentions. The baby is to be given back to God, but not yet. She will confidently go to the temple, but not yet. Not until she has weaned her beloved baby.

We can only imagine this precious period Hannah and Samuel have together—a stop-breath of time known so well by any mother who has watched her infant loll back its head, a surfeit of warm milk dribbling from its soft, still-sucking mouth.

She joins many working mothers in only having a short time solely with her little one. Whatever decisions we are to make or have made in respect of our children, today let us celebrate the mother-continuers of our kin.

Dear Father, we thank you for the special time set aside by you for your mothers and babies.

1 SAMUEL 1:24–29 (GNB)

The promise

She took Samuel, young as he was, to the house of the Lord at Shiloh... to Eli. Hannah said to him, 'Excuse me, sir. Do you remember me?'

Hannah is now quite remarkable, isn't she? Here she is with a weapon to protect her for ever from Peninnah's insults, her relationship with her husband strengthened and with a period of bonding that will involve an emotional tearing apart from her beloved son, yet she never wavers from her promise to the third vitally important person in her life, her God. I wish I could crawl inside her head at this point. Surely she must have been tempted to argue that Eli was hardly likely to remember an incident at least a couple of years ago where a distraught woman was seen muttering to herself? He didn't even know what she was asking. He'd thought she was drunk.

The courage and determination it must have taken to walk up to the temple steps and gently prise Samuel's trusting little fingers from hers is unimaginable. I know I couldn't and wouldn't have done it, and it does sadly remind me of promises I have privately made to God. Promises which I have not kept when the storms are over and the sea is calm. Vows made at times when I have been overflowing with gratitude. Unlike Hannah, I haven't made it impossible to forget my promises. From the word go, she reminds herself of her promise. Her son is to be called Samuel, shem-el—the name of God, and here related to sha-al, to ask. Can we learn something from this? Maybe we should reinforce our promises with some sort of knot in our proverbial handkerchiefs, like telling someone what we have told God we would do, or privately putting it solemnly into writing. For each one of us it will be different. Let's try to find our way.

Dear Father, show me a way that will help me remember my promises to you. Help me find the courage to carry them through.

⁘

1 SAMUEL 2:1–3 (GNB)

What a prayer

Hannah prayed: 'The Lord has filled my heart with joy; how happy I am because of what he has done! I laugh at my enemies; how joyful I am because God has helped me!'

This wonderful prayer has the hallmark of the Holy Spirit. It is an utterance of joy and confidence in a God who cares, who looks after the poorest, and who will give strength to his anointed, however humble they may appear. Hannah cannot know that her gift will be of so much use to her God; that it will be this tiny child who will be used to choose a shepherd-boy to be the second most famous king in the Bible. What she does know is that when she was at her lowest, hating herself, everyone else, even God, he heard her.

Many years ago, a dear friend of ours found that he couldn't continue in his marriage for reasons that are irrelevant here, except to say that there were genuinely irreconcilable differences. He and his wife did try but it was his decision that there was no hope. He was a Christian with a deep-rooted belief that marriage vows were taken for life, so it was not easy, but the thing that he found more difficult than anything else was the loss of self-respect. 'How can I live with myself, knowing that it was me who finally severed the tie?' There was no helpful answer.

'God doesn't care about me.' There is an answer. Even if at the moment we hate ourselves and feel there is no good in us, God has his door open. Some years ago, Adrian felt as if he'd been driven right back to the starting line in life. He wrote these words on feeling the first stirrings of new progress.

I watch
Frightened
Helpless
But secretly willing
As my foot rises, moving forward with my weight,
And I realize
That at last
I am going to walk.

✣

1 SAMUEL 2:3–11 (GNB)

A shaggy dog tale!

Stop your loud boasting; silence your proud words. For the Lord is a God who knows, and he judges all that people do... a man does not triumph by his own strength.

We have a dear old shaggy dog called Rosie and a kitten called Pepsi (hardly in the Samuel category of names). Recently Rosie had a rather drastic haircut. She always loves coming home after she has been beautified because she knows she will be in for lots of fuss and laughter and praise, so she bounded into the house to show off not only to us but also to Pepsi, whom she loves. Imagine her surprise when the kitten arched her back and spat and hissed and ran away, terrified by this glossy stranger. Poor Rosie! Her new shiny image had lost her a relationship that mattered. She lay down and put her head on her paws and for a whole day tried gently to convince her little friend that she was the same old shaggy dog friend inside.

We may get a bit uppity and sure of ourselves with an elevated expectation as to how others should respond. We may even cause those who loved us in our old raggy state to feel frightened and unsure of us. Fortunately God knows us. He has known us longer than anyone—since we were in the womb, in fact. He is not going to be too impressed by our efforts to do things in our own strength when everything he has ever tried to do is to bring us to him for help. He not only knows everything we've ever done but also everything we've ever thought of doing! God isn't in the business of bashing everything we try to achieve, but if he knows that what we really need is our old relationship with him, he may crash down pretty heavily on those things that are dominating our lives and keeping us from him.

Dear Father, bring us back to our old relationship with you, however drastic the measures that may be needed.

1 SAMUEL 2:12–18 (GNB)

God's treasures

The sin of the sons of Eli was extremely serious in the Lord's sight, because they treated the offerings to the Lord with such disrespect.

Hidden deep in my mother's dressing-table are her treasures. If you're a burglar, please don't get excited. Her treasures consist of drawings and tiny gifts and things that my brother and I made her for birthdays when we were small. One of her favourites is a hanky I made when I was six. Right in the middle is 'sewn' a large artificial violet. One out of ten for usefulness, but in terms of shiny-eyed pride and absolute conviction that my mother would appreciate my gift, ten out of ten. Nothing I could buy or make now could symbolize more love or represent as much lip-chewing, finger-puncturing concentration and commitment as my silly hanky!

It was never that God greedily demanded his dues. He wanted our first fruits because he wants us to give him our best out of reverence and love. The sin of Eli's miserable sons was that they despised the offerings made in earnest by ordinary people like us. No wonder God was angry. If my older brother had mocked my hanky, I would have been mortified and my mother furious. Jesus never laughed at the widow's mite or the boy's loaves and fishes. But are we valuing in the same way the contributions made by our church family? If the youth group writes and performs what to them is a genuine love offering to their God, isn't it up to us to honour it? (If they haven't really bothered and arrogantly assume that the rest of their church family are too lacking in the Spirit to understand, then maybe they need to rethink their offering.) The same applies to our church stewarding, our flower arranging, even our coffee brewing. If it's half-hearted, we should all be sad but if it's our very best then heaven will rejoice and we should too.

Dear Father, help us today to give you our very best, knowing that it will give you pleasure.

✣

1 SAMUEL 2:18–35 (GNB)

Trust betrayed?

The boy Samuel continued to grow and to gain favour both with the Lord and with people. A prophet came to Eli with this message from the Lord… 'The time is coming when I will kill all the young men in your family.'

This whole period of Samuel's life sends a shiver of fear through me. I think of Hannah honouring her promise and, as far as she is concerned, placing her little son in the best place possible, the temple of the Lord, to be cared for by priests. She came each year with his new little sacred coat, made with love and prayers. Yet far from being the safe, secure environment she pictured, he is in fact growing up under the influence of one of the worst families imaginable. So evil have Eli's two sons become that God has decided to go back on the promise he made to Aaron that his clan would serve him as priests for all time. The brothers are to die and God is to choose a new priest, but in the meantime, unbeknown to his parents, this vulnerable child is living under their contaminating influence.

At some point we have to let go those we love, don't we? Whether it's seeing our three-year-old child into playgroup or our 80-year-old parent into a home, we experience enormous anxiety about their safety and we have to put our trust in those looking after them. Of course we can check their credentials but we can't know exactly what will go on when we are not there, and credentials, as this story proves, don't always represent safety. There has always been danger and temptation in our world and it is impossible to shield our loved ones. We need to pray continuously for their protection. Is it not encouraging that in the midst of the atrocious goings-on of Hophni and Phinehas and the lax guidance of elderly Eli, little Samuel is kept both physically and spiritually safe?

Dear Father, please father those we love when we are not able to be there for them. We ask this with all our hearts.

✣

1 SAMUEL 2:27–32 (GNB)

Rare sightings

In those days, when the boy Samuel was serving the Lord under the direction of Eli, there were very few messages from the Lord, and visions from him were quite rare.

A couple of years ago, we had two wonderful ministers to stay from the township of Soweto, where our family had had the stunning privilege of attending a service in 1996. At the time, we had been bowled over by the singing, the number of new converts and the preaching. Now, strolling down a leafy lane near our home, we wanted to hear more.

'Do you see any actual miracles?' Adrian asked.

'Of course. We have a notebook and I write each one down carefully with the date of the healing or deliverance. We have filled several notebooks. What about you? How do you record your miracles?'

Well? What would you be able to say truthfully? How many blind are seeing? Lame walking? Maybe you would have cited some examples of visible miracles or maybe, like us, you would have had to talk of lives changing slowly, of people increasingly caring for each other, of the church giving increasing. These things are truly to be rejoiced over, but most of us, if we're honest, don't see the same level of overt miracles in a decade as this tent mission in Soweto is experiencing in a week. Why? Does the clue lie in Hophni's and Phinehas' contempt for their Lord, and in Eli's indifference?

Let us look at what God said through his prophet Malachi: 'You cover the altar of Yahweh with tears, with weeping and wailing because he now refuses to consider the offering or to accept it from you.' We want to see miracles but we don't connect our being refused with our corporate behaviour. The naivety and gratitude of congregations such as that in Soweto must make it possible for God to shower them with blessing. Our self-sufficiency and demanding nature must make the process difficult.

Dear Father, teach us to seek first the kingdom of God.

THE RIGHT PEOPLE

GENESIS 12:1 (NRSV)

Abram—moving on

Now the Lord said to Abram, 'Go from your country and your kindred and your father's house to the land that I will show you.'

In Genesis so far we have had the stories of the creation, the fall from God's ideal of Eden, Cain murdering his brother Abel, the great flood and the tower of Babel, but now God moves again to take control. Human beings by themselves haven't done too well! Abram (later to be renamed Abraham) receives the great promises—a future nation from his descendants, a close relationship with God, and a land chosen by God.

But first Abram must change his life, and move from his home in Haran, many miles north of Palestine. Abram just does it. God tells him to move, and he moves, with all his family and possessions. They had no idea of what was going to happen, but they trusted God, and set out into the unknown. And Abram was already 75!

Not many of us are like Abram, willingly embracing change! Most of us love security and being in control. So we resent change, dig in our heels and feel threatened. I remember the weeks when our elder daughter (then about six years old) invented a precarious route up our stairs: she wouldn't walk on the new stair carpet because she liked the old one! She's now just got married, so many exciting changes will be in store! But changes at work, in church, in relationships are all demanding, and often we need a push from God to be flexible.

Sometimes, too, change is forced on us, and we have to be prepared to learn acceptance and to put resentment to one side. A lady I know who is housebound through serious illness has used her situation as an opportunity to engage in prayer for her church and community. Many people have been inspired by her.

God is a God of change. If we can really trust him, we can learn to cooperate with change. The God of Abram goes before, and leads us on.

Help me to follow your leading, Lord.

✣

GENESIS 17:17 (NRSV)

Abraham—a long wait

Then Abraham fell on his face and laughed, and said to himself, 'Can a child be born to a man who is a hundred years old? Can Sarah, who is ninety years old, bear a child?'

More than twenty years have passed since Abram was promised an heir, to found the great nation of which God had spoken. Sarai, his beloved wife, believing she could never have a child, had given her maid to Abram as a sort of surrogate mother. But the son Ishmael who resulted didn't seem quite the right sort of character to be the child God had promised. Now God spoke to Abram again, renamed him and Sarai, and for the first time told Abraham that Sarah was to be the mother of the longed-for son. There was only another year to wait!

Abraham just fell about laughing. God really had a great sense of humour! Abraham hadn't lived this long without recognizing a silly idea when he heard it. But God was serious, the child Isaac was born, and the story went on through the ages.

There are many times when we have a long wait to see God's plans put into action. Maybe it won't even be in our lifetime. A great missionary spent all his life working in Sudan and didn't see a single convert. But he laid the foundations for the great growth in the Christian faith that was to sweep the country after his death.

What are the things we are waiting to see happen? Maybe it is something to do with our children, our place of work, our parents, our neighbourhood. We may be tired of waiting, or be tempted to blame ourselves for the slowness of results. Abraham, in verse 1, was instructed by God to 'walk before me and be blameless', in other words to trust God and be the person God wanted him to be. The results would then take care of themselves, maybe not in a hurry, but in God's time and in God's way.

Help me to be patient, Lord, and to look for encouraging signs of new beginnings.

✣

GENESIS 41:15 (NRSV)

Joseph—right person, right place

And Pharaoh said to Joseph, 'I have had a dream, and there is no one who can interpret it. I have heard it said of you that when you hear a dream you can interpret it.'

Joseph was his father's favourite, so his brothers resented him and he fanned their jealousy. They plotted to kill him, then sold him into slavery instead. Initially successful, Joseph fell prey to the amorous designs of his Egyptian master's wife, and when he didn't respond to her she lied about him and had him thrown into prison. He became known as an interpreter of dreams, but life must have felt pretty grim. But now, at last, Pharaoh had sent for him. By his interpretation of Pharaoh's dream, Joseph was able to save Egypt from suffering during the coming famine, and was himself elevated to high office.

Each part of Joseph's life was preparing him for the future. The naïve young man at the start of the story couldn't handle his own brothers, never mind the whole Egyptian nation! Through his life experiences, many of them bad, he had learned to trust God, handle people and understand what it felt like to be at the bottom of the heap. Only then was he ready to do the work God had planned for him.

Our lives may not have been as dramatic as Joseph's, but perhaps we can see some pattern in our experiences and how we have been developing over the years. We may still have a way to go! But like Joseph, each one of us is the right person in the right place at the right time. We are all 'right people' because we are loved by God, and he can use our gifts wherever we are. Our task may be much more ordinary than saving Egypt, but there will be things each day that would not happen if we didn't do them—and we can do these things to the glory of God.

Thank God for the things that only you can do today.

⁜

GENESIS 50:17 (NRSV)

Joseph—puts the past behind him

'"Say to Joseph: I beg you, forgive the crime of your brothers and the wrong they did in harming you." Now therefore please forgive the crime of the servants of the God of your father.' Joseph wept when they spoke to him.

Joseph's brothers had done awful things to him. However much he had provoked them, there was still no excuse for dropping him down a well, fishing him out to sell to some passing traders, then faking his death to convince his devoted father that he had been eaten by wild animals. That's on a rather bigger scale than most of our family troubles!

Joseph had turned out well despite a rocky start, and was now rich and famous. The brothers needed his help, and had demonstrated a change of heart and genuine family loyalty, but they were by no means certain that Joseph could put the past behind him. He now had the power to obliterate them (and good reason to do it). It's a measure of how all have grown during this story, that Joseph can see God's hand in what has happened and look on his brothers with pity and emotion.

Joseph's brothers had intended him harm, but we often cause unintentional hurt in our families. Some years ago, one of my students took an overdose because she felt that her parents loved her sister more than they loved her. Luckily she admitted this in time, and her parents had the chance to show her that she too was very special. But the hurt often goes unmentioned until it leads to silence and big barriers.

Some situations are not in our power to heal, but if an opportunity comes along, what can we learn from Joseph's story? It had taken many years to reach the point where both sides could show a real desire to start again without recriminations, and great strength of character was needed to seize the moment. So we should never despair of the possibility of remaking relationships, but should hold them all—and ourselves—up to God for his patient healing.

Pray for those you know (maybe yourself) facing family problems.

✣

JUDGES 6:15 (NRSV)

Gideon—feeling useless

He responded, 'But sir, how can I deliver Israel? My clan is the weakest in Manasseh, and I am the least in my family.'

Fancy being asked, out of the blue, to become company chairman and lead the takeover negotiations. All you are at the moment is the office junior, and now God is telling you that you're the only person who can do this. It's the stuff of feel-good movies! Understandably, Gideon is a little reluctant to accept that he's heard the message right. Maybe he's been able to fool the locals that he has ability, but surely God can see through him!

And that's just the trouble, because God can see through him, and, despite Gideon's reluctance, God knows he is the right person for the job. I suspect that many of us would sympathize with Gideon's position, and would much prefer to be passed by when it comes to leadership roles. We think other people are mistaken when they recognize our talents, and we run ourselves down much too easily. Maybe we should try asking 'Why not?' instead of the usual 'Why me?'

Most of us are not called to great responsibility like Gideon was, but we could perhaps do more to encourage, support and pray for those who are—and not just the people at the top, but those who care for our children and are responsible for the health of our communities.

Yet whatever role we have been given, God values us for what we are, and knows our potential for good. We don't need to be important in the world's eyes to be important in God's. He doesn't only work with the rich and famous, with good degrees from top universities and a string of television appearances to their credit! Most of the Old Testament heroes started off by protesting their inability to do the job God had in mind, yet it is only in our weakness that we can hand over to him and let him take control and transform us.

Can you try to pray regularly for someone you know who has a leadership role?

✣

JUDGES 6:37 (NRSV)

Gideon's fleece

I am going to lay a fleece of wool on the threshing-floor; if there is dew on the fleece alone, and it is dry on all the ground, then I shall know that you will deliver Israel by my hand, as you have said.

Poor Gideon! He was really worried by all this 'deliver Israel' talk. He's tried to wriggle out of it, and now God in his infinite patience is allowing Gideon to play games with him, in order to give him the confidence he needs. Often in the Old Testament, God's specific word was sought about the outcome of a battle, but here Gideon is taking that to extremes.

I must admit to having tried 'laying fleeces' in my youth! Something on the lines of 'If the next car that comes round the corner is red, then I will take the job. Sorry, I didn't give enough warning of that. If the twelfth car that comes round the corner is red, I'll take the job.' We keep on moving the goalposts until we get the result we want anyway!

But Gideon isn't using God as an alternative to making his own decision. God has given us a brain, and he intends us to use it. Here Gideon knows exactly what God wants him to do; he just doesn't have the confidence yet to go through with it. It's not a decision he wants, but reassurance. God is under no obligation to jump through these hoops of Gideon's making, but he demonstrates his loving care for Gideon and his knowledge of his character by giving him all the reassurance he needs.

We often find ourselves facing things we would rather get out of, and need God's loving support to carry us through. Maybe it's an exam, a hospital appointment, a difficult meeting, an apology to make. Our God is there with his arms outstretched to support us if we ask for his help, and there's no need to invent hurdles for him to jump over in order to demonstrate his love for us!

Read Judges 7:1–23 to see how the battle was won.

✣

1 SAMUEL 23:16 (NRSV)

David and Jonathan—friendship

Saul's son Jonathan set out and came to David at Horesh; there he strengthened his hand through the Lord.

David is in hiding, pursued by the present king, Saul, who has become murderously jealous of David's military success and his popularity with the people. Saul cannot find David, but Saul's son Jonathan, David's closest friend, knows exactly where he is hiding. Jonathan urges David not to fear, and encourages him about the future. Jonathan has risked his own life in coming to see David, but he knows how much it will mean to David in this dark time. This is the last recorded meeting of the two friends: both Jonathan and his father Saul were later killed in battle with the Philistines, and David became king.

Jonathan recognized the moment when David most needed encouragement. A friend of ours has just the same gift, but her modern-day method is to send encouraging cards. When she knows someone is facing exams, they get a cheerful card to keep them going. When a friend is having a difficult time, she sends them a card saying they are in her prayers. When she knows a speaker has put a lot of effort into a talk, she sends her thanks. We could all follow her example!

Jonathan knew the right things to say to support his friend. He assured David that he would be king, a role that Jonathan might rightly have expected to fill himself after the death of his father. But Jonathan knew that David was the king chosen by God, so he assured him of his unshakeable loyalty. This relationship gives us something to measure ourselves against—and something to aim for. We may not have much influence in the world in general, but we are of vital importance in the smaller sphere of our friends and family. Here we can offer encouragement and support when it is most needed, because we can spot the needs that others may miss. Maybe, like Jonathan, we can make all the difference.

Can you encourage or support a friend or family member today?

✣

2 SAMUEL 11:2 (NRSV)

David lets himself down

It happened, late one afternoon, when David rose from his couch and was walking about on the roof of the king's house, that he saw from the roof a woman bathing; the woman was very beautiful.

By now David is a popular and successful king, and a devout and loyal follower of God. The perfect man now does a nose-dive off his pedestal. Instead of going to war with his army, David has stayed at home in Jerusalem. Missing the action, he sees the beautiful Bathsheba bathing. The situation gallops towards tragedy, as Bathsheba becomes pregnant and David tries to make it appear as if her husband Uriah is the father. But Uriah is too loyal a soldier to go back home to his wife, and David in desperation arranges for Uriah to be killed in battle, so that he can quickly marry Bathsheba and make the child legitimate.

The prophet Nathan then tells David a story which helps the king to realize his guilt. He is desperately sorry, offers no excuses for his behaviour, and throws himself on God's mercy.

We are all capable of letting ourselves down and falling from our own ideals of behaviour. Once the first wrong step has been taken, it becomes increasingly difficult to get off the path. Yet it is not impossible, and we all know of marriages that have been rescued from the brink of collapse. But both parties must want to start again, and much forgiveness and painful understanding is necessary.

It is easy to identify with the poor murdered Uriah, feeling wronged and mistreated, but we all have within us the possibility of behaving like David too. In every sphere of our lives we can make wrong turnings and let ourselves down. Recently I hurt a colleague at work by not consulting him properly—and I really should have known better. But David didn't try to justify his actions or invent excuses. He acknowledged his mistakes and asked for God's forgiveness. We need courage to do the same.

Read the whole story: 2 Samuel 11:1—12:25.

⁜

2 SAMUEL 16:12 (NRSV)

David—coping with criticism

It may be that the Lord will look on my distress, and the Lord will repay me with good for this cursing of me today.

David was being followed by a man who was determined to humiliate him, making David look ridiculous in front of his men. Most kings in David's position would have removed this irritation from the face of the earth without any hesitation. Indeed, David was urged to do just that. But part of David's greatness lay in his ability to relate all his experiences back to God, knowing that maybe some good could come from them. David knew that he wasn't always in the right, and that even kings needed to be reminded of their faults.

Humility is a virtue that is out of fashion nowadays. We're encouraged to be confident, self-assertive individuals. We must make decisions and live with them. But sooner or later, we will do something that someone else feels is wrong, and then how do we cope when we're on the receiving end of criticism?

The art teacher I had a few years back had to convince her class that the work we were taking ages to produce was still rather far short of Rembrandt standard. If she had only ever praised us, and not pointed out our faults, we would never have improved. We had signed up for criticism when we joined the class, and we had to swallow any misplaced pride and face our shortcomings honestly.

Criticism isn't always justified or gentle, though. Unfair criticism can make our confidence sink through the floor, or rouse the desire to retaliate—echoing David's adviser's wish to 'let me go over there and take off his head'. David's better way was to see if God could bring something good out of the discomfort, and that might help us to cope too. And maybe facing criticism constructively ourselves can help us to be more sensitive to others. Above all, remember that in God's eyes we are all infinitely valuable, whatever anyone else may think.

Pray that others may be sensitive to you, and you to them.

✣

1 KINGS 18:22 (NRSV)

Elijah—standing alone

Then Elijah said to the people, 'I, even I only, am left a prophet of the Lord; but Baal's prophets number four hundred and fifty.'

King Ahab ruled the prosperous and successful northern kingdom. His foreign wife, Jezebel, had introduced acceptance of the storm-and-rain god Baal, and there were hundreds of priests of Baal who went colourfully about their business, tolerated and unhindered. True religion had dwindled, as had the number of the prophets.

Elijah was the only prophet with the courage to face Ahab and challenge the priests of Baal to a head-on contest. God dramatically sent fire to consume the soaking wet offering of Elijah, while the priests of Baal were unable to get any response at all from their god. What amazing courage Elijah showed! He was one man alone, against all the priests of Baal and a crowd that would support whichever side won. There was no more isolated position than this.

Many Christians today feel alone, as Elijah did. It is hard to be the only member of your family who goes to church or who has different priorities. I met a Christian woman who could never stay to coffee after her church service, as her husband tolerated her going to church on Sunday only if she had the traditional roast promptly on the table at one o'clock. She managed, and kept the peace! It is hard to be the only Christian at work when your attitudes towards company decisions may be different from your colleagues'. It is especially hard for young Christians to maintain their integrity, faced with pressures from their friends to do as the others do.

Whatever our circumstances, we need the courage that a close relationship with God can give if we are to cope with the stresses of standing alone, without compromising our beliefs. If our lives can be sensitive and consistent examples to others, showing that we are living by a different value system that really works, then in our own way we too can be ambassadors for God.

Read the whole story: 1 Kings 18:17–40.

1 KINGS 19:4 (NRSV)

Elijah—why bother?

But he himself went a day's journey into the wilderness, and came and sat down under a solitary broom tree. He asked that he might die: 'It is enough; now, O Lord, take away my life, for I am no better than my ancestors.'

Queen Jezebel was incensed at Elijah's triumph over the prophets of Baal. She sent her death squads after him and, sensibly, Elijah fled. After such a victory, the ignominy of flight, the lack of support from the people, and the seeming impossibility of his task were too much for him. He wished to die, resigned to failure like other prophets before him.

But God had other plans. Refreshed by food and drink, Elijah made for Mount Horeb, a hundred miles away across arid country. Still depressed, he found a cave for shelter. But this was the mountain where God had first appeared to Moses, and now Elijah was summoned out to be given a fresh revelation of God's power. Unlike the nature gods of the region, God was not limited to wind, earthquake or fire. He demonstrated his power by absolute silence—not the gentle image conjured up by the translation 'still small voice of calm', but an intense awareness of the overpowering presence of the mighty Lord.

Reminded again of the awesome nature of his God, Elijah may have hoped for all his problems to be resolved, and Israel sorted out once and for all. No such luck! God just sends him back in there, with a new mission to accomplish, and fresh problems to face. God has things for him to do, and opting out is not an option.

Under stress, I wonder how many of us mutter the well worn phrases, 'I don't know why I bother!' or 'What's the point of doing all this when nobody appreciates it?' The idea of running off to a nice quiet cave, somewhere remote, sometimes sounds quite appealing! But like Elijah, we are all expected to play our part, and the incredible power of God is there to hold us up.

Read the story in 1 Kings 19:1–18.

⁜

2 KINGS 6:16–17 (NRSV)

Elisha—the forces of God

He replied, 'Do not be afraid, for there are more with us than there are with them.' ... So the Lord opened the eyes of the servant, and he saw; the mountain was full of horses and chariots of fire all around Elisha.

The king of Syria (Aram) had sent out a large group of men, horses and chariots to surround the city where Elisha was staying and seize him. But God's forces were on the prophet's side, and Elisha led the temporarily blinded soldiers straight to the king of Israel. Elisha asked that they be given a big feast, then be set free, this generous treatment bringing peace again for a while between the two countries.

Elisha prayed for sight for his servant, to see the forces of God. Just imagine a hillside covered with horses and chariots of fire: Elisha's God is no feeble old man on a fluffy cloud! This is mind-blowing stuff, images of terrific force and visual reminders of the awe-inspiring power of God.

Christians down the centuries have found strength from the thought of the unseen forces of God to help and protect them. Every minute of every day, prayers are being offered to God by faithful Christians around the world, including dedicated communities of monks and nuns, and these prayers can encircle and uphold us. One nun described her work of prayer as sinking a bore-hole down into the rich oil of God's love, so that it could burst up to the surface.

Many people also take comfort and encouragement from the thought of the millions of faithful Christians who have died and now are with God, joining with him in his remaking of the world. We are unlikely to have to face a foreign army single-handed, but when we face our own opponents—depression, self-doubt, self-pity, even flying in an aeroplane or dealing with spiders—we can rely on God's unseen forces to be there protecting us and fighting on our side.

Thank God for his victorious power, and claim his help for anyone you know who is in trouble.

RUTH

RUTH 1:1–7 (NIV)

Rootless

With her two daughers-in-law she left the place where she had been living and set out on the road that would take them back to the land of Judah.

After ten years or more in one place, Naomi was on the move again. It was not the first time she had been uprooted. Famine had forced her husband to seek a livelihood away from home, and of course she had gone with him. How many of us are living in a place we don't quite recoognize as 'home'? Perhaps because of our husband's job, or our own career, or a family tie. Sometimes we can feel locked in by circumstances to the place where we are. When a crisis occurs, or sadness spreads over us, we may feel helpless, a victim. Naomi was bitter (v. 20). Nevertheless, she took what action she could, and it was to be the first step of a new life.

It requires bravery to make a decision when you are in a no-win situation. If Naomi had stayed, she would have lived with the loss of those she was closest to, and without financial support. Yet going meant facing the unknown, and having to acclimatize again to the home of her youth, where things might have changed. What might you have done in her position? Are you more likely to bury your head in the sand and hope things will turn out all right, or take courage in both hands and make a move for something new? Notice that it was the hand of the Lord at work which enticed her back. Perhaps she would find a new reality in her faith as well as material security in her homeland.

Commit to the Lord any circumstances in your life by which you feel trapped and ask him to help you take a new look at them. Do you have an ongoing resentment of them or do you simply 'go along with' what life has brought you? Are you able to change anything, or to accept your situation with both hands, rather than blaming someone else or the Lord?

Read Psalm 37:3–5.

✣

RUTH 1:11–22 (NIV)

Faithful friends

But Ruth replied, 'Don't urge me to leave you or to turn back from you. Where you go I will go, and where you stay I will stay. Your people will be my people and your God my God. Where you die I will die, and there I will be buried. May the Lord deal with me, be it ever so severely, if anything but death separates you and me.'

This is Ruth's beautiful expression of loyalty. Like Naomi, she has made her decision. Orpah decided differently, but there is no suggestion that either daughter-in-law made a wrong choice. Christians can be very good at deciding what others should have done, without knowing the full circumstances or having to take any responsibility for that person's decision. Like Naomi, too, Ruth was embarking on more than she knew. A relatively small step for her was to bring in new happiness. It was also part of God's plan for humankind, as she was an ancestor of Jesus in human terms.

Do you ever feel that the things you do are insignificant and unnoticed? Are you a background person, or someone's assistant, or overshadowed by a seemingly more gifted or prominent spouse, colleague or friend? Don't under-estimate the significance of your actions and your faithfulness. Ruth has set an example of loyalty which generations of the Lord's people have recognized and admired. It is her song, her epitaph. Did she feel that Naomi could not manage without her, and that somehow she would be able to provide for her—or that to add further to her pains of separation would be too much? Ruth gives no apparent thought for her own preferences. There is also a spiritual dimension. She is to share Naomi's God, and wants to be loyal to him too for herself.

Lord, am I the kind of friend you want me to be? Help me to be a friend who 'loves at all times' (Proverbs 17:17). Help me to take whatever steps are necessary to take the needs of those closest to me seriously.

RUTH 1:19–22 (NIV)

Bitter water

'Don't call me Naomi,' she told them. 'Call me Mara, because the Lord Almighty has made my life very bitter.'

Naomi certainly lets her feelings out in these verses. She does not think of what she should say, what would be 'correct'. Life has dealt her bitter blows and she is not afraid to say so. She does not stop short of blaming the Lord. Things are at a very low ebb. Do we speak too politely of our negative feelings in Christian circles? Naomi could have said, 'I have had some very difficult circumstances but I will praise the Lord anyway, and it will get better.' That may be true, but it is not how she feels, and such dishonesty would not help her to get over how she feels. She would have struggled much longer with her suppressed feelings. It may have turned to deeper depression, which could have crippled her, so that she was unable to act. As it was, she stated her true feelings, and never failed to look for opportunities to improve her situation, although that meant uprooting for the second time.

These words of Naomi offer us the opportunity to look into our own hearts. Has some past hurt always lingered because we didn't deal with it properly or express it—even to ourselves? If we did acknowledge it ourselves, did we talk about it to someone else—perhaps the person we feel caused the problem, or someone we could trust to listen to us? If you are protecting such feelings in yourself, you are not unusual. Bitterness expressed loses some of its sting. If we take action to remedy the situation, then the negative feelings can slowly turn into hope, and we are the stronger for it. Situations are not always transformed to the extent that Mara (Naomi) experienced, but every situation has an element of potential for good, whether in our own growth or that of others.

Lord, turn my bitterness to hope.

✣

RUTH 2:1–23 (NIV)

Life with mother-in-law

Then Ruth told her mother-in-law about the one at whose place she had been working. 'The name of the man I worked with today is Boaz,' she said.

You may not feel you could begin to share your secrets with your mother-in-law (if you have one). But this passage shows that it need not be a bad relationship, even if your mother-in-law does not have to be your best friend.

Intertwined in this friendship is the working of the Lord. Ruth has 'happened' on the field of one who would perhaps be in a position to marry her, as a near relative. Both are agreed as to his kindness in protecting her and seeing that she had plenty, and this meeting is to be the next piece in the jigsaw of God's plan for Ruth and Naomi.

Neither seems to be hampered by the possible tensions of a modern relationship: Ruth does not resent Naomi's questioning, and Naomi's advice is for Ruth's welfare. What are the factors that make our relationships more complicated? There's no need to feel chastened if your dealings with your mother-in-law are less ideal than this. But it may help to see how a better link could develop, especially if the hand of the Lord is evident in both of your lives, as a basis for sharing.

You may have someone other than a mother-in-law whom you trust for help and advice. Whoever it is, commit them to the Lord for his hand in your life and theirs, and bear in mind that if their advice goes against what you think pleases God, your first loyalty is to the one who shapes the present and future.

It is precious when there is such harmony with another human being. Take a look at your closest relationships and, if there is any area of friction and tension, pray for wisdom to know how to restore harmony and peace.

'Be kind and compassionate to one another, forgiving each other, just as in Christ God forgave you' (Ephesians 4:32).

RUTH 3:1–17 (NIV)

Awakening love

'And now, my daughter, don't be afraid. I will do for you all you ask. All the people of my town know that you are a woman of noble character.'

This is one of a number of love stories in the Bible. It is particularly pure and wholesome. A man and a woman beginning to admire and respect one another, yet showing great restraint and propriety! But for its time, the story has some unconventional elements. Ruth dared to go to Boaz in the night, an action that would have been easily misconstrued if others had known. The request for him to spread the corner of his garment over her was a clear signal that she wanted him to marry her.

The story is a celebration of love. The Bible is more matter-of-fact about love than we imagine: 'Daughters of Jerusalem, I charge you by the gazelles and by the does of the field: Do not arouse or awaken love until it so desires' (Song of Songs 2:7).

The gentle way the budding relationship develops is in stark contrast to our society's tendency for haste. How many of us would wait until someone else was consulted before making our decision to marry? Translated into our culture, there are questions to ask about the person's suitability, his character. How others see him can be a helpful guide. A lifelong relationship needs great forethought and it is an opportunity to glow with pride and respect for the one you are getting to know, as you hear what others think about his suitability.

This may be a time for you to remember the early days of your relationship, and thank God for that stage of your getting to know each other, and for the more mature love that you now enjoy. It may be a time to pray for such a relationship to develop under the hand of God. For others it may still be a time of waiting. Commit that to the Lord, and trust his wisdom. Or you may be able to celebrate with others who enjoy this kind of relationship.

Thank God today for your own circumstances and friendships.

✣

RUTH 3:18—4:12 (NIV)

You are my witnesses

'May the Lord make the woman who is coming into your home like Rachel and Leah, who together built up the house of Israel.'

Marriage was not just a private business. There were (and are) implications for others in the family and for the wider community. Some of the people affected were:

- the other relative who could have chosen to marry Ruth, and had a decision to make.
- Naomi, who was to have the bitterness removed of a family name cut short.
- the community as a whole, represented by the elders, who blessed the match.
- the 'house of Israel', who were to have a very special heir through Ruth.

We can under-estimate the importance of the public aspect of marriage. This is partly what sets it aside from a partnership without marriage. It is a relationship honoured and blessed by the whole community. Depending on custom, the marriage may be entirely the choice of the two people concerned, but they want their relationship to be a recognized part of their society. While the effects may not at first be obvious, in the long run it makes for a healthy society and, in their lifetime, for the support of the couple.

If you are married, think of the people who are affected by your relationship, and any children you may have. It is a wide circle, with the church as the community that stands for the house of Israel. Pray that you and your children can be a blessing to those whose lives they impinge upon. If you are not married, you may want to pray for the married people in your church, to be able to withstand the pressures and make an impact on the world around them, with a model of good relationships that younger people can learn from. Notice in this verse the respect given to the wife-to-be. Looked at like that, the role of mother is seen as the foundation of society, not a sideline, as some would view it.

Read Proverbs 31:10–24.

✣

RUTH 4:13–22 (NIV)

A kinsman-redeemer

'Praise be to the Lord, who this day has not left you without a kinsman-redeemer. May he become famous throughout Israel!'

Here is a lovely picture of contentment. Hope is restored for Naomi. Bitterness has gone. She takes care of her grandson. (Perhaps his mother goes out to work.) Another group of onlookers, 'the women', recognize the Lord's hand in this, and give him the praise.

The importance of a kinsman-redeemer was quite literally to rescue the redeemed from the poverty which they otherwise would have suffered, and from the shame and stigma attached to being without an heir in those days. But the picture is even more beautiful than the women can see, because this kinsman-redeemer, Boaz, is the ancestor of the great kinsman-redeemer, Jesus, who rescues his people from the poverty and shame of their sins. Our situation would have been even more desperate than that of the destitute Ruth and Naomi if he hadn't come to help us.

Can you feel the relief and joy Naomi and Ruth must have felt when they knew that Boaz was coming to their rescue? More than that—because Boaz was not acting out of a mere sense of duty, but in love for Ruth, the story reminds us of the extent of Jesus' love for us. That very human situation led to spontaneous praise to the Lord. To understand the depth of the need that led to our rescue by Jesus is to know the extent of his love. There is no situation too hard or that he doesn't know about. He comes to us in the difficulty and helps as he sees fit, in his wisdom. And ultimately, he saves us from our worst selves and the death which would be the result of our sin. He has not left us without a kinsman-redeemer.

If this story has touched you, take a moment to praise God for his love in not leaving us helpless, without a kinsman-redeemer.

THE WOMAN AT THE WELL

JOHN 4:3–4 (NIV)

A detour?

When the Lord learned of this [the Pharisees hearing of how he had baptized more diciples than John] he left Judea and went back once more to Galilee. Now he had to go through Samaria.

On the surface, not the most propitious start to his ministry—espcecially as the Pharisees had got their facts wrong and it was not actually Jesus who was doing the baptizing. It might appear a somewhat cowardly retreat, with Jesus seemingly determined to avoid confrontation at all costs. However, as his enforced detour through Samaria is about to crack a taboo dating back to the time of Jacob, it is worth consideration.

I find interesting the apparent ease with which Jesus accepts the need to change his plans. Most of us find obstacles thrown in our path a reason to despair and even question God. You know the scenario: you book a dynamic visiting speaker who you are sure is going to revolutionize your town. You pray and plan carefully. The big hall is not free on the only day the speaker can come and you end up in the scout hut. Mrs H. sprains her ankle and can't do the teas, the neighbour you felt was ready to make a commitment is on holiday and half the youth group have had the audacity to prefer a birthday sleepover that night. There are usually problems of one kind or another and most of us spend a great deal of time bemoaning our sad lot. If only...

For Jesus there never seemed to be one right way forward. He saw all his circumstances as God-given opportunities for glorifying his Father and teaching about the kingdom. He was infuriatingly flexible, as his disciples were to discover.

Perhaps we have to face the fact there there may be a problem with our spiritual map reading, in particular that a straight line is not always the best route from A to B. Let's face it, we would never have chosen the stable or the cross. God did.

Dear Father, help us to see our walk with you as an adventure where all detours may be part of your plan for us.

JOHN 4:6–7 (NIV)

A simple request

Jesus, tired as he was from the journey, sat down by the well... When a Samaritan woman came to draw water Jesus said to her, 'Will you give me a drink?'

On the surface, this is the most innocent and universally recognized request any of us can make. Water, the essence of life, is one need we all share, and the only reason many of us would ever go to knock on a stranger's door in a foreign country.

Not in Samaria! Here the question is a loaded one. The cup, the woman, the conversation—all were forbidden areas of communication between Jew and Samaritan. The population of Samaria was made up from remnants of northern tribes who had been taken captive when Israel was conquered by Assyria in 722BC and, although they worshipped the same God, the Jews abhorred them for being such mongrels, both in religion and race.

So why has Jesus asked her? Is he so tired and so thirsty that he just doesn't care? Is it a deliberate show of vulnerability, to put her at her ease? Is it for our benefit, to show us that it's all right to let our weakness be seen by those who don't know us? Is it because he didn't care about archaic, sterile rules? It's probably a bit of all these, but perhaps the main reason might be that he is using shock tactics to set a challenge and give her a chance to respond.

His request creates an immediate change in the dynamic, and swaps their roles, putting her fully in charge of the situation. It doesn't bully or coerce. It introduces an element of intrigue. It opens up the possibilities of this encounter in a way that chat about the weather never could. There never was any pussy-footing about with Jesus.

Dear Father, thank you that you never bully us into doing what you want. Thank you too for this image of you as tired and vulnerable. So many of us are feeling like this today. And thank you for this reminder that it's more than OK to receive help from those who do not yet know you, instead of feeling that, for your sake, we have to be strong all the time.

✣

JOHN 4:9 (NIV)

On dangerous ground

The Samaritan woman said to him, 'You are a Jew and I am a Samaritan woman. How can you ask me for a drink?'

I wonder what my response would have been to Jesus' request. I have a feeling I would have had a quick glance around to see if anyone was looking and slipped him a drink. Not very commendable, I'm afraid, but I've always been a bit of a coward!

I love the Samaritan woman's response. Very sure of herself and decidedly not intimidated by this unusual request, she fires straight from the hip. She knows the rules. She isn't going to get caught out—not her!

Many years ago, when I was a second-year student at the Bristol Old Vic Theatre school, I had an encounter that I will never forget with a new first-year student. 'What do you hope to do while you're here?' I asked, expecting him to tell me which options he had chosen, and hoping to show off just how much I belonged. 'I want to start up a Christian Union,' he replied. Weird or what? How could I let him down gently? 'I'm afraid I can't really see that catching on here. Most of us feel we've grown past that phase in our lives.'

Never had I felt so sure of my ground, and in a way I was proved right. He never did start a Christian Union. However, he did unearth in me wells of loneliness for the God I had left behind years ago, he did bring me to Christ, and eventually he married me. Yes, this strange, unconventional (loopy?) young man was Adrian, my husband!

The Samaritan woman was sure of her ground too. She was putting him right, or so she thought. Actually she was being lured into a sort of benevolent quicksand. How wonderful for her. Only in Jesus do we allow ourselves to be on dangerous, insecure ground in order to be completely safe.

Dear Jesus, you always were ingenious in your dealings with those you met. Please meet us and topple us off our little safe perches so that we too can be shocked into beginning to open our hearts and minds to you. We need you so much.

✣

JOHN 4:13–14 (NIV)

Opening the doors

Jesus answered, 'All who drink this water will be thirsty again, but those who drink the water I give them will never thirst.'

There is something decidedly Pinteresque about the conversation these two are having. I can't help sympathizing. I wouldn't have had a clue what he was on about either. So why does Jesus do it? Why does he so often communicate enormous truths to people who haven't a hope of understanding him? What seems to be going on is twofold. First, there is the sort of lunge and parry that often takes place at the beginning of a relationship, an establishing of common ground and differences. She unconsciously reveals her lively spirit, her anxious will to understand, her good-heartedness, her simple but solid commitment to her God. There is more to this woman, and that brings us to the other thing that is happening.

Recently I took my daughter and a friend to EuroDisney. Among the attractions was a Star Wars simulator ride where we were encouraged to believe that we were off on a nice safe ride through the space station with an android who had just passed his driving test. Of course, within a few minutes our novice driver pressed the wrong button, huge metal doors opened before us and we were thrown out into utter chaos for what seemed like eternity.

Certain things have the same effect of opening the doors to our chaotic inner selves. Death does it, fear does it, and, in a more gentle way, things we don't understand, like this disturbing riddle-like communication, have the same effect. Our world is suddenly tilted on its axis and we are forced to look at the familiar from what seems an alien perspective.

The Samaritan woman may not understand what Jesus is saying but somehow a key is gently being turned which will unlock the door to the chaos within in order for healing to take place.

Dear Father, help us to recognize that the fact that we don't understand what you are saying to us immediately doesn't mean we should close ourselves to it. Help us also to be aware of those times when we need an expert to help us with the locks.

JOHN 4:16–17 (LB)

Tricky situations

'Go and get your husband,' Jesus told her. 'But I'm not married,' the woman replied.

Interpreting dialogue is rather tricky, isn't it? So much depends on the tone of voice. I know the way it would be dealt with in some of the epic films of the life of Jesus. Lots of significant background music and close-ups of intense, soul-searching eyes. I confess our family finds most interpretations of our Lord rather lacking in wit and whimsy. Here, I suspect, he is very relaxed and actually enjoying himself as, having completely confused her with all the stuff about water, he suddenly and unexpectedly gets to the point, and, by catching her unawares, neatly causes her to tie herself into a knot.

We see from the following conversation that Jesus discerns perfectly well that she has no husband, but wants her to tell him so herself. I wonder what would have happened if she had lied? We'll never know, of course, as she gives an honest reply, thereby setting herself up for stage three of this intriguing drama. One thing is for sure. At the point where the spiritual dimension is most apparent there is no swelling background music.

If Jesus can deal with ordinary people with humour and normality, and if he has no difficulty in relaxing with those who are in a ness, why do we have so much difficulty in doing the same? I'm sick of meeting people who, at a time in their lives when they are obviously failing, have been subjected to humiliating ordeals at the hands of Christians who consider themselves to be set apart for that purpose. It's as though they are afraid it will seem as though they are taking neither the sin nor the gifts of the Spirit seriously if they appear too laid-back.

In future dealings with those whom God puts temporarily in our care, let's try to remain who we are and leave the clever stuff to the Holy Spirit!

Dear Father, we are reallysorry if we have ever made someone feel worse about themselves because we have felt out of our depth and resorted to silly posing and ways of speaking. Help us to relax and entrust the real work to you.

✣

JOHN 4:18 (LB)

Unpleasant truths

'All too true!' Jesus said. 'For you have had five husbands, and you aren't even married to the man you are living with now. You couldn't have spoken a truer word.'

I'm glad Jesus doesn't host Surprise Surprise. I suspect that there would be rather less saccharine and rather more salt! This must have been a nasty shock and, on the surface, seems a bit unfair.

Recently I have been finding life quite hard going, but I didn't realize quite how unreasonable I had been getting until one of my sons, in the middle of my having a go at him, shouted, 'You just don't realize what a cushy number you've got. You've done nothing but moan about how hard done by you are recently. Other people would give their eye-teeth for what you've got.'

My defensive reaction was to get even crosser, but later when we met up rather snuffily in the garden, he apologized for being rude. 'Yes, you were pretty foul,' I said, 'but you were also horribly right.' I had been getting things badly out of perspective and feeling ludicrously sorry for myself. It was a great relief to acknowledge it, say sorry to God and reflect on all the good things I have.

It's not always easy. We want to like ourselves, and coming unexpectedly face to face with our sins is rather like being at a wedding and bumping into someone you have let down in the past, or being caught out in a lie. It makes us feel grubby and small. We don't like it and we don't like the job of making someone we care about feel bad in this way. But in the case of this woman it is the beginning of a new way of life for her as a respected member of her community and a follower of Jesus. The truth is about to set her free.

If we had been there, would we have been so kind?

Dear Jesus, give us the sensitivity not to crash around in someone's life when it isn't appropriate, but also give us the courage to serve up the truth when it is really necessary, even if it is unpleasant.

✣

JOHN 4:23 (NIV)

True worship

'A time is coming and has now come when the true worshippers will worship the Father in spirit and truth, for they are the kind of worshippers the Father seeks.'

Having worshipped in many different styles of church and frequently felt like someone lost and agonizing over which is the 'right' way to get to the kingdom and getting horribly tired and hot in the process, these words offer a resting place, an oasis, a place of refreshment and the chance to relax.

If we want to sit chatting to God in the shade, that's all right. If we want to leap and shout in dazzling pools and waterfalls, that's OK too. There are only two rules: be true to yourself and allow yourself to be at home with your loving Father.

Do you have a special place where you feel particularly comfortable being with God? We do. It's a place called Carberry Towers in Scotland, and the other day Adrian and I were trying to decide why it is so special. We decided that it was the sight of children sliding down the banisters! I know that sounds silly, but this is a magnificent castle, built for royalty with a history of hosting such eminent persons as the Queen Mother. Yet here we feel free to play and relax in total trust.

Our family have slept in the Queen Mother's bedroom. Our dirty socks have cluttered the royal carpet! We have played French cricket on croquet lawns and rolled down the hill where Mary Queen of Scots was captured. Carberry is a place where everybody is equal in a place they don't deserve. We are awed by its grandeur but, paradoxically, there is nowhere where we feel more at home.

Surely a glimpse of heaven on earth? A model for the ideal place of worship. Whatever form of worship we choose, please allow it to acknowledge the awesomeness of God and also let us feel free to do what comes naturally.

Dear Father, can it be true that we are allowed *to relax with you? Most of us could do with sliding down some banisters. Help us to do it today.*

✣

JOHN 4:25 (NIV)

Christ revealed

The woman said, 'I know that Messiah (called Christ) is coming. When he comes he will explain everything to us.' Then Jesus declared, 'I who speak to you am he.'

This is the stuff of fairytales, isn't it? The frog you kissed becomes a prince, the wild swan you cared for is your long-lost brother, the old woman you let sit by the fire is your fairy godmother. The disguise slips away and, in typical fairytale style, it feels just right.

This is no fairytale. It is the glorious truth that the ordinary young man sitting with his back against her well, drinking from her cup and telling her things about herself that he couldn't possibly have known, is the Messiah she has been longing to meet.

There is a truth hidden here as great as any. It is the truth that Mother Teresa understood when she first began caring for beggars on the streets of Calcutta. It is the truth that Jesus tried to explain to his disciples again and again: 'I was hungry and you gave me something to eat, I was thirsty and you gave me something to drink.' ... 'Lord, when did we see you hungry and feed you, or thirsty and give you something to drink?' ... 'Whatever you did for one of the least of these brothers of mine, you did for me' (Matthew 25:35, 37, 40).

I don't think the idea is that we go sailing around delivering largess like Victorian gentry. The key seems to lie in the fact that whoever Jesus was with was made to feel that they were the most important person in the universe and that whatever was troubling them mattered to him. If we start trying to see people we meet in the same way, I think we will automatically want to do our best to help them.

Whom will we have the honour of meeting today?

Dear Jesus, please forgive us for the many times when those we meet have not also had the pleasure of meeting you! Help us to see those we meet today with your eyes, and give us a little bit of your perception, courage and ease so that we can be useful to them.

✣

JOHN 4:27 (NIV)

The living God

Just then his disciples returned and were surprised to find him talking to a woman. But no one asked, 'What do you want?' or 'Why are you talking with her?'

I wonder why the disciples were so silent. After all, they weren't normally. Look at the time when the women tried to bring their children to see Jesus. They didn't have much difficulty in saying what they thought then.

Obviously they were shocked by this major break with tradition. In fact, it was potentially scandalous. Was it this that silenced them? Or did they sense something special going on and were loath to disturb it?

I think maybe it was the latter. A few times in my life I have known without a doubt that I was in the presence of the living God. Although I've never seen tongues of fire or heard a rushing wind, I have been aware of being in the presence of something far greater than me, something truly awesome. And it silenced me, albeit temporarily!

The other day I watched a news report from Florida where a new hurricane was ripping through the seaside towns. They called it Danny and were talking about it rather indulgently as if it was a mischievous toddler who had just knocked down his friend's tower of bricks. 'Old Danny has been out on the rampage, knocking down as many houses as he can lay hands on. He is at present resting out to the west but we expect to see more of his handiwork tonight.'

As this was followed by footage showing traumatized families clinging tearfully to each other in the debris of their homes, clutching the few possessions they had been able to salvage, it felt to me as though Danny had a few behavioural problems. Hurricanes are huge, terrifying and awesome. So is God. He is not a tame God. When we gather in his name, we should expect that sometimes we will glimpse his power, even if on the surface all seems quiet.

When that happens, we need to shut up, watch and learn.

Dear Father, thank you for being all-powerful and almighty as well as loving and forgiving. Open our eyes to see more of your glory.

JOHN 4:28–29 (NIV)

Come and see

Then leaving her water jar the woman went back to the town and said to the people, 'Come, see a man who told me everything I did. Could this be the Christ?'

One of my favourite hymns lists all the complexities of our faith, then finishes the verse with one definite statement: 'But this I know, that Christ was born of Mary.'

The woman of Samaria knew just one thing about the stranger at the well. This was 'a man who told me everything I did'. Hardly the greatest miracle that Jesus ever performed, some might say, but enough for her to abandon her precious water jar and rush back to her village to persuade others to come and hear as well. The rest of the story shows that she succeeded. But how?

A few weeks ago, I was greatly amused. My 18-year-old son and his friend were engrossed in a fishing programme on the television. The intricacies of the correct way to place a lugworm on the end of the line were fascinating to them. Yet I happen to know that neither of them is the least bit interested in fishing, the only thing my son ever having caught being my husband's ear.

I couldn't resist finding out why they were so captivated, especially as the friend looked embarrassed. 'It's the bloke doing it, I s'pose. So keen! While I'm watching him I feel as if fishing's the best sport in the world. I even feel as if I am a fisherman—or could be. Silly, really.'

Oh but I know! I adore 'Gardeners' Question Time'. After all, what could be more fascinating than a plant I've never heard of, with a name I'll never remember, suffering from a disease that's unpronounceable, which I can't see anyway because it's radio? Perhaps silliness is hereditary.

In order to pass on the good news of Jesus, we really must not worry that we don't know all the answers, especially the ones that are incomprehensible, obscure or difficult to put into words. Sheer enthusiasm is extraordinarily catching. Wonderfully silly, really!

Take what I know and what I am and help me to show how much I love you, so that I can catch an ear for you.

JOHN 4:30 (NIV)

Delicious curiosity

They came out of the town and made their way towards him.

Why? Well, I suspect they came out of sheer curiosity. We all love the opportunity of being diverted from the humdrum. We crowd to the office window at the slightest excuse. We are particularly intrigued by anyone who knows something that they can't—apparently—possibly know.

But have you noticed what bad press the quality of curiosity gets? 'Mere' and 'just' usually precede the word, as though it's a rather base or superficial desire, to be quelled where possible.

Children are reprimanded for undisciplined peering at people, for eating things they find on the floor, taking lids off saucepans and poking the sleeping dog to see what happens. 'Curiosity killed the cat,' we say, and of course it is true that it could lead to danger.

However, it is also the means by which, from babyhood, we learn about our world, the reason we have penicillin, and the basis for exploration. It is what makes travelling fun, and antique shops and cookery programmes popular. It is one of the most exciting and fundamental inbuilt gifts that God has given us—an eye-shining hunger for knowledge that only the abused and starving lose.

Curiosity led the shepherds and the wise men to the stable where Jesus was born, and is here leading a whole village to come and hear the good news that God does not care less for them than for the Jews.

So what are you still curious to know about Jesus? Are there burning questions you are dying to ask him? Can you imagine yourself as part of this crowd jostling for the best place from which to see and hear the stranger? Or have you 'grown up', feeling you know as much as you need to and that you are far too disciplined to want to explore territory beyond the sensible boundaries you have set yourself?

Dear Father, look into our eyes. Do they shine, or have they become dulled with common sense and the cares of the world? Give us today not only our daily bread, but also a slice of that delicious curiosity we had as children, so that our life can become an adventure again.

JOHN 4:31 (NIV)

In the team

Meanwhile his disciples urged him, 'Rabbi, eat something.'

I feel sorry for the disciples sometimes. They try so hard to look after him, to keep the crowds away so that he can rest and eat. These are the tasks of support teams, and their efforts are often ignored in just the way that Jesus ignores the efforts of the disciples here. Completely absorbed, the idea of sitting down to eat is clearly nothing more than an irritant. As a mother, I know this situation all too well. Trying to get children to eat something sensible on the day of their exam, first day at senior school or first driving test is usually a pretty thankless task. I know I'll probably get accused of fussing, nagging and not understanding how they feel!

The disciples would have been failing Jesus if they hadn't continually nagged him throughout his ministry to sit down to eat something nourishing and have an occasional day off. Perhaps he specially chose those who had been fishermen because of these very qualities of loyalty, dogged dedication and practicality, learned during their years engaged in that hard craft.

It is easy to feel defeated when you see someone you care about getting utterly worn out. When efforts to help seem insubstantial and are sometimes ignored, it is not uncommon for the frustration to turn into resentment. The 'what about me?' phenomenon is often a direct result of feeling undervalued. I know because I've been there, done that—and never even got a T-shirt. I came to feel very deskilled in the role that God gave me as my husband's 'support team' and I meet so many women who have felt the same.

Many of us don't feel we're building anything for God most of the time, just mopping up the mess left behind by the 'real' workmen, but let those of us who bash on in this way try to keep in mind the kind of dear, loyal, non-geniuses who were used—albeit with a little help from the Holy Spirit!—to build the Church.

Dear Jesus, sometimes we get fed up with our role in the lives of others. Today help us to remember that in supporting those we care about, we are your team.

✣

JOHN 4:34 (NIV)

Being obedient

'My food,' said Jesus, 'is to do the will of him who sent me and to finish his work.'

A mind-blowing thought in our consumer age, isn't it? This is the era of eating. We talk a lot about being 'fed' in the church. I've heard it a good deal in reference to the actual service. Worship is described as 'stodgy' or 'frothy', sermons as 'indigestible' or 'bland'. We want lots of cream on our pudding, lots of goodies. We look around and see others with more goodies than us and we bang our spoons for more.

Others of us want our services to be like fast food, made to a formula, attractively packaged, cheap and easy to digest, so that they don't trouble us after we leave the service but allow us to get on with the 'real' stuff of life. I've also heard this metaphor used again in connection with people deciding to leave one church and go to another: 'I just wasn't being fed.'

The inference is that their spiritual needs were more mature than most and that, whereas the rest of that church are still at the milk stage, they are on to meat.

All this looks rather silly in the context of what Jesus is saying. Our food is to do the will of the Father. I don't think this means we have to have services that are like the worst school dinners, chewy and tasteless. But if worship really does mean that we offer him the very best of ourselves, and teaching means that we learn more about how he wants us to live our lives, then being obedient will automatically be on the menu and we won't need to feel hungry or want more than we have.

Food for thought, eh?

Dear Father, we are really sorry for the times when we have greedily looked at what others have on their plates or despised what we have on our own. Help us to live in your delightful upside-down way, trusting that you will look after our needs.

✣

JOHN 4:35 (NIV)

Ready for harvest

'Do you not say, "Four months more and then the harvest"? I tell you, open your eyes and look at the fields. They are ripe for harvest.'

Every year I look at our apple trees and vow that, this year, I will pick every apple before it falls. Every year I end up with a lawn covered with windfalls, resulting in boxes of 'please eat me' outside the gate for the children going to school, and a garden full of apple cores! It is amazing how easy it is not to open our eyes and see the fields ripe for harvest, and it has a lot to do with the fact that harvesting is jolly hard work.

I have a friend who has recently started running an Alpha course. 'I thought it was just going to be really easy,' he said. 'I thought anyone can have a few people round once a week for a while.'

He was wrong. It is tough. It is also rewarding, as those who do pick their apples and store them neatly and eat them all year round tell me!

Just a word of caution that is not an excuse. Jesus says, 'Look at the fields.' Sometimes we try to reap where not even a seed has been sown and wonder why we are so unsuccessful. In the case of the woman of Samaria, Jesus has carefully established that she is indeed ready. She may have sinned but she is aware of it. She has a longing to meet her Messiah and an open heart to hear what Jesus has to say to her. She may not understand it yet (we don't have to be theologically fluent before we come to Christ), but she wants to hear more and wants everyone else to hear it as well.

What can we learn from this? We learn the need to pray that our eyes will be opened to see who is ready for harvest, and, if the time is right, to be open to working hard to bring the harvest home.

Dear Father, open our eyes to see what you see, and please keep nagging us if it is time for us to use our scythes.

PART FOUR

Transformed!

When autumn's fruitfulness ends and the plants die back, it's hard to remember what spring is like. Winter can seem so long and gloomy. Then suddenly snowdrops, crocuses and daffodils spring up. Brown earth and bare branches become a riot of colour. A spring week of sunshine and showers transforms everything as sap rises and buds burst into leaf. The world is green again.

Life's like that too. Years of prayer and faithful service to friends can seem fruitless. Then, all of a sudden, there's life. Your friend suddenly knows what you are talking about. Jesus becomes real to her; his irrepressible life is springing up, changing her heart.

God has promised, 'As long as the earth endures, seedtime and harvest, cold and heat, summer and winter, day and night will never cease' (Genesis 8:22, NIV). Just as he has set a pattern for the seasons, he puts seasons into our lives. As well as times of joy and new life, there are times to trust that God is still in control when life seems barren and fruitless. There are times of sorrow and endings, times when trouble seems overwhelming.

It can take those darkest times to turn us towards God. It's as if we can't see the light until it's really dark. Then light breaks in and life springs up. The tiniest seeds of hope, half-whispered prayers, become reality. Death and decay give way to resurrection life.

In this last series of readings, we will be looking at what it means to be changed by God:

What marvellous love the Father has extended to us! Just look at it—we're called children of God! That's who we really are. But that's also why the

world doesn't recognize us or take us seriously, because it has no idea who he is or what he's up to. But friends, that's exactly who we are: children of God. And that's only the beginning. Who knows how we'll end up! What we know is that when Christ is openly revealed, we'll see him—and in seeing him, become like him. All of us who look forward to his Coming stay ready, with the glistening purity of Jesus' life as a model for our own.
1 JOHN 3:1–3 (*THE MESSAGE*)

As John says, Jesus is our motivation for purity: because he loves us and we want to love him, we live God's way, looking forward to the day when we will see him face to face.

FRUIT OF THE SPIRIT

JOHN 15:1–8 (NIV)

Growing fruit

'I am the vine; you are the branches. If you remain in me and I in you, you will bear much fruit.'

We seem to hear a great deal more about the gifts of the Spirit today than we do about the fruit—perhaps because the promise of instant power from on high seems more in tune with the age in which we live than the whole lengthy business of growing and producing fruit.

Just thinking about all that weeding, pruning, fertilizing and watering reminds me uncomfortably of all the problems multiplying in the garden. But if I don't get out there soon, everything will just become a tangled, unrecognizable mass of undergrowth beneath which no one will even see the lovely fruit and flowers that grow when they are given enough space and nourishment.

Paul writes in Galatians 5:22–23 and 25, 'The fruit of the Spirit is love, joy, peace, patience, kindness, goodness, faithfulness, gentleness and self-control... Since we live by the Spirit, let us keep in step with the Spirit.' As this passage reminds us, it is only possible for the fruit of the Spirit to grow and be seen in us if we spend enough time with Jesus to actually 'keep in step' with him, allowing our lives to be filled to the brim with his wonderful love. But unfortunately, in the rush of today's world, we can just go through the motions of our faith, attending all kinds of meetings and church services, not allowing enough time alone with him in the stillness of our hearts just to drink in his presence and hear what he is trying to say to us.

When we really listen to Jesus, then the wonderful fruit of the Spirit, such as love, joy and peace, can actually be seen and recognized in our lives. Try to ask yourself honestly, when others look at you, how much of Jesus can they recognize?

Lord, please help me today to 'remain in you', to grow the fruit that you want me to grow, and to become daily more like you. Amen

✣

JOHN 15:9–11 (NIV)

Finding real joy

'As the Father has loved me, so have I loved you. Now remain in my love. If you obey my commands you will remain in my love, just as I have obeyed my Father's commands and remain in his love. I have told you this so that my joy may be in you and your joy may be complete.'

I find it hard to believe that these words were spoken shortly before Jesus went to his death, almost as a last will and testament to the followers he was leaving behind. And here at this most agonizing moment in time, he talks about, of all things, joy!

Have you ever noticed how people who radiate the most remarkable joy are often the very ones who have been through the most trouble? There is nothing plastic or insincere about them, but somehow they seem to be drawing from a secret well that many of us have not yet begun to discover, for the genuine spiritual fruit of joy is not dependent on outward circumstances.

A few years ago, I came across a delightful woman. I assumed that she must have come from a happy, secure home where there was plenty of love on offer. To my astonishment I discovered that her mother had been an alcoholic who had often beaten her black and blue during a very painful childhood. She had experienced very little human joy throughout this time, but, as Psalm 126 reminds us, she had discovered for herself the wonderful truth that 'those who sow in tears will reap with songs of joy'.

The true joy of the Spirit can carry us through the darkest of days, though not denying the pain that we are experiencing, or feeling that we have to keep a stiff upper lip. If we draw close to him and cast our cares on to him, we will experience that joy for ourselves.

Read Isaiah 35 and ask God to give you a sense of real joy at the promises he has in store for you.

✣

PHILIPPIANS 4:6–7 (NIV)

Real, lasting peace

Do not be anxious about anything, but in everything, by prayer and petition, with thanksgiving, present your requests to God. And the peace of God, which transcends all understanding, will guard your hearts and your minds in Christ Jesus.

A few years ago, we lived on a South Pacific island where enormous waves pounded up into our garden during the monsoon season. At other times we could dive and snorkel in the clear, deep blue water, wondering at the amazing beauty stretched out below us. I found it fascinating that however much the winds and the waves were lashing on the surface of the water, deep down among the corals and the beautiful fish and plant life very little ever changed or moved. It remained beautiful. That is a picture of real spiritual 'peace'.

The peace of God is about a very deep, secret area of our lives where we can live in safety with him, clinging to the certainty of his love and protection, however terrible the storms and difficulties that may be raging over us. This is, of course, easier to say than to do.

Possibly, like me, you are a natural worrier: 'Will my children be safe? What are the teenagers up to now? Is my husband's job going to last?' If so, then you will no doubt find this concept of peace quite a difficult one to hold on to. And even if you do manage to give your worries to God, then you may well find yourself snatching them back again only moments later. Just remember that God's sign in the water of peace says, 'No fishing.'

Once, my daughter stayed with some Christian friends and was astonished to find that they were simply not allowed to worry about anything, but had to give the problem to God in prayer—but after all, that is exactly what this verse says.

In this troubled world, please help me to find the peace that you promise and to bring this same peace to others I meet.

✣

JAMES 5:7 (NIV)

Learning to be patient

Be patient, then, brothers and sisters, until the Lord's coming. See how the farmer waits for the land to yield its valuable crop, patiently waiting for the autumn and spring rains.

None of the fruit of the Spirit sounds more out of tune with the age in which we live than patience. 'Take the waiting out of wanting,' our television screens urge us. 'Buy now, pay later.'

I am afraid I am not naturally a very patient person and developing this particular fruit in my life has been a very painful, drawn-out process. I have found myself crying out to God, 'How much longer, Lord? I seem to have been praying about this for ever, and yet there is absolutely no sign that you have even heard my prayers.'

My experience of answered prayer has all too often been at the eleventh hour or when there seemed to be absolutely no hope left, and many times I have been driven to ask, 'Why?' Sometimes it seems as if the Lord is saying to me, 'You have to learn to trust and be patient because this is the only way for you to find out that you can safely leave things with me. Trust in my love and I will answer when the moment is exactly right.'

I once tried desperately to find a suitable couple to lead some children's work on a Christian houseparty, when no one seemed available. Then suddenly at the eleventh hour our prayers were answered. It may not surprise you to hear that, rather like the best wine that Jesus miraculously produced at the wedding feast in Cana, this was one of the most successful children's weeks we ever experienced.

Dear Lord, you know how many times I have begged you to hear my prayers about .... Please help me now to find the patience to trust you with this, to believe that you have heard and you will answer, and to leave this concern with you. Amen

✣

DEUTERONOMY 7:9 (NIV)

On being faithful

He is the faithful God, keeping his covenant of love to a thousand generations of those who love him and keep his commands.

The virtue of faithfulness can sometimes sound like something from a foreign language programme in today's world. Marriage promises get broken so often that couples will sometimes reluctantly admit to making their vows of faithfulness to each other with some kind of 'let-out' clause in the margin of their minds. 'I promise to be faithful unless and until...' Small wonder, then, that many hesitate before committing themselves to marriage.

True faithfulness is a thread of pure gold that runs like a treasured seam deep in all relationships and situations dear to the heart of God. Faithfulness when everything seems to be going wrong. Faithfulness when your loved ones seem to be at their most difficult, and faithfulness when humanly speaking you have every opportunity to walk away from that very painful situation.

We all know how we would like our husbands and friends to behave towards us when we let them down or fail to be there when they need us, but somehow it seems different when we feel hurt or rejected. True faithfulness both to God and to our families and friends is all about hanging in there when the going is tough and when there is very little sign of daybreak on the horizon.

In Proverbs 31 it says of the ideal woman that 'she is worth far more than rubies [and] her husband has full confidence in her', and that 'she speaks with wisdom, and faithful instruction is on her tongue'. Pray that the Lord will help you to be this faithful to the family and friends he has entrusted to you.

Lift to God those areas of your life in which he is asking you to be faithful at the moment and ask him to help you, however difficult the circumstances. Remember that underneath are his everlasting arms.

✣

MATTHEW 11:28–30 (NIV)

A gentle God

'Come to me, all you who are weary and burdened, and I will give you rest. Take my yoke upon you and learn from me, for I am gentle and humble in heart, and you will find rest for your souls. For my yoke is easy and my burden is light.'

The image I like best is that of a strong, protective shepherd bending down to pick up and cherish a tiny, struggling lamb. It is a gentleness that I often see in my counselling work as our loving and gentle God reaches down to rescue and protect someone whose life is in a terrible mess, for whom he will go to any lengths to save and heal. 'A bruised reed he will not break, and a smouldering wick he will not snuff out,' says Isaiah 42:3.

In the book A Shepherd Looks at the Twenty-Third Psalm, Phillip Keller shows, from his years of experience as a working shepherd in

New Zealand, just how much we are in need of the loving, gentle care of our almighty creator God. Living with the technical and scientific advances of the early 21st century, we may not always fully realize this fact.

It is this same fruit of gentleness that we are called to show in our own lives as we seek to be like God. Gentle loving care, despite the aggressive pushiness of the age in which we live; gentleness when we are dealing with those who have needs that stretch us to the very limits of our patience.

Lord Jesus, my loving shepherd, please give me your gentleness and your deep concern for those around me in greater need. Help me not to trample on other people's feelings when I am under pressure of time or just tired. And may my presence bring your strong gentleness into every situation in which I find myself, so that others may actually sense your presence in my life. Amen

EZEKIEL 47:9, 12 (NIV)

Good growing conditions

Swarms of living creatures will live wherever the river flows... Fruit trees of all kinds will grow on both banks of the river. Their leaves will not wither, nor will their fruit fail. Every month they will bear, because the water from the sanctuary flows to them. Their fruit will serve for food and their leaves for healing.

I have always loved the river of life in Ezekiel as it is such a wonderful parable of what gives our lives power and hope and meaning. The fruit of the Spirit will only grow on the banks of this river where the pure water of life can reach and nourish the growth.

I wonder how much of the nourishing river of life is reaching your world at the moment. Maybe your times alone with God are being drowned out by the demands of home and family, or you feel too overburdened trying to hold down a career at the same time. Even in the best of churches, there may not always seem to be a great deal of nourishment available, and life quickly becomes a matter of doing, and endless activities, rather than just being and allowing the fruit of the Spirit to grow and develop in our lives.

In this passage, the trees are simply planted by the water; they are not doing anything except soaking up the water of life.

How can you draw closer to God to find this water of life for yourself? I need to find a place where I can see out into the garden and drink in the beauty of his creation. Then again, some people have special music that speaks to them, or a particular passage from scripture that they have grown to love. As you come before the Lord today, ask him to show you something new that will bring the waters of life to you in a fresh and wonderful way.

Read Psalm 92:12–15. Just think—the promise is that you will still bear fruit in old age and remain spiritually fresh and green.

TAKE HEART

MATTHEW 22:37 (NIV)

Matters of the heart

Love the Lord your God with all your heart and with all your soul and with all your mind.

When we read anything, including the Bible, most of us use mainly our minds—we're taught that way in school. But we're going to focus now on matters of the heart—and I don't mean either triple bypass operations or the Valentine 'lurv' of the magazines and soaps.

When a fledgling blackbird flew at top speed into the glass of our patio doors a moment ago, my heart beat faster and my stomach lurched. I tiptoed forward, willing it still to be uninjured, somehow. The sight of its stiff little body made me wince for its hardworking parents. They even fought off magpies that attacked their nest!

Our bodies react in physical ways to emotions as well as to danger—guts churn and hearts beat faster. Down-to-earth Hebrews often referred to 'guts' in Old Testament passages which modern Christians have translated as 'heart'. The Hebrew word for compassion doesn't pull any punches. It means 'a churning of the bowels'!

Heart (or gut) reactions matter and the Bible has a huge wealth of things to say about them. Our hearts/guts are described variously as hard, proud, perverse or calloused; as contrite, responsive, happy or secure; as anxious, humble, broken or faint; and as pure, faithful, upright and even 'circumcised'! Why are they so important? Because they govern our relationships with God and with one another. Jesus said, 'Out of the overflow of the heart the mouth speaks. The good man brings good things out of the good stored up in him, and the evil man brings evil things out of the evil stored up in him' (Matthew 12:34–35).

Lord, help me to understand, and to feel, more of the heart of the matter—of your heart, of my heart, of my neighbour's heart. Help me to understand, and work out in practice, how all of these can meet, and beat, together.

⁘

HOSEA 11:8–9 (NIV)

God's heart

How can I give you up, Ephraim? How can I hand you over, Israel? ... My heart is changed within me; all my compassion is aroused. I will not carry out my fierce anger, nor will I turn and devastate

Ephraim. For I am God, and not a human being—the Holy One among you. I will not come in wrath.

Listen to some sermons and you'd think that Christianity's main concern was sorting out complicated details of theology and background—so that we can believe six impossible things about God, if not before, then after, breakfast.

But we're not following some system of philosophy. We may try to understand God with our minds but in the end it will prove impossible. He's so much bigger than we are! He gave us brains to use, but we'll only truly begin to get to know him as we worship and walk with him. That's the totally amazing part! Christians are people who, through no merit of their own, form a relationship with God and begin to discover more about his heart.

And what a heart! Never remote or impassive, throughout the Old Testament God demonstrates heart-feelings of anger, exuberance, love and compassion far stronger than ours. Yet as various human beings whom he trusts speak and interact with him, he'll change heart, sparing a city, forgiving an individual, extending a life.

In today's passage, yet again God's chosen people Israel had refused to turn back to him. By rights, God said, he should destroy them utterly, yet, 'It was I who taught Ephraim to walk, taking them by the arms; but they did not realize it was I who healed them… I lifted the yoke from their neck and bent down to feed them' (Hosea 11:3–4). How can anyone with such a tender father's heart give up his children? God asks himself. We feel his agony. And we catch a glimpse of what is at the heart of his being.

May I not grieve your heart, Lord, but make it glad!

✣

JOHN 12:27 (NIV)

Jesus' heart

Now my heart is troubled, and what shall I say? 'Father, save me from this hour'? No, it was for this very reason I came to this hour.

Jesus had the biggest heart, reaching out to all kinds of people—family, friends and enemies; strangers, children and women. He revelled in parties but also needed time alone with his Father to share emotions ranging from anger to sadness, joy to compassion. But of himself, the amazingly great Son of Almighty God said, 'Take my yoke upon you and learn from me, for I am gentle and humble *in heart*, and you will find rest for your souls' (Matthew 11:29, my italics).

Most Christians relate more easily to Jesus than to the Father. I've always found it the other way round, but recently have been looking closer at this extraordinary God-man. Was it because Jesus responded so exactly to God's heartbeat that he did such surprising things on earth, rarely choosing the way people expected him to go? Some of the things he said and did, I still don't understand, but I do know that, as 'God with us', Jesus came to live among ordinary people, sharing their joys and despair, loving both them and his Father with all of his heart. Being a 'bridge too far' between sinful man and a holy God brought him in the end to Gethsemane. His heart troubled way beyond the stomach-churning stage, he sweated agonizing drops of blood there. Finally he gave his heart, quite literally. From it, water and life-blood flowed as the Roman soldier's spear pierced his side shortly after he died on the cross. Even today, that water and blood wash us clean, making us fit to stand before the Father and share his life.

Jesus endured all that, Hebrews says, for the joy that was set before him. What joy? Surely not being in heaven with his Father, or he wouldn't have come to earth at all. No, his death brought him the joy of knowing us better.

What heart-love! Thank you, Jesus!

⁘

ACTS 13:22 (NIV)

A man after God's heart

I have found David son of Jesse a man after my own heart; he will do everything I want him to do.

Do we want to be women after God's heart, not just following his rules, going to church and being good little Christians, but people who listen to God's heartbeat and begin to 'do the things we see him doing'? If so, aren't we in danger of sounding a bit big for our dainty little shoes? After all, both men and women have always failed to come anywhere near God in holiness or love.

Well, yes—but David is described as a man after God's own heart and he wasn't very holy when he slept with Bathsheba, nor very loving when he sent her husband to his death. He wasn't doing what God wanted then, surely? He, his family and nation certainly suffered the consequences of David's wrongdoing, yet at the end of the day he was judged a man after God's heart. Why? He repented. In his brokenness he turned from the dangerous fantasy that a king could do what he liked. He cried out to God for help and found the strength to bring his thoughts, feelings, reactions and actions back into line with God's heart, God's thoughts and God's ways—to worship God again.

God knows what is in our hearts: 'Immediately Jesus knew in his spirit that this was what they were thinking in their hearts, and he said to them, "Why are you thinking these things?"' (Mark 2:8). Yet that doesn't stop God from believing in us. Once we've repented, his heart is huge enough to restore us to the joy of our salvation again.

Thank you, Lord, that you know what is in our hearts, both good and bad, and yet still you yearn to have deeper heart-relationships with us, like the relationship that you had with David. You remain convinced that we can be women whose hearts are like yours!

✣

1 KINGS 11:1–13 (NIV)

Hearts unlike God's—divided

So Solomon did evil in the eyes of the Lord; he did not follow the Lord completely, as David his father had done.

One way our hearts often differ from God's is that ours are divided. We'll 'buy' the gospel as we buy 'pick and mix' sweets, taking only the selection that we like.

David's son Solomon had everything going for him—wisdom, riches, God's promises. He even met directly with God, twice. Yet he let his weakness for women (1000 of them, which seems excessive, to say the least!) seduce him into following their gods. God took objection to his heart-attitude, which had strayed a long way from the humility, gratitude and desire for righteousness that had been so outstanding in his father. God told Solomon, 'Since this is your attitude and you have not kept my covenant... which I commanded you, I will most certainly tear the kingdom away from you' (v. 11).

What's my weakness? What, like a wedge, has the potential, little by little, to divide my heart from God's? Do I buy into materialism for the security or the kudos? Do I put 'religious' observance before unselfish love? There's a sweatshirt slogan which reads, 'I'd rather be fishing!' Whatever it is that God has asked me to do, am I begrudging about it because there is always something else which I'd rather be doing—and does that 'something' take priority at times when I know it shouldn't? Does fear, or longing, cause me to put my faith (only half-seriously of course) in horoscopes or similar things? Do I trust lotteries or pension and insurance schemes more than God? Or do I trust and worship him with an undivided heart, at least for most of the time, returning wholeheartedly when I've strayed, as David did? Is my love for God as unconditional as his for me?

'Teach me your way, O Lord, and I will walk in your truth; give me an undivided heart, that I may fear your name' (Psalm 86:11).

MARK 3:1–6 (NIV)

Hearts unlike God's—stubborn, deceitful

He looked round at them in anger and, deeply distressed at their stubborn hearts, said to the man, 'Stretch out your hand.'

Late one hot Sunday afternoon, when we lived in a terraced house, a horrible thing happened. Our neighbour's oldest child, a loving and sensitive girl of about ten, had brought her class's rabbit home for the weekend. The whole family had been making a fuss of it, much to their dog's annoyance. When someone left the back door open, the inevitable happened. Dog pounced on rabbit—and rabbit was dead within seconds.

The whole family was distraught. It would have been bad enough had the pet been their own, but a whole classful of children loved this one! The mother, who had long resisted weekend rabbit entertaining on the grounds that this might happen, blamed herself for giving in. All three children, wailing loudly, accused each other of leaving the door open. The dog howled—why did no one love him any more? Unfortunately, though, we couldn't stay to comfort our neighbours as we were off to church. Next day we learnt that Sue, who lived two doors the other side of us, had been there for them all evening. Sue had only just become a Christian but, as she said, 'No point going to church to hear about loving people when you have an opportunity to actually do it!'

Ouch—my heart can be as stubborn and uncaring as a Pharisee's! When God's Son came among them, healing the sick, they quibbled about ways in which he might have broken the Sabbath law—which was there to help people anyway. Jesus must have felt as Jeremiah prophesied, 'The heart is deceitful above all things and beyond cure; who can understand it?'

Lord, sometimes my heart is apathetic. When I don't care enough, I've even used you as an excuse. I can be cynical and perverse, deceitful and stubborn—so unlike you. Sometimes I do feel 'beyond cure'. Give me a new heart, one more like yours!

✣

PSALM 95 (NIV)

Hearts unlike God's—hard

Today if you hear his voice, do not harden your hearts as you did... that day at Massah in the desert where your ancestors tried and tested me, though they had seen what I did.

What if Jackie Pullinger hadn't obeyed God's voice to get off a ship where he told her—in Hong Kong? What if John Wesley hadn't listened when God told him the world was his parish—if he'd stayed put instead of riding thousands of miles on horseback, preaching the gospel to ordinary people? What if Lord Shaftesbury hadn't listened when God told him to keep up the fight to improve conditions for the mentally ill and for children down mines; or Nelson Mandela hadn't listened to what God was telling him about forgiveness? If they'd all hardened their hearts and opted for a quiet life, maybe others would have stepped in, but meanwhile, how much extra suffering would the world have seen?

Each of those obedient people had first experienced the supreme heart-softener of God's grace. The hearts of those who resist grace can grow so hard that they become impervious to God. As Jesus said in Matthew 13:15, 'For this people's heart has become calloused; they hardly hear with their ears, and they have closed their eyes.' I'm writing this on holiday in Austria, where the tour guide told us that the prince-archbishops who used to rule over the rich Salzkammergut area expelled all the Protestants who lived there. A month ago I stayed in a house with a priest hole, where Catholic priests, fearing for their lives, once hid from Protestants. Often the church persecuted gospel preachers and those who translated the Bible into languages which ordinary people could read. It doesn't make Christianity sound like wonderful news, does it?

Help me never to become so proud and hard-hearted that I'm shut off from your grace, Lord. For I need to turn and repent, to find healing and rediscover your way ahead so many times each day.

✣

PSALM 61:1–5 (NIV)

Faint-hearted?

From the ends of the earth I call to you, I call as my heart grows faint; lead me to the rock that is higher than I.

They say that faint heart never won fair lady. Presumably the same applies to gentlemen(!), fame, fortune or whatever. 'Go get—and may the strongest win!' says our culture, but God as usual takes the opposite view. 'A broken and contrite heart you will not despise,' says Psalm 51:17. Our society may despise the timid ones, who think they can't do anything worthwhile, the ones who say, 'I am poor and needy and my heart is wounded within me.' But the ones who know that they need God are the very ones to whom his heart reaches out.

My heart grew faint, along with my voice, last month. I'd been asked to lead a women's prayer retreat, something I've never done before. On the Wednesday beforehand I developed a temperature and began to feel ill. By the Friday when the weekend was due to begin, I'd all but lost my voice. The women, who'd accepted that their speaker was a bit of a nervous novice, arrived to find that she couldn't speak, or even think straight. The vicar's wife, a nutritionist, thrust echinacea drops down my throat. The women were already praying and encouraging me like mad, while I was whispering to God, 'I've done all I can; over to you!' It's not a bad feeling, to be helpless in his hands. And thanks to him and the lovely praying women, we all had the most hilarious, moving and special weekend!

Lord, you are revolutionary. You came to bind up the broken-hearted and preached good news, not to the successful, but to the poor. Thank you that, though you live in a high and holy place, you choose also to live with those who are 'contrite and lowly in spirit, to revive the spirit of the lowly and to revive the heart of the contrite' (Isaiah 57:15).

ACTS 16:11–38 (NIV)

Heart surgery

One of those listening was a woman named Lydia... a worshipper of God. The Lord opened her heart to respond to Paul's message.

Not the misogynist that people think he was, Paul was speaking specifically to women here—women who had gathered to pray outside the city gates of Philippi. Lydia, a rich businesswoman, worshipped God. But if she had heard about Jesus before, the message hadn't struck home until God 'opened her heart' that day. I'm sure we've all known times when God has opened our heart in a similar way, causing us to respond to some new aspect of himself.

In a more dramatic example, after being knocked around by husbands and lovers, 'Sal' was abandoned with various children. My friend 'Lin' had become her friend. For ten years she told Sal about Jesus. Sal came to believe, but drew back from the implications of committing herself. Finally she agreed to attend an Alpha course. In the final few hours of the course weekend away, she allowed Lin and me to pray for her. But then, 'You'll have to stop!' she gasped. 'I'm having a dizzy spell or something.'

'That's the Holy Spirit,' explained Lin.

'Really?' Suddenly her troubled look was replaced by a huge smile. She'd met God! As he did with Lydia (an altogether different type of woman), the Lord opened Sal's heart in that moment and afterwards there was no stopping her. She told everyone she knew, she joined the church, got baptized and slowly, with the help of God and Christian friends, she began to work through some of the huge problems in her life.

Thank you, Father, that whether we're respectable, religious people or not, you're willing to send Christ to dwell in our hearts. Then you put your Spirit in our hearts as a deposit as well, guaranteeing what is to come. You're surely the greatest heart surgeon of all, since you take away our hearts of stone and give us hearts of flesh.

✣

ACTS 7:51 (NIV)

Circumcised hearts!

You stiff-necked people, with uncircumcised hearts and ears! You are just like your ancestors: You always resist the Holy Spirit.

A neighbour had recently given birth by Caesarean section, so she couldn't drive. As I took her to collect a prescription, she explained that their rabbi had circumcised the tiny baby two days before and that their GP thought his worsening infection stemmed from the home-operation. We both winced as she described the process. As it turned out, the illness had nothing to do with her baby's circumcision, but I still thank God that he's dropped that particular requirement for Christians!

We don't escape entirely though. Circumcision never was about a purely physical operation. Romans 2:29 talks about 'circumcision of the heart, by the Spirit, not by the written code'. Whatever does that mean? In scripture, sometimes an uncircumcised heart and a stiff neck are paralleled. I know that a stiff neck makes me inflexible—for example, when I'm driving, looking both ways at road junctions becomes difficult. The words from today's reading are spoken by Stephen, the first Christian to be stoned to death for his faith. The Jews who threw the stones wouldn't allow their hearts to be opened to the gospel truth he proclaimed. In effect, they thought they knew the law better than God. Proud and inflexible, their actions became terrible. As for circumcision of the ears(!), look again at Jesus' words in Matthew 13:15.

Jewish males are marked physically by circumcision as a sign of their faith, of their Jewishness. In theory they're marked as ones who will obey God's law, but God had always wanted their hearts to be marked too, like David's. Today he practises special non-invasive heart-surgery on the hearts of Christian men and women, if we co-operate. But what kind of a new, improved, marked heart is he after? We'll have a brief look at some of the qualities in the next few days.

In the meanwhile, consider the kind of heart-qualities you'd want in a husband or lifelong friend.

⁂

PROVERBS 15:13 (NIV)

Happy hearts

A happy heart makes the face cheerful, but heartache crushes the spirit.

If you've been thinking about what heart-qualities you might look for in a lasting friendship, you might find it interesting to glance at one of those lonely hearts pages found in freebie local papers. Many people specify not only age, looks, background, interests and so on, but something called 'GSOH'. This intrigued me. Having cynically assumed that the letter 'S' stood for a three-letter word ending in 'x', I had real problems trying to work out the rest. In fact, the initials stand for 'good sense of humour'—which, as any right-minded person knows, is far more important than sex in a lasting relationship!

It's not just hilarity—wouldn't we all choose to spend time with people who believe the glass is half-full, rather than half-empty, with people who look cheerful rather than miserable? I have a friend who sees good in everything. Occasionally this makes me want to hit her, but most of the time I love to be with her. Even her e-mails lift my heart. Though not a Christian, she makes every effort to seek out and appreciate beauty and goodness in little things and to encourage everyone. Since her sister died young, she's felt it is her mission in life to spread happiness around her. I think God likes that!

However, some people have experienced such heartache that their spirits end up crushed, and that's a terrible thing. Jesus promised to be there for such people, not to despise or break them but to nurture and mend over time.

Lord Jesus, you were anointed with the oil of joy above your companions and crowds wanted to be with you. Give us something of your happy heart and cheerful face—make us attractive for you. And for those whose hearts ache and whose spirits are crushed right now, you've known that too. Will you bring into their lives people who will share a little bit of happiness with them, as much as they can bear at the present time?

⁘

PSALM 51 (NIV)

Pure hearts

Create in me a pure heart, O God, and renew a steadfast spirit within me.

David wrote this psalm after the prophet Nathan had confronted him over his sin with Bathsheba. Few of us will have done anything as wicked as causing the death of our lover's spouse, but there again, if asked, few would feel that our hearts were pure or our spirits steadfast. We'd all acknowledge, it's vital to any relationship that each partner remains true and trustworthy—that they don't betray each other.

Certainly God sees it that way. He's really tough about it. Jesus said it is the pure in heart who will see God! (Matthew 5:8).

But the word translated 'pure' here means 'clean'. Dirty, impure things can be made clean! From the same word comes 'catharsis', which has the sense of being purged, as when emotions are brought to the surface and released through watching a tragic drama. We can 'take heart' from David who, despite knowing none of the benefits bought for us by the drama of Jesus' death on the cross, asked that God would 'create' a pure heart and 'renew' a steadfast spirit within him.

We all waver; we're not always pure or steadfast; but we do have times when our hearts are right with God, when we love him and long to serve him with all of our being. He notices when we serve him faithfully through the petty irritations and setbacks of everyday life. And when we become impure, when we run off doing our own thing, afterwards God can clean our hearts, recreating and renewing the bits we've spoilt.

David didn't stay wallowing in the grief of his repentance for ever. After turning from his sin, he set his face firmly in God's direction and, with God's help, moved forward. May we do the same after transgressions great or small.

Is there any area of your heart which you're not allowing God to renew, because you're too ashamed of it?

✣

2 CHRONICLES 32:16–26 (NIV)

Responsive hearts

But Hezekiah's heart was proud and he did not respond to the kindness shown him; therefore the Lord's wrath was on him and on Judah and Jerusalem.

Hezekiah must have been fantastic at praying. There he was, king of little Judah, with his capital city, Jerusalem, under siege to the ridiculously strong armies of the superpower of the day—Assyria. Then Hezekiah prayed and God's angel slaughtered all the enemy troops overnight. The mighty Assyrian king, Sennacherib, had to limp back home in disgrace. It's comparable to all the US armed forces being annihilated under mysterious circumstances while attacking Andorra!

Shortly after this astounding victory, King Hezekiah fell ill, seriously ill. About to die, he prayed, and again God heard and gave him a miraculous sign. 'Wow,' thought Hezekiah, 'I've done it again—my prayers are really something!' Spiritual success gives a heady feeling of power but also heralds a dangerous time. Maybe our church prays, someone's miraculously healed of cancer and we're all over the moon—got healing sorted now! It's easy to take our eyes off God and assume that we ourselves are the answer to all kinds of problems.

We can respond to God's kindness rightly, with gratitude and humility, or we can respond wrongly, in pride. In the end Hezekiah proved to have the right kind of responsive heart. He repented in time to prevent God's anger turning on him and his people. God healed him and he continued to reign as one of the best kings to grace the pages of the Old Testament. Hezekiah faced testing times—a massive enemy attack and serious illness. Yet after a serious setback caused by his mistaken heart-attitude, his responsive, praying heart released God's goodness again.

'Blessed are those whose strength is in you, who have set their hearts on pilgrimage. As they pass through the valley of Baca [weeping], they make it a place of springs' (Psalm 84:5–6).

God, we don't want to have proud hearts, but responsive hearts, pilgrim hearts, hearts touched by you.

✣

JOHN 16:33 (NIV)

Take heart!

I have told you these things, so that in me you may have peace. In this world you will have trouble. But take heart! I have overcome the world.

One small word causes Christians a lot of trouble—the word 'should'. After reading these Bible notes, it will be all too easy to think, 'Oh dear, I should have a pure, godly heart, steadfast, responsive and without pride. I should be happy, and today's verse implies that I should be peaceful too, even though it promises me lots of trouble as well! I don't stand a chance!'

But that doesn't take into account Jesus' heart for us. His words in the verse above aren't some kind of cruel parody of the song: 'Though there's trouble ahead, you'd better face the music and dance... or else!' No, he tells us to 'take heart'. Why? Because he has (not 'we should') overcome the world, with all its sin and sorrow. In the end we're secure not in the rightness of our own hearts, but because he holds us close to his heart.

Isaiah 40:11 reminds us, 'He tends his flock like a shepherd: he gathers the lambs in his arms and carries them close to his heart; he gently leads those that have young.' Sheep can race about in wild-eyed panic, doing themselves all kinds of damage. They have peace only because they follow the shepherd who looks after them, shields them from danger, overcomes their enemies and leads them to food, water and shelter. If their hearts follow the good shepherd, who knows their silly ways but still cares enough to give his life for them, they can't go very far wrong.

May we forget about the 'shoulds'. May we nestle close to your heart, where everything begins to make sense. As we begin to appreciate the love that's in your heart, may ours melt and change, becoming more like yours. May we, whatever our circumstances, take heart in all that you are, in all that you have done and will do. Amen

ROMANS 12

ROMANS 12:1 (LB)

Jesus look-alikes

I plead with you to give your bodies to God. Let them be a living sacrifice, holy—the kind he can accept. When you think of what he has done for you, is this too much to ask?

'Who does he take after?' That's what we usually ask when a baby arrives, and if we want to please the proud father we'll say 'it' looks like him! Paul tells us twice that God hopes we'll all take after Jesus as we grow up as Christians (2 Corinthians 3:18; Romans 8:29). He wants us to be Jesus look-alikes in every situation, in the way we think, speak, act and relate to others. 'Some hope,' we might think, 'in our materialistic, pleasure-loving age!' Yet when Paul was writing to a group of new Christians in a remarkably similar cultural setting, he gave them some practical tips that we might will find helpful. Over the next two weeks we'll be looking at them in detail, but today Paul starts by telling us that the process of becoming like Jesus will cost us everything. We need to give our bodies to God as a living present—and our personalities, desires, dreams, feelings, thoughts, time, activities—everything! Jesus did that for us when he stepped down into our world, so to become like him we start by doing exactly the same.

When I was a child, my favourite daydream was imagining myself as a brave and noble missionary, dying a martyr's death in a jungle. I've since realized that it is a lot easier to die for God on one dramatic occasion than it is to live for him through the ordinary little hassles of every day. Jesus spent 30 out of his 33 years doing unimportant, boring little jobs in a small family business—but he did every single one of them for God.

Father God, I do want to be like Jesus but, when I look at the mess that's me, the idea seems utterly ridiculous. Please take every cell of my body and every detail of my life so that you can start the job of moulding me into his image. Amen

✣

ROMANS 12:2 (LB)

Thinking like Jesus

Don't copy the behaviour and customs of this world, but be a new and different person with a fresh newness in all you do and think. Then you will learn from your own experience how his ways will really satisfy you.

It is one thing to give our bodies to God as a present, but of course we also have to give our minds. Most of us don't realize how easily we are influenced by this world's thinking patterns. A friend of mine watched TV for a whole evening and told me she'd counted 88 occasions when she had seen God's rules or principles for our behaviour flouted or broken.

It's not just the media who are to blame. We 'catch' our culture's value systems and coping strategies from our families in early childhood, and from our friends and workmates as we grow up. We absorb popular catchphrases that are totally contrary to God's way of thinking—statements like 'Oh, it's OK, everybody does it', or 'You must look after number one', or 'I've got a right to be happy'. When we finally hand over our minds to God, they are so cluttered up by this kind of stuff that it seems to take him a lifetime to alter our thought patterns.

Perhaps his job could be speeded dramatically if we spent as much time absorbing Jesus through the Bible and Christian books as we spend absorbing the world through videos and the telly.

My mind is always slipping into 'worry mode', but one of my favourite verses in Isaiah 26:3: 'You will keep in perfect peace those whose minds are steadfast, because they trust in you' (NIV). When I start panicking, it is usually because I'm concentrating on all my problems and letting them dominate my thinking. If I can mentally turn away from them and concentrate on the Lord, and all the promises he has made to me, I soon get my peace back again.

Lord, my brain buzzes with so many negative thoughts, I feel sick of living with myself sometimes! Please help me to think about life, myself and other people the way you do. Amen

✣

ROMANS 12:3, 10, 16 (LB)

Acting like Jesus

Be honest in your estimate of yourselves, measuring your value by how much faith God has given you. Love each other with brotherly affection and take delight in honouring each other. Work happily together. Don't try to act big. Don't try to get into the good books of important people, but enjoy the company of ordinary folks. And don't think you know it all!

Today Paul describes the kind of attitude towards others that we need if we want to be like Jesus. I guess he would heartily approve of the preacher who, looking sadly at a drunk in a gutter, said softly, 'There but for the grace of God go I.'

We ask God to change us, but when he does we take the credit and start feeling so pleased with ourselves that we look down on everyone else. You only have to listen to a few after-church conversations to realize how prone we all are to pride—the worst sin of all. Have you heard this kind of thing? 'Don't ask her to help; she's only a new Christian, she hasn't a clue!' 'My husband isn't nearly as far on as I am.' 'Oh, she's the sort who lurches from one problem to another!' 'I can't stand happy-clappies!' If we treat one another like that, no wonder non-churchgoers label us as judgmental.

Jesus had a lovely way of making everyone he met feel they really mattered to him. One day, a half-naked woman was dragged to him by a crowd of respectable citizens. She had been caught in bed with someone else's husband and they were out for her blood. Instead of despising her, like everyone else, Jesus looked at her with such uncondemning love that she was completely changed. His attitude gave her the confidence to start a new life (John 8:2–11). People can be crushed by our disapproval or set free by our encouragement.

When you think about other people, would you say you were more likely to look up at them in admiration for their good qualities, or down on them for their failures and mistakes?

ROMANS 12:4–5 (LB)

Relating like Jesus

Just as there are many parts to our bodies, so it is with Christ's body. We are all parts of it, and it takes every one of us to make it complete, for we each have different work to do. So we belong to each other and each needs all the others.

I was hanging around London, killing time before an important interview. Feeling scared and lonely, I went to a kiosk for a hot drink. I'll never forget the face of the lady who served me: her smile was so radiant that her face positively shone. Without thinking, I said, 'You must be a Christian!' 'I sure am!' she replied, and the moment she gripped my hand I stopped feeling alone or afraid. After chatting for five minutes, we felt we'd known each other for ever.

Paul tells us today that the bond between Christians is closer than family; we are part of the living, moving, hearing, speaking, loving body of Jesus here on earth—a body so vast that it stretches right over the globe, yet it is linked together by a network of invisible 'veins and arteries'. Paul was so pleased with this 'body' idea that he expanded it when he wrote to a church in Corinth (1 Corinthians 12:12–31). We don't know how the Roman Christians were relating to each other, but in Corinth they were fighting like dogs and breaking Paul's heart. God wants us to be as close to each other as two toes on a foot, yet it seems as if we Christians are always quarrelling. We form ourselves into a lot of small, mutually exclusive groups, declaring that we are the only ones who've 'got it right'.

We can't mend the broken body of Christ worldwide, but we are responsible for our own broken relationships. Has someone upset you? Jesus deliberately sat next to Judas Iscariot at the last supper and went out of his way to show him special kindness and courtesy. Could you treat your 'enemy' like that?

Could you write a list of the people you find difficult, and ask the Lord to help you treat them as Jesus would?

⁘

ROMANS 12:6–7 (LB)

Serving like Jesus

God has given each of us the ability to do certain things well. So if God has given you the ability to prophesy, then prophesy whenever you can—as often as your faith is strong enough to receive a message from God. If your gift is that of serving others, serve them well. If you are a teacher, do a good job of teaching. If you are a preacher, see to it that your sermons are encouraging and helpful.

Peggy sat in church feeling utterly miserable. 'We all have a gift we can use to serve God,' said the voice from the pulpit. 'Except me,' thought

Peggy. Everyone else in church seemed so talented but, since her children had left home and her husband had died, she felt so useless and too shy to get involved with church activities.

'We'll spend a moment in silence,' concluded the vicar, 'so everyone can ask God what is their spiritual gift.'

'There!' thought Peggy at the end of the prayer. 'That proves God never speaks to me.' The only word that had come into her head was 'soup'! On the way out of church, the vicar said, 'Peggy, some of us take food to the homeless in London on Saturday nights. Could you make some soup next week?' It wasn't long before Peggy was not only making soup each week, but going with the team to ladle it out. As her confidence has grown, she's made some special friendships with her 'regulars' and recently she told me, 'What they need, even more than hot soup, is someone who's got time to listen to them.'

So often, we think it's the 'up-front' people who are important in our church communities. Today, however, Paul gives the private unseen gifts, like serving others, equal status with the public gifts of prophecy, preaching or teaching. A body needs hands and ears just as much as it needs a mouth.

Lord, I don't have much in the way of time or natural talents to give you, but, like the little boy who gave you his picnic lunch, please take what I have and use it to help others. Amen

ROMANS 12:8b, 13 (LB)

Giving like Jesus

If God has given you money, be generous in helping others with it... Those who offer comfort to the sorrowing should do so with Christian cheer. When God's children are in need, you be the one to help them out. And get into the habit of inviting guests home for dinner or, if they need lodging, for the night.

That advice is all very well if our families share our Christian commitment, but taking it too enthusiastically nearly finished Jemma's marriage. She discovered that her gift was caring for people in trouble. She was an excellent listener and very generous with her time, energy and resources. Then one day her husband erupted. 'I work my guts out for this family, but when I come home tired, there's always some lame dog here telling you a sob story. Supper's never ready because you've been out hospital visiting, and you keep giving my hard-earned money to a load of spongers!'

'Surely God wants me to help people? Jemma asked her friend.

'Of course he does,' she replied, 'but perhaps your priorities are in the wrong order. Your personal relationship of love and friendship with God himself always comes first, then your family and after that the things you do for God. You've been so busy working for him that you haven't had enough time to spend with them, and your family feel they come last for you nowadays. No wonder Tom's stroppy!'

Juggling priorities is always difficult. Some people so enjoy worship and being with God that they don't notice the sad, lonely people in the world around them. Others are so absorbed by husband, children and job that God gets lost under the smart new furniture. Jesus gave all his time and energy to other people, but for the first 30 years of his life he gave everything he had to his family.

Lord, the demands of other people pull me in all directions. Please keep on filling me up with yourself, because on my own I've got nothing left to give. Amen

ROMANS 12:8 (NIV)

Leading like Jesus

If your gift... is leadership, then govern diligently.

Before we all start bristling at the way Paul links the word 'leadership' with the word 'man', let me say that being a Christian leader isn't only about wearing your collar the wrong way round. It applies to anyone who influences others, whether it's helping with an Alpha group, Sunday school class, ladies' meeting or college or school Christian Union, or being a mother or child minder.

The job of making God real to others is a serious one. Hebrews 13:17 says that leaders will have to give an account of their work before God's throne one day. As we've already seen this week, it's no good saying, 'But I'm only there to make the tea (or soup). In God's eyes our gifts are all equally important, so we are all equally responsible for the people we serve, whether that's thousands or just one. Jesus was the greatest leader of men ever, but he spend lots of his time with just three of his followers.

His leadership assignment was to show a group of people what God was really like and prepare them to go and share that information with the world. If you are a mother, or help to run any kind of church activity, that is your commission too.

It wasn't so much what Jesus said about God that influenced his group, but the way he modelled God's love to them in the little practical details of life. Few of us realize how intently we are being watched by others all the time, and our children are the most critical observers of all. My mother never told me how vital it is to spend time alone with God each day, but every morning, however early I toddled into her bedroom, she was always reading her Bible. Similarly, I don't remember anything my Sunday school teacher said, but I'll never forget how incredibly kind he was to me when my dog died.

Lord, help me to model your love to the people who watch me today. Amen

✣

ROMANS 12:9 (LB)

Loving like Jesus

Don't just pretend that you love others: really love them. Hate what is wrong. Stand on the side of the good.

I often struggle with how to act towards people I don't love—or even like. Selwyn Hughes once said, 'You can't always feel your way into actions but you can always act your way into feelings.' I find that statement helpful, yet it seems to contradict what Paul is saying. Surely acting is pretending? Just a week after she became a Christian, Janet joined a little nurture group I helped to run. She had never read the Bible before, but was determined to obey it to the letter. When we were talking about the knotty question of love, she suddenly looked very worried. 'But I could never love the woman who stole my dad from Mum. She ruined my childhood. I won't even speak to her.'

We calmed her down, saying that God never asks us to do anything without offering to help. Then, a few days later, Janet rang me. 'My dad's just phoned out of the blue,' she said tearfully. 'He's in the district and wants to pop in. He asked if he could bring Velma with him. I do want to love her, but how can I?' I told her to ask God to put his love in her heart. 'Then, even if you don't feel any love of your own, you will be able to love her with God's love. Just act out his love to her.'

'That's hypocrisy,' she protested.

'But you won't be insincere,' I replied. 'You actually will have love in your heart for Velma—not yours but God's. Just treat her as Jesus would.'

Very doubtfully, Janet agreed. Three hours later, she burst through my front door, looking radiant. 'It worked!' she said. 'At first it felt very odd, fussing around her, chatting and smiling, but before they left I caught myself thinking how nice she is. Acting loving really did make me feel loving—well, a bit, but it's a start, isn't it?'

Lord, please fill my heart with your love towards ....

✣

ROMANS 12:11 (LB)

Working like Jesus

Never be lazy in your work but serve the Lord enthusiastically.

Life seemed to have gone badly wrong for Amanda. She'd always wanted to be a missionary, but when she met her husband at Bible college she decided to settle for being a pastor's wife. Somehow he never made the grade, and now he worked in a biscuit factory. Amanda was fed up, overweight and stuck at home with three children. She couldn't even find a role at church because of her husband's awkward shifts. The house was a tip and somewhere under all the mess she had mislaid her joy.

'You know what, God?' she said belligerently one night when the baby had earache. 'All I wanted to do was serve you! I would have gone anywhere in the whole world, put up with anything and worked round the clock, but you landed me in this dump, doing absolutely nothing!'

Isn't it strange how God seems to meet us at our lowest moments? Amanda was giving the baby yet another drink when she suddenly felt that the Lord was speaking to her. 'You are giving this cold water to me. You serve me by serving your family and I want you to know that I appreciate the way you care for me.' Amanda's tears splashed down on to the baby's head as she began to see her life from a totally new perspective.

It is easy to admire people who do exciting things for God while we plod on in a boring job or care for elderly or very young relatives. Yet, surely, serving the Lord full-time means doing the next small job for him, whether that means preaching to thousands or comforting one baby. To Jesus it is not what we do that counts but how we do it—and who we do it for. His aim was to please his Father in everything he ever said or did and I'm sure that applied when he tidied the carpenter's shop or raised the dead and preached the Sermon on the Mount.

Lord, show me how to work for you today, and help me give it my best shot. Amen

⁘

ROMANS 12:12 (LB)

Rejoicing like Jesus

Be glad for all God is planning for you. Be patient in trouble.

When my six children were small, I was taken seriously ill, and for the next eight years I was trapped in a wheelchair. Life was extremely tough and sometimes I just did not want to go on living. The pain and frustration of that illness seemed so ghastly at the time, but now when I look back I can see how much good God was able to bring to me and my family through that experience. I also guess that when I look back after a few billion years in heaven, those difficult years will seem like a few brief unpleasant seconds in comparison with all the fun I'll be having.

We don't tend to look at our problem-dominated lives from the perspective of eternity. Heaven, however good it's going to be, seems a long way ahead when we feel ill, can't pay the bills or have lost someone we loved dearly. Yet Paul tells us to fix our attention on the future and be glad because of all the good things God is planning. I think he is talking about this life as well as heaven. Earlier in this same letter he says that God wants to bring good out of all the nasty things that hit those of us who love him and are willing to fit into his plans (Romans 8:28).

A few years after Paul wrote this letter to the Christians in Rome, their emperor, Nero, went mad. He began throwing them to his lions or burning them alive to light the city streets at night. I guess they must have remembered what Paul told them in today's verse because the patient, even joyful, way that they died impressed so many people that Christianity spread even more rapidly around the Roman empire.

'Let us fix our eyes on Jesus, the author and perfecter of our faith, who for the joy set before him endured the cross, scorning its shame, and sat down at the right hand of the throne of God' (Hebrews 12:2, NIV).

✣

ROMANS 12:12 (LB)

Praying like Jesus

Be prayerful always.

I used to get mad with Paul for saying we should 'pray without ceasing'. He obviously didn't have six children! Yet it does seem as if Jesus, in spite of his pressured lifestyle, was in continuous contact with God, as well as spending those early mornings alone with him (Mark 1:35). But is it possible in today's world to 'be prayerful always'?

Obviously, talking to God in words all the time is impossible. People in the office or supermarket would think we were nutty and we simply wouldn't cope if we didn't keep our minds on the job. I think I'm beginning to realize that prayer is a relationship that doesn't depend on words. Perhaps when the person you love most is always there with you, you get so close that words lose their importance. You just love them through everything you do, say or think.

We all know we need to spend a few moments each day 'plugging into God', but it's vital not to sign off with a final 'Amen'. We need to stay in his presence as the day unfolds, acknowledging that he is there by wordlessly referring everything to him. When the phone rings I don't say, 'Almighty Father, please assist me to communicate appropriately during this conversation.' My heart simply sends a 'help' in his direction as I lift the receiver. When I'm hoovering, or driving to work, my thoughts are all over the place, but I keep reminding myself to bring God into them. I'm not asking for anything; I just share what I'm thinking.

Whenever I get the nagging feeling that I've fouled up and need his forgiveness, I don't wait until my next official prayer session to sort it out, because I loathe feeling out of sync with him.

Sharing the little enjoyments of each day is important too—new buds on a house plant or the rich taste of the soup I'm cooking.

Lord, my days are just a string of small actions, leading on from one another. Show me how to keep on invoking your presence as I move through each of them. Amen

✣

ROMANS 12:14, 17a, 20a (LB)

Reacting like Jesus

If someone mistreats you because you are a Christian, don't curse him; pray that God will bless him... Never pay back evil for evil... Instead, feed your enemy if he is hungry, if he is thirsty give him something to drink and you will be 'heaping coals of fire on his head'.

We all know this is how Jesus behaved. When people yelled abuse at him, he kept quiet; he even healed one of the thugs who arrested him. But what about us? I think it's humanly impossible to love and treat kindly someone who has abused you, deserted you or ruined your life. Forgiving is too tough on our own—we need God's help. All he needs is our willingness to spit out the hate and, in its place, breathe in his love and forgiving grace. I find I have to do that every time the bad memories come back into my mind. Perhaps I'll have to keep at it for the rest of my life.

Julie's daughter was traumatized when a neighbour exposed himself in the park. For three years Julie couldn't look out of her front windows in case she saw this man, who lived opposite. 'But I had my revenge,' she said. ' I kept bringing the subject up in conversations with my neighbours, working them up against him until no one would speak to him—or his wife.'

Then Julie became a Christian and after a talk on forgiveness she made the decision to try it, 'so long as I never have to speak to him'.

One day his wife was taken ill, and he went to see her in hospital each evening after work, returning late and tired. Julie kept feeling that God wanted her to plate up an extra meal at supper time, and take it over to him when he returned. The very idea revolted her, but the night she finally managed it, he thanked her with tears pouring down his face. They both knew it was much more than a plate of supper.

Lord, forgive me that I can't forgive, but I want to want you to make me willing. Amen

✣

ROMANS 12:19, 21 (LB)

Forgiving like Jesus

Never avenge yourselves. Leave that to God, for he has said that he will repay those who deserve it. [Don't take the law into your own hands.] ... Don't let evil get the upper hand but conquer evil by doing good.

Once, in my wheelchair days, one of my sons behaved so badly that I wished I could get up and commit murder, but I was helpless. I could only say, 'You just wait till your father comes home.' God isn't a sentimental old grandpa, beaming indulgently down on the world. He gets violently angry when one of us (whom he calls the apple of his eye) is hurt by someone else. Hellfire was not a medieval invention; Jesus often talked about it. If hell and punishment didn't exist, then there would have been no need for him to die on the cross. Of course we don't like the subject, but the Bible tells us just as much about God's wrath as it does about his compassion.

If he simply patted the heads of people who selfishly destroy others, and let them off, it would be impossible for us ever to forgive. We would feel it was our responsibility to make them suffer, but knowing that we can leave their punishment to God on judgment day sets us free from the obligation. The trouble is, we want to pay them back ourselves so that we can see them squirm. It is that kind of vengeful anger that destroys us, and we have to bring it to God for his forgiveness, or we're in danger of forfeiting our own forgiveness and also facing God's wrath (Matthew 6:15).

Have you ever thought what a ghastly punishment God might have planned for those heartless soldiers who banged nails through his Son's hands, laughing at his agony? Hell would be too good for them. But we may meet them all in heaven one day, simply because Jesus prayed for them. 'Father, forgive them' meant 'Father, let them off.' Forgiving is one thing, but praying that God will also forgive goes far beyond that—it could set them free from punishment.

Are you willing to forgive as Jesus forgave?

✣

ROMANS 12:15, 18 (LB)

Feeling like Jesus

When others are happy, be happy with them. If they are sad, share their sorrow... Don't quarrel with anyone. Be at peace with everyone, so far as it depends on you.

Empathy is not like sympathy, which feels for others. Empathy takes us right inside someone else and feels the pain with them. It understands because it identifies, but it isn't just an emotion—it does something positive to help. Jesus cried for Mary when her brother died, but he did more than weep—he raised him from the dead. Jesus could have stayed in heaven, feeling sad for the mess we're in, but he felt strongly enough to come and do something about it.

Feeling like Jesus means more than just listening to someone's problems after church and then saying a quick prayer and telling them to keep smiling. It means identifying so completely that you know instinctively what practical help they and their family will need during the coming week—and then giving it.

Pippa never went to church and was too shy to make friends. At first she did not know that her neighbour Carol was a Christian—she just thought she looked nice. One day, without warning, Pippa's husband left her with three children. She was so shocked that she took an overdose. As she came round in hospital, she saw Carol's face.

'Don't worry about the kids,' Carol said. 'I've got them round at my place. And when you're better I'd love you to come and stay too, for a bit.' Over the next few weeks Pippa felt totally surrounded by the love and care of Carol's church. Suddenly she had the friends she had always wanted and it wasn't long before she met Jesus himself.

He must sometimes look down at desperately sad people like Pippa and long to help and comfort them—but how can he, unless one of us acts for him?

Lord, I want to feel the same about people as you do. Send me out into the world you love, and let me be so like you that people will be drawn to your love, which fills my heart. Amen

TRANSFORMING LOVE

PSALM 23 (NIV)

Old yet ever new

The Lord is my shepherd, I shall not be in want.

This psalm is the most recited and the best loved. Even though the words may be familiar, they still have the capacity to move, to challenge and to comfort. It is full of intimate detail and reads as a conversation between David and his loving Lord. Just recently, when I read this psalm again, I made it into my prayer, my conversation with him.

'Dear Father, because you are the shepherd of my soul I have everything I need, I lack nothing. You enable me to stop, even though the effort of doing so is harder than keeping going. But you have a place of safety and comfort for me where quiet waters flow and nothing hurries me or drowns out your still small voice. It is there that you restore my aching soul and heal my damaged body.

'And even if the way ahead is through the darkest of valleys, nothing will frighten me for you will be with me just as you said, and even though all seems harsh and unyielding, comfort will come.

'You have lavished your provision upon me even in the most difficult of times. I am overwhelmed by your love and my life knows blessing upon blessing.

'Because of your grace I am pursued by goodness and love—they are my constant companions and will abide and remain with me all the days of my life.

'And as if this weren't enough, I will be where you are—at home in heaven, for ever. Amen.'

The familiar words of the Bible can transform our lives daily. The words are as relevant, as challenging as when they were first spoken because they were spoken to and by people just like you and me who faced the same situations we face. His words may be old, but they remain ever new!

Father God, may your word be real and relevant, challenging and comforting. May it find a place in our hearts and be lived out in our lives. Amen

✣

HEBREWS 12:1 (LB)

Go for it!

Since we have such a huge crowd of men of faith watching us from the grandstands...

The 'huge crowd' refers to those commended for their great faith in chapter 11. What a wonderful picture of a grandstand inhabited by the likes of Enoch, Noah, Abraham, Jacob, Joseph, Moses and countless others cheering us along in the race marked out for us!

The experiences and examples of the saints of old are in the pages of the Bible to encourage us along. But what of today? Do we have those around us to cheer us along? Are we part of a crowd or 'cloud of witnesses', as in the NIV version, cheering others along?

Regardless of our ability, we still have a part to play in others' lives. My days of participating in sports or most other activities are long gone. I spectate rather than participate. Initially it was difficult to be still and to watch. But the Lord reminded me of the words he spoke to the disciples: 'Watch and pray.' I could pray. I could cheer them along as I 'watched' their lives.

A story is told of a little boy who auditioned for a part in the school play. On the day the parts were awarded, his mum went to collect him, fearful that he would be disappointed at not being chosen again. As she neared the school he rushed out to meet her. Wide-eyed with excitement, he exclaimed, 'Mum, Mum! I've been chosen to clap and cheer!'

As I pray for friends, perhaps in some small way I can 'clap and cheer' them along. I can join with others in forming our own 'cloud of witnesses' to pray, to clap and to cheer. We all have a part to play, and it isn't dependent upon our ability, only our availability.

Father God, help us to watch and pray, to clap and cheer for those around us and to play our part in each life. Amen

✣

HEBREWS 11:1 (KJV)

Here and now

Now faith is the substance of things hoped for, the evidence of things not seen.

Society seems to be inhabited by 'now' people. Yesterday is gone; tomorrow may not even dawn; all we have is the 'now'.

Recently I was phoned by a young friend asking if he could visit me. As I reached for my diary he quickly said, 'I'm here now! I'm on your doorstep.' The wonders of mobile phones!

Sometimes I simply cannot keep up with the 'now' generation. My life may not be able to keep up, but my faith can. I love the idea of changing the emphasis on the way we say these words. Try it: 'Now faith...' What about now faith?

Now faith is as new and exciting as the first day it dawned upon us.

Now faith is fresh and new each day, like manna from heaven.

Now faith gives life substance as it focuses on God.

Now faith helps us to trust in the evidence of the things we cannot see. At times there seems little evidence that God is at work in our lives, unlike the days when he dwelt among us—wherever he went there was evidence that he had passed by! People were healed of every kind of disease and disability. Today, what evidence do we have? What evidence do we need?

Sometimes the biggest challenge we may ever face is to trust him; to trust that he is still with us, working in and through us, despite there being no outward evidence. Dare we? My answer is a resounding 'Yes!' I have all the 'evidence' I need: an empty tomb and a risen Lord is all that I need, to know that he is alive and that the faith that I have in him enables me to face every 'now' and every new day with all its challenges and opportunities.

Dear Father, help us to see that 'now' faith is the substance of things hoped for, the evidence of things not seen—yet! Amen

✣

2 CORINTHIANS 12:8–10 (NIV)

The plea of the helpless

Three times I pleaded with the Lord to take it away from me.

Paul was in good company—Jesus prayed three times in the garden of Gethsemane for the 'cup' to be taken from him. We don't really know what Paul's 'thorn in the flesh' was. But it drove him to plead with the Lord three times to take it away.

I have lost count of the times I've pleaded with the Lord to take the MS away—it seems more like three hundred or three thousand times! But just as Paul received his answer and Jesus received the strength he needed, we too can know something of the sufficiency of his grace to help us and to hold us through the most difficult and horrid of times—and to understand something of the paradox of his strength being made perfect in our weakness.

Many things in our Christian lives are topsy-turvy and yet can reveal something wonderful about his grace. The list is intriguing and challenging. As A.W. Tozer said, 'We are strongest when we are at our weakest and weakest when we feel strong. We are often at our highest when we feel at our lowest. We can often do more by doing nothing and can go furthest while standing still. We have more when we have given all that we have away and have the least when we "possess" the most' (The Best of Tozer, Christian Publications Inc., 1978).

Only the Lord can make sense out of some of the things we face. Only he can turn our weaknesses into something useful, something worthwhile. We fear weakness and illness and having to depend on others. Yet even weakness, illness and dependency can be turned around for good if we allow his grace to flow through our lives.

Father God, your grace is indeed sufficient in all of our needs. Help us to know your strength even in our weakness. Help us to see the wonder of the paradox of trusting you. Amen

JOB 2:10 (NIV)

The harbour of acceptance

He replied... 'Shall we accept good from God, and not trouble?'

This question has taxed minds for centuries—how can we accept what often seems totally out of keeping with God's character and love? We are comfortable with good, but what about the hard times?

Some years ago, as I was tussling with the loss of function in my legs and the realization that I may soon need to use a wheelchair, someone used the term 'harbour of acceptance'. I had never heard of such a thing, but began to be drawn towards learning this most wonderful of lessons.

I had been in London as part of my job and had struggled all day long to get around. Now safely back on the train I began my journey home. I let my mind wander and remembered how I used to be—active, involved in everything. I was afloat on the high seas of life and enjoying every moment, even when things were rough. I loved it. I loved life! But now it was time for me to head into calmer waters, back to the 'harbour' where I could take stock of all that had happened over recent months: the diagnosis of MS, the changes physically. Once there, it seemed as if it was time to bid farewell to legs that functioned as I wanted them to; to a body that worked normally, properly. I closed my eyes and imagined myself on the harbour wall. From there I waved farewell to the life I loved, to the function I had, and began the process of acceptance, of being willing to accept this 'new' way of doing things.

I had no idea what lay ahead of me, only that in those brief moments on a train journey home I was facing a different sort of journey into a life I could never have imagined—but with the sure knowledge that the Lord would be with me and would keep me safe.

Dear Father, when we face those things we find difficult to understand, draw us into that safe place where acceptance comes. Amen

✣

EZEKIEL 37:1–3 (NIV)

Dry bones

He asked me, 'Son of man, can these bones live?' I said, 'O Sovereign Lord, you alone know.'

I cannot be the only one who has had hopes and dreams that have died and become almost like this valley of dry bones Ezekiel saw in the vision. He saw the nation of Israel rise up again and become a vast army. Some of our hopes and dreams can come to life again, have new life breathed into them, as God once again begins to move on our behalf.

Jesus spoke about a seed falling to the ground and dying so that new life could come. His death brought us life. It is a paradox of the Christian walk that from death can come life; from a seemingly impossible situation can come something good .

Sometimes when I look at my life it seems as if the hopes and dreams I had—to marry, to have children, to be healthy and active—lie before me like dry bones, lifeless. Yet somehow and in some way God has effected a change in my attitude to the loss of my job, my home, and friends who could no longer cope with all that was happening to me. Ability has been replaced by disability and the 'death' of so many things, but as Jim Elliot said, 'We lose what we cannot keep, to gain what we cannot lose' (Elisabeth Elliot, Shadow of the Almighty, STL Books). At times things aren't quite how we would want them to be—but whatever lies at your feet today as dry old bones can be revived, can even be changed into something altogether different. Just as the bones became flesh and sinew, hopes and dreams can be transformed and can turn out to be far better than we ever dared imagine.

Dear Father, may your breath gently blow over our lives. Let us allow you to revive, regenerate, renew our hopes and dreams. 'Can these bones live? O Sovereign Lord, you alone know.' Amen

✣

JOHN 17:3 (NIV)

To know him

Now this is eternal life: that they may know you, the only true God, and Jesus Christ, whom you have sent.

I became a Christian when I was eleven years old. I was intrigued and mystified by the concept of 'eternal life'. Some years earlier I had made the horrifying discovery that people die—a young friend had drowned in a local stream and for the first time in my life I realized that people don't last for ever. So when I met Jesus and heard about eternal life through him, I grabbed him—and it—with both hands.

As the years passed, my concept of eternal life changed—it isn't only the life that awaits me in heaven but a life to be lived here. Eternal life began that day I met Jesus, and is a lifelong journey into knowing him.

It seems all too easy these days to create a God in our image, a loving, kind God who wouldn't dare declare war on our concept of him. We can often allow our intellect to create a God who is very intelligent and reasonable; who is very scriptural and wonderfully easy to put in a 'box' and who complies to all our wishes and awaits our hurried prayers; a God who wouldn't allow illness and loss to come our way.

Eternal life is purely and simply knowing him—knowing him in the wonder of life, in the joys and the delights it brings. But it is, more importantly, knowing him when we have nothing to base that knowledge upon except the faith that comes from him alone, that holds us and sustains through the darkest of times.

But what matters supremely is that he knows us! We are graven on the palms of his hands, we are never out of his mind. His is the initiative, ours the response. We know him because he first knew us and continues to know us—as friends!

Dear Father, thank you for my eternal home in heaven. Help me to enjoy eternal life knowing you here and now, day by day. Amen

DELIGHT IN GOD

PSALM 149:4 (NIV)

God delights in you

For the Lord takes delight in his people; he crowns the humble with salvation.

What a marvellous antidote to a low self-image! The idea of God loving me as part of the teeming mass of humanity doesn't always make me feel particularly special, whereas the thought of God 'delighting' in me throws a fresh and exciting light on the relationship. Some synonyms of 'delight in' are 'appreciate, enjoy, feast on, relish, revel in'.

I use those words to describe sticky toffee pudding, bluebell woods, sun-drenched bank holidays and my adorable great-nephew (aged 2)! Something that is delightful brings pleasure, amusement, a desire to linger and prolong the experience.

Spending time with me is not a duty for God; not a time when he inwardly groans at the mess I get myself in and wonders how he is going to extricate me from it. It is a delight to him. He is thrilled to meet with me. He is enchanted by my conversation. He is satisfied with my spiritual growth. He appreciates what he sees of Jesus in me. He looks forward with great anticipation to my arrival in heaven. This is mind-blowing... but how could it possibly be true?

Let's think back to creation. God created you and me in love and in his own image. Although that image is very marred, it is still there and, because God did it, it is wonderful—altogether delightful. We more often focus on the things we do wrong. Have you ever berated yourself in exasperation: 'I'm so stupid!' God doesn't think you're stupid. He delights in you. His opinion of us is not dependent on how well we perform. It is based on the reality that he lovingly and intricately created us and therefore we are delightful. Let's revel in that today.

It's incredible to think, Lord, that you delight in me. Help me to focus on what you say about me, and not on what I think about myself.

⁜

MICAH 7:18 (NIV)

God delights to show mercy

Who is a God like you, who pardons sin and forgives the transgression of the remnant of his inheritance? You do not stay angry for ever but delight to show mercy.

What does God do with all the sin that erupts in our world every day? I'm sure he gets utterly sick of the horror of it all. So how can he be delighted to show mercy? Wouldn't it be acutely painful to a holy God to acknowledge the reality of grotesque acts of wickedness as well as the more everyday sins that we all commit? Even on our own level, shame makes us feel sick, dirty and unwilling to face God and admit what we've done. If only we could go back and erase those awful moments.

In forgiveness, one party has to own up and the other can then offer or withhold the liberating words, 'I forgive you from my heart for the hurt that you caused me.' The Christian religion stands alone in having a remedy for guilt and sin, all because of Jesus and his death on the cross. This must be part of why God is delighted to show mercy. It is an act that honours Jesus and brings his life, death and resurrection into the full beam of the spotlight. The cross's dynamic message is shouted out to all the principalities and powers in heaven and on earth. Jesus did it all! We can be forgiven!

Anything that honours Jesus delights God the Father, so although this in no way gives us a licence to sin, it does mean that we need have no fear that God is sitting on his throne with a severe frown on his face and reluctance in his heart to forgive us. He delights in showing mercy.

Father, thank you that I can be forgiven for anything I've done wrong. Thank you that you don't begrudge this gift, but you delight in forgiving me. Help me not to hide from you or from others when I feel guilty, but to come to you for release and freedom.

✣

2 CORINTHIANS 12:10 (NIV)

Delighting in difficulties

That is why, for Christ's sake, I delight in weaknesses, in insults, in hardships, in persecutions, in difficulties. For when I am weak, then I am strong.

This sounds masochistic! Paul had a mighty big job. He strove to get the gospel out to the whole Gentile world. Surely difficulties and weaknesses that hindered his effectiveness should have been a total frustration to him. I get really irritated when things slow me down.

On one occasion I had to return from the mission field because of illness. I had an important job to do in Africa, so why was God allowing this? Didn't he see the needs? Well, of course he did, but he also saw needs in my life. Over the months, he gently helped me face up to and repent of wrong motivations in my heart. Eventually I got to the point of agreeing with Paul. 'Yes, Lord, I delight in my weakness because through it I've experienced more of your love.' In my weakness I became stronger in the Lord.

I guess when you've had as many trials as Paul you learn to turn more quickly to God and regain his perspective. I still struggle with hindrances. My immediate response is to groan, and only in hindsight do I think about what God might be doing.

Is there an area where you feel weak? Are you being persecuted or insulted? Are you in difficulties? No one is suggesting that you should be thrilled to be ill or thwarted in some way. To delight in these things means looking to God and trusting him to work through them. Just as infra-red goggles enable James Bond to see in the dark, so looking at trials with God's perspective will enable us to see something to delight in.

Lord, I don't want to be a triumphalistic Christian in the wrong sense and not be real when things hurt. But I do want to trust you so that in my weakness I become stronger in you.

PSALM 1:2 (NIV)

Delighting in God's word

But their delight is in the law of the Lord, and on his law they meditate day and night.

The mark of whether we delight in, enjoy, savour, relish and appreciate God's word seems to be that we meditate on it day and night. The word 'meditation' conjures up images of undisturbed hours of contemplation. At first glance this appears to be OK for nuns and monks in cloisters but a bit unrealistic for busy people in the 21st century.

A synonym for 'meditate' is to chew the cud. Cows munch grass to extract every atom of nourishment. As they swallow and start the digestive process, it then becomes part of them. To meditate on God's word means to focus, think, mull over and seek with the Holy Spirit's help to discover new meanings, and then to apply it to life in some practical way. It then becomes heart-and-mind experience and not just happy thoughts and theory. It is digested. God's word and his values then govern life decisions and influence attitudes at home, in work and socially.

This sounds great, but how does it work in reality? Let's look at Jesus. He delighted in God's law. His life radiated godly values and attitudes. How did he manage to meditate day and night with all the competing demands facing him? We know he took extended times with God on occasions, and made time for prayer. He was so steeped in God's word that he was able to draw on these reserves when he was confronted with needy people and difficult situations from morning to night.

Can we so organize our lives that we are able to take extended time with God regularly? This would provide a wellspring for the rest of life. A way of topping up this wellspring on a daily basis is to choose one or two verses (like these readings) and keep mulling them over during the day whenever you have a free moment. Memorizing the verse helps.

Lord, 'open my eyes that I may see wonderful things in your law' (Psalm 119:18).

✣

ISAIAH 58:13b–14 (NIV)

Sabbath—a delight?

If you call the Sabbath a delight and the Lord's holy day honourable, and if you honour it by not going your own way and not doing as you please or speaking idle words, then you will find your joy in the Lord, and I will cause you to ride on the heights of

the land and to feast on the inheritance of your father Jacob. The mouth of the Lord has spoken.

In our media-saturated age we are constantly assailed by extravagant promises—some explicit, some implied. For example, this beauty cream will restore your youth; this new kitchen will make you and your family happy; this wardrobe is easy to assemble! No wonder we get a bit cynical.

God's promises are wildly extravagant, and are founded on his utter integrity. He promises joy—a vivid emotion of pleasure, extreme gladness. He says the Israelites would 'ride on the heights': that is, that they would control the land. They would be victorious and not defeated by their enemies. They would feast—they would be amply provided for. Joy, victory and abundance—what more could we want?

But these are not unconditional promises. In order to experience these goodies, we need the right attitude towards God. The Sabbath goes right back to the dawn of time. God rested after all his creative work and he made the day holy—a special, set-apart day. Do we have a Sabbath that leaves us refreshed physically, mentally, emotionally and spiritually? Is it an honourable, holy day, when we focus on God and what he wants of us, rather than doing our own thing?

Many of us have to work on Sundays. The particular day is not the issue, it's the attitude that is important. Do we make time in the week to stop, rest, listen to God and allow him to energize us for what lies ahead? God can safely entrust great things to people like this.

Lord, help me make Sabbath a reality in my life.

✣

ISAIAH 55:1–2 (NIV)

Delight for thirsty souls

Come, all you who are thirsty, come to the waters; and you who have no money, come, buy and eat! Come, buy wine and milk

without money and without cost. Why spend money on what is not bread, and your labour on what does not satisfy? Listen, listen to me, and eat what is good, and your soul will delight in the richest of fare.

In the past, when desires for fulfilment and satisfaction have come into my mind, I have berated myself as being self-centred. I've told myself that I should not think about my own needs but give myself in serving others. These verses cast a different light on the dilemma. The fact that I'm thirsty and hungry and seeking satisfaction is not a problem to God. He created me with these needs. They are part of being human.

Whatever our need is—peace, joy, fulfilment, love—God says, 'Come. Don't try to get your needs met by any other means. The world has no answers to the deep emptiness in your heart. Come, listen to me and I will satisfy you—not just with enough to get by, but with the richest of fare—an abundance you can barely contain.'

When God speaks to us, his message is one of love, forgiveness and mercy. He brings us to the cross of Christ where all our needs are met. Our foundational relationship is restored, which then puts all other relationships into context. If we look to people to meet our needs for love, acceptance, intimacy and comfort, we will be sadly disappointed and put our friends and family under grossly unfair pressure. They cannot be God to us—only God can fill that role. God does sometimes use other people to show us his love, but we need to recognize that he is the source and the person is merely the channel.

Lord, I come to you with my hunger and thirst. Thank you that you do not expect me to be a super-saint, but that you want me to live in dependence upon you each day.

✣

1 SAMUEL 15:22 (NIV)

Obedience delights God's heart

Does the Lord delight in burnt offerings and sacrifices as much as in obeying the voice of the Lord? To obey is better than sacrifice, and to heed is better than the fat of rams.

This verse contains a salutary warning. King Saul had been given a clear commission by God. He returned from the battle confident that God would be pleased with him. 'I have carried out the Lord's instructions!' he exclaimed. But he had changed those instructions to suit himself, so his obedience was only partial. God was not pleased, and for that disobedience Saul lost his crown.

In this incident Saul revealed that he thought his battle plan was better than God's and that God probably wouldn't notice if he bent the rules a little. This was arrogance of the highest order. Yet do not some of us fall into the same trap? God says, 'Do not lie,' but sometimes it seems expedient to be economical with the truth. Jesus says, 'Forgive those who've hurt you,' but sometimes we nurse our grievances and expect others to make the first move. We need to recognize that God has given commandments for our good and he does know best. Total obedience delights his heart and it will delight our own hearts also, even if it is painful at first. Disobedience will inevitably result in grief, loss and heartache.

Total obedience! That sounds an impossible task. Another commandment God has given is that we should confess our sins as soon as we are aware of them. King Saul protested his innocence and did not initially face up to what he had done wrong. This compounded his guilt.

We have a forgiving God to whom we can come for cleansing. Let's do it, so that our obedience can delight him.

'The blood of Jesus, his Son, purifies us from all sin' (1 John 1:7).

THE NEW HEAVEN AND THE NEW EARTH

ISAIAH 60:1–5 (NIV)

Millennium promises

Arise, shine, for your light has come, and the glory of the Lord rises upon you.

When my neighbour's third child was born, one of her toddlers, watching his sister in the bath, asked in a puzzled way, 'But what's Amanda for?' We can all sometimes wonder why we dig gardens, paint walls, take photographs, worry about buying presents, when we are all going to die and someone else is going to throw the photographs away and dig up our plants. Somehow we need to know what we are for, and part of that is to know what is going to happen to us all in the end.

Over the next two weeks we are going to be reading from the last chapters of Isaiah in the Old Testament, and from Revelation, the very last book of the New Testament. In these chapters we are given a vision, a picture of the future, a promise that one day we will know all the answers, that we will discover what our lives were for.

We begin with a rousing call that sounds a bit like the bugle waking campers as the dawn breaks in the eastern sky. The Lord is calling his people to wake up because a wonderful day is beginning.

Can you remember waiting for something wonderful to happen? I can still just about remember the feelings I had when, as a child, I went to bed on Christmas Eve, knowing that the next morning there would be a knobbly sock and a pile of wrapped presents by my bed. 'Arise, shine,' the Lord says. The moment you have been waiting for has come.

Wake me up, Lord; show me as I read these verses that you have promised a wonderful future for those who follow you, and may that promise give a rosy tint to all I do.

✣

ISAIAH 60:18–22 (NIV)

Big promises

No longer will violence be heard in your land, nor ruin or destruction within your borders, but you will call your walls Salvation and your gates Praise.

Many people were waiting for the start of the new millennium. The digital clocks were clicking forward to a big party. But by 6 January, when we all went back to work, a lot of people were wondering why they had been so excited. It would be different if we thought the millennium was bringing an end to violence!

The Lord's words here are being spoken to 'Jerusalem', to his chosen people, in their city, where the Lord was worshipped in his temple. Only things had not turned out too well. Jerusalem had been conquered by foreign armies, its people exiled, the temple knocked down. But even before that, the people had stopped praising the Lord and had disobeyed his laws. The prophets told them that they had brought ruin and destruction on themselves.

But now the Lord promises a wonderful restoration—no more violence, no more tears, but rebuilding, a new start, a glorious dawn with every hope fulfilled. Some people were desperately hoping that the new millennium would bring a new start for our world.

Imagine reading these words today on the morning after your church has been burnt down and Christian friends attacked, beaten and killed, in Sudan, in Indonesia, in northern Nigeria. Do these promises mean anything now in today's world?

As we read on, we will begin to see that the Lord fulfils his promises in two ways. As we trust in him, we see them being fulfilled partly here and now. (Jerusalem's temple was rebuilt. Later it was demolished again.) But the final and tremendous fulfilment is still ahead of us, when the day of the Lord comes at last.

Pray for those Christians who live in violent parts of our world, that they will be able to put their trust in these promises today, even though they have to wait for them to come true tomorrow.

✣

ISAIAH 61:1–7 (NIV)

Fulfilment in Jesus

The Spirit of the Sovereign Lord is on me, because the Lord has anointed me to preach good news to the poor. He has sent me to bind up the broken-hearted, to proclaim freedom for the captives and release from darkness for the prisoners.

Most people long for freedom for captives, gladness instead of mourning, praise instead of despair. Isaiah says that there is someone who can bring this new life, new joy and new start, someone with the Spirit of the Lord in him.

We can imagine the shock and surprise in the synagogue at Nazareth around two thousand years ago when Jesus read these verses and then said, 'Today this scripture is fulfilled in your hearing' (Luke 4:18–21). Jesus claimed that he is the one who fulfils all these great promises of God that we have been reading about. He is the new dawn—the wonderful Christmas morning present.

The most important moment in history, when God begins to save us and restore us, does not come with great armies but with a man who lives and dies on earth. So the fulfilment of God's promises of enormous light and glory begin with a small, vulnerable human baby. His death brings forgiveness, new life and the promise of a wonderful future. And the first sign that this has begun is that he came back from death.

What are our longings for a new start? Relationships we long to see on a better footing? Healing for people we love who are unhappy or hurt? Putting right damage we have done or has been done to us? As you pray, bring these longings to Jesus, sent to bind up the broken-hearted.

Perhaps we will see these prayers answered soon, but we may have to wait, seeing them partly answered now. Write down all you have prayed for, and keep watch. We are sometimes too preoccupied to notice that there are some answers now, even if we have to go on waiting for the final wonderful dawn.

✣

ISAIAH 62:1–5 (NIV)

The marriage we were made for

As a bridegroom rejoices over his bride, so will your God rejoice over you.

Running through the Bible in the Old and New Testaments, there is a lovely series of pictures that describes the relationship between the Lord and us as a marriage, a covenant of love. It can be very powerful and very physical. There is a dark side as God mourns over his people's betrayal of love, calling it adultery. Here in this passage, the message is that we are wooed, loved and chosen just as a lover chooses his bride. We are clothed in bridal dress, wearing a royal diadem (v. 3). Our (single) name is changed, from Desolate and Deserted to My Delight is in Her, and Married (v. 4, NRSV).

Remember that Jesus too talked of himself as the bridegroom (Mark 2:19–20). Like an engagement, this relationship can start for us now if we turn in love to our Lord. But the final wedding feast will come when heaven opens for us and all the promises of our betrothal are fulfilled.

The Lord speaks of his relationship to his people as the deep, passionate, committed love of a husband in the best possible marriage. Some of us have known such love for a time; others have glimpsed what it could be but sadly have never found it, or have lost it far too soon. But the Lord is our lover now and for ever, and we can look forward with total certainty to all the rich fulfilment of the wedding feast one day.

Lord, help me to remember I am chosen, loved and cherished by you—today, tomorrow and for ever.

✣

ISAIAH 62:8–12 (NIV)

I won't let it happen again

Never again will I give your grain as food for your enemies, and never again will foreigners drink the new wine for which you have toiled; but those who harvest it will eat it and praise the Lord.

'I have worked so hard to make this business really successful and now in one week it's been taken over, and I've been made redundant.'

'I did my very best for my son, and now he's dropped out of college, gone to Nepal and doesn't even phone us any more.'

Working very hard at something and having it snatched away happens to lots of people—to farmers whose crops fail, to those whose health fails when they are still young, to refugees who have to leave everything behind. Because we live in a fallen and unfair world, these things will happen and not just to those who deserve it. But God says, 'I will put it right.' 'Your Saviour will come and he brings reward and recompense' (v. 11).

Injustice, disappointment and unfairness are hard to bear and sometimes the resulting bitterness and resentment can eat us up. We need to hold on to the promises of God that he knows what has happened to us and will certainly put it right one day. 'Never again' is his promise to us. Jesus tasted defeat, betrayal and injustice and knows what they are like. He doesn't say they won't happen, but he does promise that we will one day hear heaven shout, 'Never again.' 'Never again' is the message of the resurrection.

Sometimes we need help to begin to forgive those who have hurt us, and to let go of resentment and the desire to pay them back. We may need someone we can trust to help us bring it all to the Lord. 'Father, forgive them. They don't know what they are doing,' Jesus prayed. Are we able to pray that?

✣

ISAIAH 64:1–9 (NIV)

Waiting for the great day

No eye has seen any God besides you, who acts on behalf of those who wait for him.

However busy we are with a very full life, when we know that something wonderful is going to happen, we are also waiting. We wait for a holiday, a visit, an appointment. We wait for Christmas morning, for our wedding day. We wait for someone we love to come home after a long time away. We may be waiting and worrying that it might not happen. Sometimes we can be very impatient, like children who want their presents now, and cannot wait for Christmas morning. God's promises come but we have to wait for them.

In these verses, the people of God are being impatient. They cannot wait for the promised dawn when everything will be put right, the presents opened and the feast begun. 'Why don't you come? Why do we have to wait?' Then they answer this question for themselves. 'You have hidden your face from us and made us waste away because of our sins' (v. 7). Why do they have to wait? Because they have turned away from God. He is not teasing by promising presents that he then keeps hidden. He is waiting for us to ask for them—to admit that we have been wrong and to ask for his forgiveness.

These great promises are not for those who do no wrong. They are for those who have done wrong and have been forgiven. The Saviour who died for us and came alive again brings the fulfilment of God's promises to us, by making our forgiveness possible, so that we can wait knowing the promises are for us.

So we wait, Lord, loved and forgiven and doing right, with these wonderful promises about to come true. Lord, give me a sense of your glory just round the corner so that waiting for your coming brings colour and excitement to all I do.

✣

ISAIAH 65:17–25 (NIV)

A new heaven and a new earth

Behold I will create new heavens and a new earth. The former things will not be remembered, nor will they come to mind... the sound of weeping and of crying will be heard in it no more.

In our last verse from Isaiah, the Lord promises us not just heaven, but a new earth.

All the delights of the world around us will be restored and recreated—sunsets and rainbows, roses and redwoods, mountains and hedgerows, human love and music, poetry and language—all this will be ours to enjoy, unspoilt. We live on a spoilt earth, but God gives us enough glimpses of beauty to hint at what the new earth will be like.

All the bad things will be gone and forgotten. No more sadness, resentment, pain, disablement, prejudice and cruelty. They will not even be remembered. The 'never again' promise is repeated. No babies that die, no building things up to see them torn down, no planting crops that we do not harvest; no old people finishing their lives in misery. There will be no more damaged earth, no more killing and hunting: even lions will eat straw beside the oxen.

We live in a world where bad and good are completely mixed up together, where good things that God gives us to enjoy are spoilt. We paint in beautiful colours, but the paint flakes off. He puts the beauty of gold and diamonds into the rocks, but humans fight and kill to find them, and cheat and steal to possess them.

When we pray, 'Your will be done on earth as in heaven', we are promising to do all we can to put things right. Our work, filled with his Spirit, is to make our earth more like his heaven until he comes in glory to create new heavens and a new earth.

Praise him for all the glimpses of heaven that we have on earth, especially as we worship our Lord Jesus who was made man on earth.

✣

REVELATION 19:1–10 (NIV)

Heaven opens up to us

Then I heard what sounded like a great multitude... shouting, 'Hallelujah! For our Lord God Almighty reigns. Let us rejoice and be glad and give him glory! For the wedding of the Lamb has come and his bride has made herself ready.'

I am writing these words on a cold November day. The sky is heavy and grey. The light is poor, even at midday. There is enough rain in the air to chill the bones. The hills are dim grey against the darker grey of the sky. The trees are dripping and lifeless. The world is muffled, colourless, cold and silent.

Imagine it suddenly all changing in a flash to blazing, tropical, midday sunshine—and not just sudden light, warmth and colour, but noise too. That is what John is describing. It is heaven opening up.

We have read in Isaiah the promise of a future heaven for those of us on earth. Here we glimpse heaven itself. We see the shining, piercing light of the glory of God. When the Lord said to his people, 'Arise, shine, your light has come', this is where the light came from.

Heaven is here and now, although we cannot see it at the moment.

The sun is the other side of the clouds. All its joy and glory is real now, waiting for the right time to break through into our world. The multitudes of heaven are shouting in a wonderful Hallelujah chorus, 'The wedding of the Lamb has come, and his bride has made herself ready.' When he comes there will be no more doubts. We will be there in the bright sunshine of heaven. It will be greater than anything we have ever known, but we won't be in the back row craning to see; we are the guests at the wedding, but we are also, as the Church, the bride, taking pride of place next to the bridegroom.

Help me to be ready for you when you come, Lord, as a bride for her husband.

⁘

REVELATION 19:11–16 (NIV)

The warrior judge

I saw heaven standing open and there before me was a white horse, whose rider is called Faithful and True. With justice he judges and makes war... He is dressed in a robe dipped in blood, and his name is the Word of God.

Jesus the Lamb, whose wedding feast is prepared for his people, is also the warrior judge on a white horse, whose robe is dipped in blood. The word-pictures John draws are vivid and shocking, and sometimes not easy to understand. If you look back at Isaiah 63:1–6, you can see that John uses Isaiah's words to describe this new vision of God at work.

Jesus is King of kings and Lord of lords, bringing justice and judgment. He comes out of heaven followed by heavenly armies, to strike down the nations. This is the other side of God's promised 'Never again'. If all the bad things, the pain and suffering are to be ended, then the wicked have to be brought to justice. We cannot have the love of the Saviour without his justice.

Jean discovered that her twelve-year-old son, Hugh, was involved with a gang who were stealing from younger boys at school. When she confronted him, he admitted what he had done, but Hugh was horrified when his mother took him to see the Head. She agreed with the Head about the punishment and made sure it was carried out. Hugh knew she loved him and for this reason he expected her to protect him from justice, not to help carry out the punishment. But true love does not let us get away with evil. If we do not seek the forgiveness of the Lord's love, then we will face the judgment of his love.

Lord, help me to be honest about myself and to accept your judgment on my life; to ask for your full and free forgiveness for all I have done wrong. Help me to put right any damage I have done to others, even if the consequences are hard to bear.

✣

REVELATION 20:1–6 (NIV)

The millennium again

He seized the dragon, that ancient serpent, who is the devil, or Satan, and bound him for a thousand years.

A friend was telling me that her son likes books about real things—about tractors and dinosaurs. He has little time for everyday stories, let alone fantasy and poetry. Like many of us, he will probably find some parts of Revelation hard to cope with later on. It is full of descriptions that sound like fantasy and science-fiction.

In today's passage, there are two difficult ideas. The first is the binding of the devil. John sees an angel coming down to earth and capturing Satan, using four different words to describe the power of evil in our world. The angel has a chain and a key to the prison and he locks the devil up—but for a limited time, not for ever.

God is teaching us two things here. First, evil is very powerful, and it takes a lot of holy strength to control it. Second, God is able to control the devil, who is not free to do whatever he likes in our world.

Throughout the ages, human thinking has often fallen into the trap of neglecting one of these truths about evil, either under-estimating its strength and power or believing that Satan is God's equal in the struggle to control our world. On the cross, God in Christ defeated evil once and for all, but it was a titanic battle.

The second picture is the thousand years—a millennium. Christians have wondered what this means, and some have thought that there will be literally a thousand years of human history when evil is under lock and key. But from what we know about the use of numbers in this book, it is more likely to be a symbol than literally a thousand years—a symbol standing for God's perfect heavenly time. So John is letting us know that God is in control, that evil has limited powers, and that his perfect heaven breaks through into our time-controlled world.

Thank God that he is in control of history.

✣

REVELATION 20:11–15 (NIV)

The great white throne

And I saw the dead, great and small, standing before the throne, and books were opened. Another book was opened, which is the book of life.

The final day when God blazes in splendour like the sun, and everything is put right, may happen next week or not for another thousand years. But John says that when that day comes, we will all stand before the throne of God.

And then the books are opened! I would be very interested to know what is in the books about some people, but I am not so sure I want anyone else to know what is in mine! This is John's way of saying that God knows all that we have ever done. But there is another book—the book of life, which contains the names of all those who will enter heaven. Their list of wrongdoings has been crossed out, wiped away by the mercy of the Saviour who died to cancel them.

But what of those who are not in the book of life? We may not want to face the last sentence of our reading, but people cannot turn their back on God and say 'no' to him and expect him to drag them into heaven against their will. Some of my family do not believe in God. In ordinary daily life, telephone calls and meals together, it is hard to remember that heaven is just around the corner and that people I love will stand before the throne of God and may have to face the loss of heaven. I know that the Lord is calling me to pray for them, and to live so that they can see something of God in me.

Do you know that your name is in the book of life? If you have turned to Jesus, then it is. Make a commitment now to pray for someone who does not know him.

✣

REVELATION 21:1–6 (NIV)

A new heaven and a new earth

He will wipe every tear from their eyes. There will be no more death or mourning or crying or pain, for the old order of things has passed away.

'Then I saw a new heaven and a new earth,' John says, repeating the words we read in Isaiah some days ago. John is told to write down the vision as trustworthy and true. Because John did as he was told, we can read these verses two thousand years later in English.

John tries to describe the new heaven and earth, but finding the words to do so is very hard. He is drawing a mind-picture of something outside our experience and beyond our language. Like Isaiah, John talks of heaven as a new Jerusalem, but how do you describe a perfect city? He says that the city is a perfect cube, over a thousand miles high, wide and deep. It is made of gold so pure that it looks like glass, and precious stones with wonderful sparkling names—jasper, sapphire, emerald, carnelian, topaz, amethyst and pearl.

But the most wonderful thing is that at the centre of this imagined city there is a throne and round that throne multitudes are shouting and singing, but on the throne is a God who wipes away the tears from the eyes of any person who is crying. It is not like the great throne-rooms of this world's rulers, because the one on the throne is our Father, and beside him is the Son who bears the scars of our rescue.

Let him fill you with his joy and peace as he wipes away the tears from your eyes.

✣

REVELATION 22:1–7 (NIV)

Bringing heaven to earth

Then the angel showed me the river of the water of life, as clear as crystal, flowing from the throne of God and of the Lamb down the middle of the great street of the city.

When we see programmes or read about people who do not have access to clean water, then we begin to realize that water is far more precious than gold or silver. The lands of the Bible are places that know drought, when water is short and what is available may be badly polluted. No wonder John sees at the centre of the heavenly city a wonderful river of crystal-clear water.

A couple from our church work for a water development project in Tanzania. They plan and engineer the bringing of water to villages and farms where until now the women, mostly, have had to walk many miles to carry water back home. They are working to bring the kingdom of God on earth, to begin making God's promises for the future come true now. They are making these words of God real for Tanzanian villagers. They are saying that fresh water is part of God's heaven on earth.

All the promises we have read—comfort for pain, tears wiped away, captives freed, the broken-hearted bound up, as well as the shouting and singing in worship to God, the acceptance of his love and forgiveness—are promises that will fully come true only when God brings an end to human history and everyone will see him face to face. But they are also promises for now, in part, and they can begin to come true now for you and the people round you. We can make a bit of heaven come on earth. That is the work of the disciples of Jesus Christ.

Help me to know your heaven so that I can start to make heaven on earth.

THE SECOND COMING

MATTHEW 24:1–8 (NRSV)

Don't panic

You will hear of wars and rumours of wars; see that you are not alarmed, for this must take place, but the end is not yet... Nation will rise against nation, and kingdom against kingdom, and there will be famines and earthquakes in various places: all this is but the beginning of the birth-pangs.

I expect many readers have experienced giving birth. Early labour pains may be followed by birth two hours later, or two days later, or the pains may even prove to be a false alarm and nothing immediate follows. That is what it is like, Jesus tells us, when we look for the 'signs of his coming'. 'Wars and rumours of wars... nation against nation... famines and earthquakes...' It sounds familiar: Kosovo, Northern

Ireland, Israel, the Sudan; human violence and natural disasters frequently dominate the news and make it appear that wars and disasters are on the increase. But remember Pompeii, the Crusades, the plague, Napoleon, Amritsar—war and tragedy are not new phenomena. Many have predicted the imminence of the end of the world, and have even named a date for Jesus' return. Jesus said that such events would inevitably happen. We must not be alarmed.

What is our personal response to this? How are we to behave during these times of 'labour pains'? We turn to the apostle John. 'Now, little children, abide in him, so that when he is revealed we may have confidence and not be put to shame before him at his coming' (1 John 2:28). When we are shocked at pictures of the suffering we see almost daily on our TV screens, we grieve for the sufferers, but our faith in God's sovereignty or his love does not need to be shaken, even though we cannot understand why he allows such tragedies. Job endured ghastly loss and pain, and he was angry with God; he reckoned he did not deserve such suffering. But eventually (in chapter 42) he could affirm his trust in God who was truly in control.

Lord, help me to share Job's conviction in you, the God in control.

MATTHEW 24:9–10, 13 (NRSV)

Things won't be easy

They will hand you over to be tortured and will put you to death, and you will be hated by all nations because of my name. Then many will fall away... but the one who endures to the end will be saved.

I recently visited an Islamic country in the Middle East. There I met a Christian convert from Islam. He had spent a year in prison, suffering extensive torture, in the authorities' efforts to persuade him to renounce his faith and to betray others. How relevant for him these verses are! It is hardly surprising that some do turn away from their faith. We who live in a 'safer' climate should pray for Christians who suffer such aggressive persecution.

For most of us, the negative influences are more subtle. But Jesus describes our situation too. 'Because of the increase of lawlessness, the love of many will grow cold' (v. 12). We live in a secular climate where most people ignore God and—like a salty seaside atmosphere that corrodes cars left standing outside—our Christian values are gradually eroded and our love for Christ easily fades. We rarely face outright persecution, but in a society where it is regarded as odd, no longer the 'done thing', to go to church, the Christian has to swim against the current of popular opinion. We need courage to insert into a conversation a comment that puts God's perspective on life or death, or to decline—graciously—an invitation that we know would detract from God's way for us. It is uncomfortable to be laughed at, or ignored, for your Christian faith. We all need to make sure our lights are shining as brightly as they were a year ago.

O Jesus, I have promised to serve thee to the end;
Be thou for ever near me, my master and my friend;
I shall not fear the battle if thou art by my side,
Nor wander from the pathway if thou wilt be my guide.
J.E. BODE (1816–74)

Read Matthew 24:9–13.

MATTHEW 24:14 (NRSV)

Good news for the world

And this good news of the kingdom will be proclaimed throughout the world, as a testimony to all nations; then the end will come.

Recently I spent two weeks in Borneo, a country of big rivers and many waterways through the jungle. I heard of inland villages where the good news of Jesus has never reached, and of Christians who go on mission trips upriver to share the gospel with tribal people. 'This good news of the kingdom will be proclaimed throughout the world.' It is nearly two thousand years since Jesus died, and the gospel is still penetrating into corners of the world where his name has never been heard. There are other countries where militantly anti-Christian governments have forced Christians to go underground and believers risk their lives to worship, to read the Bible, even to share their faith with others.

This extension of the gospel of Christ's kingdom is one of the preludes to 'the end', to his return. How can we help this to happen when we are not all called to go to Borneo or Uzbekistan? Before his ascension, Jesus promised to give us his Holy Spirit to enable us to be his witnesses. Maybe your next-door neighbour is totally ignorant about Jesus—you may be the only Christian she knows. Pray for an opportunity to tell her about your faith in Jesus. Make time to find out as much as you can about the church in one particular country, so that you can give prayer and financial support intelligently.

For some, there will be a call from God to work overseas in the cause of the gospel. The nature of missionary work has changed in recent years, but Christians willing to commit themselves to live and work overseas for the cause of the gospel are still needed. Living conditions will often not be easy, frustrations may abound; it may even be hard to see what difference you are making. But your reward will be in knowing that you are obeying Jesus.

Read Acts 1:6–8.

✣

MATTHEW 24:27, 30–31 (NRSV)

A blaze of glory

As the lightning comes from the east and flashes as far as the west, so will be the coming of the Son of Man... They will see 'the

Son of Man coming on the clouds of heaven' with power and great glory. And he will send out his angels with a loud trumpet call, and they will gather his elect from the four winds, from one end of heaven to the other.

Jesus' description of his return is dramatic. It will be no hole-in-the-corner affair, but like lightning that flashes across the whole sky. Read Paul's similar picture of Christ's coming, as he writes to those who are worried about what will happen to believers who have already died: 'The Lord himself, with a cry of command, with the archangel's call and the sound of God's trumpet, will descend from heaven, and the dead in Christ will rise first. Then we who are alive, who are left, will be caught up in the clouds together with them to meet the Lord in the air; and so we will be with the Lord for ever' (1 Thessalonians 4:16–17).

Those early Christians thought that Jesus would come again in their lifetime. Two millennia later, we can be confident that all who have been Christians down the centuries will together go to be with him in eternity. And, whether we are alive or dead, we can be equally confident that we will not miss this culminating event of all history. May we live in such a way that we will not need to be ashamed, however suddenly he comes.

Brothers, this Lord Jesus shall return again,
With his Father's glory, with his angel train;
For all wreaths of empire meet upon his brow
And our hearts confess him King of glory now.
C. NOEL (1817–77)

We pray with the hymn writer that we may enthrone him in our hearts, and 'let him subdue all that is not holy, all that is not true'.

Read Matthew 24:26–31.

✣

MATTHEW 24:36–37 (NRSV)

No one knows

About that day and hour no one knows, neither the angels of heaven, nor the Son, but only the Father. For as the days of Noah were, so will be the coming of the Son of Man.

'When will it happen?' Most of us like to know what future events we can write in our diaries; it gives us a measure of security. But there is one question to which not even Jesus knew the answer: when will he come back? His return will be unmistakable and sudden. The people of Noah's time were corrupt and violent and God saw that 'the wickedness of humankind was great in the earth' (Genesis 6:5). People totally disregarded God and his way, and the flood struck suddenly, without further time to change their lives. This is the abruptness, Jesus says, with which he will return. He will come without warning, like a burglar in the night.

So how can we be ready, if we too are to have no warning of his coming? John shows us how. 'When he is revealed, we will be like him, for we will see him as he is. And all who have this hope in him purify themselves, just as he is pure' (1 John 3:2–3). A life modelled on Jesus and his character: that is our response to the Father's immense love for us.

What will this mean in practice? It will mean love worked out in our relationships with family, friends, neighbours, colleagues. It will mean graciousness towards the surly, a smile towards a mother with a crying child, forgiveness towards those who wrong us, patience with roadhogs, an offer of help to the elderly, courtesy towards those who serve us, generosity to those who are worse off than we are. It will mean self-control in our personal habits and willingness to put ourselves out for other people's needs. Does that sound impossible? Not if we co-operate with the Spirit who wants his fruit to grow in our lives.

Lord, may I grow more like you and be ready for your return.

Read 1 Thessalonians 5:1–11.

✣

MATTHEW 24:42, 44 (NRSV)

Keep awake! Be ready!

Keep awake therefore, for you do not know on what day your Lord is coming… Therefore you also must be ready, for the Son of Man is coming at an unexpected hour.

Jesus loved capturing people's attention with stories—and everyone loves a wedding! So he told a story about the bridesmaids at a wedding. Among their duties, they were to meet the arriving bridegroom and escort him to the bride, lighting the way with their oil lamps. But on this occasion he was delayed, and they dozed off while they waited for him. Suddenly there was a shout: 'He's coming!' Five of them were prepared: they had spare oil and could refill their lamps. The rest had been careless: they woke with a start to find that their oil had run low. While they went to the store for a refill, the bridegroom came and the group went off. When the foolish ones arrived back, they were late; the door was shut. 'Lord, Lord, open to us!' was their cry. The reply was devastating: not just 'You're too late!' but 'I do not know you.'

We can prepare for a burglar with mortise locks and burglar alarms, but the burglar comes unannounced and takes us by surprise. Similarly, the bridesmaids had ample time to prepare for the bridegroom, but when he came he came suddenly. So it is with Jesus' return. We need to be ready now, so that when he comes he does not catch us off guard. How are we to be ready? Those words 'I do not know you' are the key. I heard of a three-year-old who has recently started to go to church. She told her grandmother, an ordained woman, 'I'm like you now. I know all about Jesus.' Granny: 'And do you know him?' Child, thoughtfully: 'Not yet.' There is a difference between knowing about a person and knowing them. If we are to be ready for Jesus' coming, we must know him as a friend, not just as a doctrine.

Read Matthew 25:1–13.

✣

MATTHEW 25:14–23 (NRSV)

Faithfulness rewarded

'Well done, good and trustworthy slave; you have been trustworthy in a few things, I will put you in charge of many things; enter into the joy of your master.'

Another well-known story! This time Jesus uses the image of a businessman who goes away on a business trip and leaves his money in the care of three employees: five talents (worth many thousands of pounds) for one, two for another, just one for the third. Although he does not give specific instructions, it is implied that they are to use the money for trading. The first two employees knew that their master would put this money to work, so by hard work, ingenuity and shrewdness, they doubled the money by the time their employer returned. 'Well done,' was his commendation. 'You have proved your reliability. I can trust you with more.'

What does this mean for us? The 'talents' do not represent either money or particular giftts and abilities (in the way we use the word 'talent'). Rather, they are the responsibilities God gives his people in the light of our abilities and circumstances. He wants to be able to rely on us to use faithfully and fruitfully the opportunities for service that he gives us. My own congregation has recently put out a leaflet for our annual 'Stewardship Sunday'. I like the acrostic on the cover: 'Christ gave everything. We give: Our time and talents, Understanding, Resources, Service, Energy, Love, Values, Earnings,

Support.' OURSELVES. Each one of us is challenged to look at our lifestyle, our situation, our individual characteristics. It may seem obvious that God has given us many good things; others may appear to be impoverished in comparison. But he asks every one of us to be faithful in using for him whatever he has given us.

Thank you, Lord, for all the good things you give me. I pray that I may know how you want me to use them for you, and that I may fulfil your desires for me.

✣

MATTHEW 25:24–30 (NRSV)

Apparent injustice

'Throw him into the outer darkness.'

The story continues. The third man sees his master in a different way from the others. 'He's a hard man. I don't want to make a mistake and lose his money. I'll keep it really safe, and hide it where no one will steal it.' When his boss appeared, he got it all out of its hiding-place; he put on a brave face as he said, 'Look, sir, here it is. I kept it safely for you. I was afraid I would lose it.' His master was furious. 'At least you could have got interest at the bank. Take him away; he's no good to me!'

This parable appears to deal with the contrast between the faithfulness and industry of some and the idleness of others. There is reward for the hard-working and severe punishment for the lazy. But behind the behaviour is belief; behind the faithfulness there is faith. The men had different concepts of their master's character. Two saw him as one they could trust, for whom they wanted to work. The third one's perception was of a hard, greedy man of whom he was afraid. Much of our behaviour is determined by our perception of God's character. Do we see him as the hard, unfeeling, distant god who (like Islam's Allah) will be merciful if we're lucky? Or is he a God whose goodness, justice and love we can really trust? That is the God we will want to serve and to please.

God has shown us what he is like, both through the Bible (the written word) and through his Son, Jesus (the living Word). This man was thrown out because, at the basic level, he did not understand what his master was like. The foolish bridesmaids were excluded from the party because they were strangers to the bridegroom. Do you want to be included in Christ's 'party' when he comes again?

Lord, I pray that I may grow in understanding of your true character, and in knowing you as well as knowing about you.

✣

MATTHEW 25:31–33 (NRSV)

Separation—can it be true?

When the Son of Man comes in his glory, and all the angels with him, then he will sit on the throne of his glory. All the nations will be gathered before him, and he will separate people one from another as a shepherd separates the sheep from the goats, and he will put the sheep at his right hand and the goats at the left.

As a teenager, I studied Matthew's Gospel for a public examination. I had no problem in believing Jesus' miracles, but there were many verses I wanted to cut out of his teaching. The clear separation of sheep from goats, wheat from weeds, good from bad fish; he used illustrations that were familiar to his largely rural audience to emphasize the finality of the judgment that awaits us: 'Collect the weeds and bind them in bundles to be burned' (Matthew 13:30). I didn't like it. It did not fit with my concept of God's character. Surely a God of love would not act in such a harsh, destructive way? Many people are reluctant to believe that God will exclude anyone from his eternal kingdom.

Later I saw that a holy God who is a righteous judge cannot just overlook the misdemeanours of those who choose to ignore him. I had a glimpse of the utter, blinding purity of a God whose 'eyes are too pure to look on evil', who 'cannot tolerate wrong' (Habakkuk 1:13). If God were only holy like that, we would all be eternally banished. But such holiness throws his love into sharp relief. Probably the best-known verse in the Bible is John 3:16: 'God so loved the world that he gave his only Son, so that everyone who believes in him may not perish but may have eternal life.' His love is seen against a backdrop of the very real possibility that we might perish. Yes, there is eternal death as well as eternal life. The separation of 'sheep' from 'goats' is a reality.

When the Bible's teaching about God conflicts with my own ideas about him, which is most likely to be right?

✣

MATTHEW 25:34–40 (NRSV)

The king in disguise

The king will say to those at his right hand, 'Come, you that are blessed by my Father, inherit the kingdom prepared for you from the foundation of the world; for I was hungry and you gave me food, I was thirsty and you gave me something to drink, I was a stranger and you welcomed me.'

At first sight, this passage seems to say that our acceptability to Christ is determined only by our good works in caring for the poor and needy—yet this contradicts much else that we read in the Bible. So what is Jesus telling us to expect when he comes in glory as king and as judge?

Jesus' first coming was in disguise, a baby born in a stable into a humble family. Throughout his life he identified with the poor, the downtrodden, the homeless: 'the Son of Man has nowhere to lay his head' (Luke 9:58). Much of his ministry was among the poor and the sick, among those who were outcast and despised. These people really mattered to him. And he expects the ways we show our love for him to include costly, practical care and love towards those who are so important to him, those with whom he identified.

Two beautiful stories are told. One is about Francis of Assisi, who came from a wealthy upper-class family. One day, out riding, he met a hideous leper. He dismounted to hug him; as he did so, the man's face was transformed into the face of Christ. We read, too, about Martin of Tours, a Roman soldier who was a Christian. One freezing day, a beggar stopped him to ask for money. Martin's pockets were empty, but he tore his cloak in two and gave one half to the beggar. That night in a dream, he saw Jesus in heaven, wearing half his cloak, and heard an angel asking, 'Master, why are you wearing that old cloak?' Jesus replied, 'My servant Martin gave it to me.'

What will Jesus say to you when you meet him face to face?

MATTHEW 25:41–46 (NRSV)

Judged—and found wanting

'Lord, when was it that we saw you hungry or thirsty or a stranger or naked or sick or in prison, and did not take care of you?' Then he will answer them, 'Truly I tell you, just as you did not do it to one of the least of these, you did not do it to me.' And these will go away into eternal punishment, but the righteous into eternal life.

Each one of us is free to live our lives as we choose, but one day God will call us to give account for our use of that freedom. Can you imagine the line-up as we wait to face our maker? Jesus had a solemn warning in the Sermon on the Mount: 'Not everyone who says to me, "Lord, Lord" will enter the kingdom of heaven, but only one who does the will of my Father in heaven. On that day many will say to me, "Lord, Lord, did we not prophesy in your name, and cast out demons in your name, and do many deeds of power in your name?" Then I will declare to them, "I never knew you; go away from me, you evildoers"' (Matthew 7:21–23). We might say, 'But Lord, I was in church every Sunday... Lord, I ran the church bazaar for 20 years... Lord, I read my Bible and said my prayers twice a day...' What if he asks us, 'But where were you when the tramp came to the door... when your neighbour was dying of cancer... when you watched the television pictures of starving Sudanese...?' Would we dare to tell him, 'Lord, I was too busy'?

The chapter ends with some very unpalatable words, a solemn warning of eternal punishment for those who have not shown his love to others. These words are not to leave us frightened, but to spur us on to love Christ and to love people.

Ask Jesus for help to be aware of the needs around you today and to respond to them.

LOOKING INTO THE FACE OF GOD

PSALM 27:1–14 (NIV)

Does God have a face?

My heart says of you, 'Seek his face!' Your face, Lord, I will seek. Do not hide your face from me.

At six every evening, a small face would appear at the window of the house opposite us, looking eagerly down the road towards the station. Then, suddenly, it would vanish and from the front door a three-year-old body would hurl itself on to the pavement. Weaving between the streams of tired commuters, she made towards a tall man with a huge ginger beard, shouting, 'Daddy, my daddy!' When he saw her, he would crouch down and open his arms wide. I loved the way she would look up earnestly into his face as she told her news. 'I found a caterpillar, I put it in a matchbox for you, and I made some sticky cakes for your tea.' All the time she talked, her little fingers would stroke the ginger shredded wheat of his beard.

The God that the Bible portrays is not merely a creative force or a vague power of good, but a person who feels, thinks, communicates and wants to be known and loved in return. His face is mentioned many times, and so are his features: 'for the mouth of the Lord... has spoken' (Micah 4:4, NRSV); 'the eyes of the Lord range throughout the earth, to strengthen those whose hearts are fully committed to him' (2 Chronicles 16:9); 'my cry came before him, into his ears' (Psalm 18:6); 'smoke rose from his nostrils; consuming fire came from his mouth' (2 Samuel 22:9).

People would 'seek the Lord's face' when they wanted to come close to him. Another frequently occurring phrase, 'enquire of God', could be translated from the Hebrew as 'stroke the Lord's beard'. God longs for us to be that close to him. He longs for the kind of intimacy that delighted my neighbour when his daughter gazed up into his face and chatted to him as she stroked his beard.

Lord, I can't see your face, but show me how to look into it by faith. Amen

✣

NUMBERS 6:24–26 (NIV)

What makes God smile?

The Lord bless you and keep you; the Lord make his face shine upon you and be gracious to you; the Lord turn his face towards you and give you peace.

On holiday last summer, it rained most days. As I sheltered in a seaside café one morning, I noticed a family at the next table. Comical but moving—that's how I would describe the doting smile on the father's face. The toddler was obviously his first child—the longed-for son of his dreams. The father's beaming smile followed him everywhere as he dashed between the tables on unsteady legs. Even when he covered himself from head to toe with ice-cream the father still smiled proudly, as he murmured, 'Just look at him feeding himself!'

People in the Bible often prayed that God's face would shine (smile) on them or be turned towards them: perhaps they wanted God to look at them as a new and besotted father looks at his firstborn! And of course that is how God looks at us. He says we are the apple of his eye, his delight. His beaming smile follows us, too, all through the day, wherever we go.

Yet the Bible also tells us that God turns his face away from people who deliberately disobey him (Deuteronomy 31:17). He never abandons his children but we can lose his smile—that sense of being close and comfortable with him. One of my children behaved extremely badly once, when grandma came to tea. Later he came up to me and whispered, 'Mummy, I'm sorry, please make your face smile at me again!'

I used to think I had to wait until I went to bed at night before going through a long list of all the things I'd done wrong that day. I've since learnt not to wait that long. The moment I feel I've upset God I ask his forgiveness—then and there. It comes instantly, so long as we ask.

Lord, I want to live constantly in the light of your smile. Thank you for forgiving me so often and so quickly! Amen

Read Psalm 31:14–20.

✣

PSALM 17:15 (NRSV)

Another way of praying

As for me, I shall behold your face in righteousness; when I awake I shall be satisfied, beholding your likeness.

My friend Dave was born blind. When people urged him to pray for healing he used to smile and say, 'If the first thing I ever see is the face of Jesus, it will be worth waiting a lifetime for a thrill like that!' Dave died recently and I often imagine him sitting there gazing! The face of God may be invisible to us on earth, but we can still gaze—by faith.

On his way to work in the fields, an old French peasant used to slip into church and sit for a while, smiling up at the rafters. He did the same on his way home in the evening. Curious, the priest asked him what he was doing.

'I just look at him and he looks at me,' was the simple reply.

Once I used to feel guilty if my mind wandered while I prayed. Now I realize praying can also mean just sitting in God's presence, basking in his love.

The more you care about a person, the less important words are as a form of communication. I adored my father and spent every available moment with him, yet we could go for long walks together or sit by the fire for a whole evening without talking. We used to say we could read each other's thoughts just by the expressions on our faces, but to get that close to someone you do have to spend a lot of time with them.

We all need to make a point of coming face to face with God every day, to open ourselves to him, and to give him the chance to open himself to us. Not just for our benefit either—he actually enjoys looking at us. He says to each of us:

'Come then, my love; my darling, come with me. You are like a dove that hides in the crevice of a rock. Let me see your lovely face and hear your enchanting voice' (Song of Songs 2:13b–14, GNB).

✣

EXODUS 33:11–23 (NIV)

I can't see his face!

And the Lord said, 'I will cause all my goodness to pass in front of you, and I will proclaim my name, the Lord, in your presence... But,' he said, 'you cannot see my face...'

Moses was said to talk to God 'face to face as a man talks to his friend'. Yet, today's passage shows that he only saw God's face by faith and not in reality. Elijah, another Old Testament 'friend of God', trudged 40 days through the desert to encounter God. Yet, when he finally stood before him on Sinai, listening to his whispery voice, he hid his face in his cloak (1 Kings 19:12–13).

In Old Testament days, God seemed so distant and powerful that people dared not even speak his name. Jesus came to show us what God is really like: 'Anyone who has seen me has seen the Father' (John 14:9). The only way to know God is to look at Jesus, and Moses and Elijah were finally allowed to do that. Once, when Jesus was standing on a mountaintop, he began to shine like the sun and the terrified disciples saw Moses and Elijah talking with him face to face (Matthew 17:1–8).

When one of my six children refused to look at me when I spoke to him it was either because he knew he had done something which would make me cross or I had done something to make him cross—such as refusing him sweets! When we don't feel like looking into God's face it may be for the same two reasons. Perhaps we don't want to let go of something we know is upsetting him: an unhealthy relationship, activity or self-indulgence might have become so important to us that it blocks out his face whenever we try to focus on it.

We can also be 'upset' with him over something he has allowed to happen to us or refused to let us have. When we are arguing with God our resentment hangs like a cloud between his face and ours.

Lord, may nothing come between your face and mine today.

✣

JOHN 1:41–42 (NIV)

When Jesus looks at me

The first thing Andrew did was to find his brother Simon and... brought him to Jesus. Jesus looked at him and said, 'You are Simon son of John. You will be called Cephas' (which, when translated, is Peter).

I wonder how Peter felt when he first looked into the face of Jesus. The big, loud-mouthed fisherman was named Simon ('reed') because he was as easily blown about as reeds in the wind. He was so weak, he changed his priorities according to the people he was with; yet, as he stared at Jesus, he knew those eyes were looking right through him, seeing not the man that he was but the man he could become.

'You may be named after a wobbly reed, but you will be known as Peter (the rock),' Jesus told him.

When we look into the face of Jesus we can't hide anything from him. That can feel unnerving, but also comforting. Most people judge us by our outward appearance, our achievements or our past record. When Jesus looks at us he sees the person he could make us into one day. He also sees all our struggles and fears. The rich young man whose story is told in Mark 10:17–23 longed to follow Jesus but he was afraid. His money made him feel safe, comfortable and a 'somebody' in this world. Jesus looked into his face, challenging him with, 'Will you trust me to provide everything you need, instead of relying on your money to do that for you?' Mark describes the expression on Jesus' face as he waited for the answer—'a look of deep love and longing' (v. 21, Amplified Bible).

Lord, I know that you look at me sadly, too, when I struggle with the issue of where I place my dependency. I want to trust you for everything in life, but I find myself leaning on other things and other people instead. I know you can see what I could become if only I were willing to let you change me. Thank you, Lord, for your uncondemning love that accepts me as I am and loves me—whatever!

✣

MARK 8:22–26 (NIV)

The hidden face

They came to Bethsaida, and some people brought a blind man and begged Jesus to touch him. He took the blind man by the hand and led him outside the village.

When Jesus had just changed someone's life, he often said, 'Your faith has healed you.' I guess faith was easier when you could look up into that face and see the strength and compassion in the eyes of Jesus. The man in today's passage didn't have that advantage. As he stood in the crowded marketplace, feeling the crowds jostling around him, all he could do was grope out towards a voice in the darkness. Suddenly, he felt his hand grasped and held tightly by the work-roughened hand of a carpenter. Was he puzzled when he wasn't healed on the spot? Everyone was expecting that to happen. Murmurs of disappointment, even anger, must have followed the blind man as he stumbled away over the cobbles beside a complete stranger.

We don't know how far they walked, how long they spent together or what they talked about, but they would have been friends and not strangers when, at last, Jesus stopped in the peace and privacy of the countryside. Even then the miracle wasn't instant but gradual! Why did Jesus take so long? Making friends with that man mattered more to Jesus than just healing him because, to Jesus, our relationship with him is of paramount importance.

Isn't it frustrating when you pray for something but nothing happens? Like this blind man, we grope towards God by faith, feeling sure he must want to help, but then the waiting begins! Sometimes he really does seem to 'hide his face' (see Psalm 102:2), yet something vital is happening in that gap between the point where we begin to ask and the moment when our prayers are answered. He is teaching us to know and trust him. He wants us to walk by faith and not by sight (2 Corinthians 5:7).

Thomas said to him, 'My Lord and my God!' Then Jesus told him, 'Because you have seen me, you have believed; blessed are those who have not seen and yet have believed' (John 20:28–29).

✣

JOHN 15:1–18 (NIV)

The laughing face of Jesus

'If you obey my commands, you will remain in my love, just as I have obeyed my Father's commands and remain in his love. I have told you this so that my joy may be in you and that your joy may be complete.'

One summer, we went to Europe for our holiday. The weather was awful! Mountain-walking was impossibly dangerous and poking round the shops was too tempting. The only places where we could keep dry, warm and financially solvent were the numerous, ornate churches. By the end of a fortnight I realized I had looked into the face of Jesus thousands of times, through icons, portraits, stained-glass windows or sculptures; but never once had he smiled back at me. The artists had all depicted him looking depressed, severe, disapproving, anorexic or downright cross!

I know Jesus was called the 'man of sorrows' and that he died in agony, but I am convinced he was also full of joy and laughed a lot. Some of the stories he told would have tickled the Jewish sense of humour of his time and had people rolling on the ground! Humans are attracted to joy but we avoid people who look stern or miserable; the crowds would never have flocked after Jesus if he had looked like all those portraits. The Pharisees would have approved of him, and he might have attracted the academics of his day, but it was the ordinary working people, like Peter, whose hearts Jesus won—and the poor, the disreputable, drop-outs and no-hopers. One look at his face would have made them feel accepted and included, not frowned on and despised.

Joy is as catching as flu! My friend Liz is always laughing; she sees the funny side of everything, and after spending time with her I always feel better. As we look into the laughing face of Jesus we, too, can catch his joy and then pass it on to a sad world that needs his kind of refreshing joy so badly.

Lord, help me to see what you are really like and then to introduce the real you to others.

✣

MATTHEW 26:67–68; JOHN 19:3 (NIV)

The disfigured face of Jesus

Then they spat in his face and struck him with their fists. Others slapped him and said, 'Prophesy to us, Christ. Who hit you?' ...

They went up to him again and again, saying, 'Hail, king of the Jews!' And they struck him in the face.

One Sunday, our six children got the giggles in church. It was the sight of the visiting preacher that started them off, and he was certainly the ugliest man I had ever seen. His face was grotesquely disfigured, but the moment he began to speak the children were riveted—tears replaced the laughter. Hesbon had been a pastor in Kenya when terrorists attacked his village, burning his house and church and murdering his family before his eyes. Finally they battered his face to a pulp with the butt of their rifles, yet, as he told us how Jesus had given him what he called 'peacejoy' in the centre of his anguish, his mutilated face shone with unearthly radiance.

The face of Jesus does not only have laughter lines but it also bears many ugly scars. Isaiah 52:14 (GNB) says: 'He was so disfigured that he hardly looked human.' His face will also be deeply lined by other kinds of suffering. He knows what it feels like to be rejected by the people you love, misunderstood by your family, betrayed, abandoned, blamed unfairly, misunderstood and excluded. He was single, lonely, poor, overworked, physically and verbally abused, taken for granted, publicly disgraced, beaten and apparently defeated. He understands, from personal experience, almost anything we go through—except, of course, the searing pain of guilt. Yet it was to spare us that—worst of all the emotions—that he died in our place on the cross.

'Surely he hath borne our griefs, and carried our sorrows' (Isaiah 53:4, KJV). Thank you that, at your cross, I can exchange my pain for your 'peacejoy'.

Read Isaiah 53:1–11.

✣

EXODUS 34:29; 2 CORINTHIANS 3:18 (NIV)

Reflecting his face

When Moses came down from Mount Sinai... he was not aware that his face was radiant because he had spoken with the Lord... And we, who with unveiled faces all reflect the Lord's glory, are being transformed into his likeness with ever-increasing glory, which comes from the Lord.

The other day, I met a friend who had just returned from a silent retreat at a convent. Her face literally shone. 'Perhaps it's fresh air and monastic soap,' I thought, but as she talked about all that the Lord had done for her I realized that her radiance came from inside. Like Moses, she had spent time alone with God—and it showed!

The small boy who played Gabriel in a nativity play I attended last Christmas froze completely at the sight of the audience. His first line was, 'Fear not!' but he was too scared to say it! The entire cast prompted him but still he stood, green with terror. Then suddenly he caught sight of his dad, smiling encouragement at him from the front row. He caught that smile, as if it had been thrown like a ball, and soon he was beaming round at us all, sharing his father's smile with everyone!

Sometimes we get very worried about what we are supposed to do for God, but I am sure he just wants us to be radiators! The one in my sitting-room stores electricity at night, while it's cheap, so in the morning it warms everyone who comes near it. If, however, I've forgotten to switch it on the night before, it remains icy cold. It is by spending time with God that we absorb and store the warmth of his love so that we can radiate it to everyone we meet.

Lord, help me to remember to keep looking up into your face, over the heads of all those who will surround me. I know you love them, even the irritating ones. Let me catch your smile, and your attitude towards them.

JOURNEY TO A DIFFERENT LAND

LUKE 2:1–7 (NIV)

Journey to Bethlehem

She gave birth to her firstborn, a son. She wrapped him in cloths and placed him in a manger, because there was no room for them in the inn.

Joseph didn't believe her! She had been so excited to see him after her three-month stay with Elizabeth, but during the terrible night that followed their painful conversation, perhaps she regretted saying to Gabriel, 'I am the Lord's servant' if it meant she had lost the man she loved so much. But in the night he saw an angel too!

Mary must have been busy during those first few months of marriage, sewing baby clothes, weaving blankets for the wooden cradle that Joseph probably would have made, and cleaning their tiny home above the carpenter's shop until it shone. But all her careful preparations were wasted when another journey was forced on her.

As they travelled towards Bethlehem, did she think, 'Surely God wouldn't allow his son to be born by the roadside!' Being 'the Lord's servant' was very costly for Mary. Perhaps, as she finally lay down in that filthy cowshed, it was fortunate that she could not see into the future. Another unexpected journey would soon begin—their escape into Egypt. And she would have seen her anguish when she lost twelve-year-old Jesus in Jerusalem, as well as the awful day when he told their local synagogue that he was the Messiah, and so incensed all her neighbours that the whole family had to leave their home and business and move to Capernaum. She would have felt the pain of her other children's refusal to believe in Jesus and her own time of wondering whether he was going mad; then the final agony of watching him die in apparent defeat. Serving the Lord wholeheartedly never makes life easy! Although Mary could not foresee these things, afterwards as she looked back over her life's journey she would have known that God had been carrying her all the way.

'The Lord your God... has watched over your journey through this vast desert... [He] has been with you, and you have not lacked anything' (Deuteronomy 2:7).

⁜

LUKE 14:15–24 (NIV)

Journeys 'to' are journeys 'away from'

Jesus replied: 'A certain man was preparing a great banquet and invited many guests... "Come, for everything is now ready." ... Still another said, "I just got married, so I can't come."'

We had packed and tightly taped the last of the boxes that held basic household necessities for moving to and living in an old Soviet apartment block in Ukraine. We were embarking on an adventure, a journey. Suddenly our home in Canada looked better than ever, glowing with comfort, 'known-ness' and beauty.

I was finding it hard to imagine what living in an apartment in Ukraine was really going to be like. We had been warned that hot water and electricity would be intermittent and possibly non-existent for extended periods of times. But worse than that, we would miss our family and friends! We would miss pushing our beautiful grand-daughters on the swings. We would miss candle-lit meals together with friends and family. We would miss deep conversation over dark cappuccinos.

But we had been invited to share a banquet of ministry that was taking place in Ukraine and Moldova—and everything was ready! 'But our friends and family are here,' we were tempted to protest. 'Our grandchildren are here. We can't come just now.'

It makes me wonder how Mary managed her journey from anonymity into being 'highly favoured by God'. Mary had not only become pregnant in a most unorthodox way, but she required personal protection by the man she was promised to in marriage. Her life journey took her away from respectability, from cultural acceptance and from the normative comfort of her home.

In the middle of all these losses, where was her journey taking her? To a great banquet that was now ready! To the birth of a king whose journey would take him from majesty to humanity, from glory to a woman's womb, from splendour to a stable.

And Mary delighted in being invited to such a banquet and on such a journey.

Dear Jesus, gives us Mary-hearts that are willing to journey from our places of comfort to the great banquet that is ready—now.

✣

LUKE 14:15–24 (NIV)

Journey to the banquet

Jesus replied: 'A certain man was preparing a great banquet and invited many guests... "Come, for everything is now ready." ... Another said, "I have just bought five yoke of oxen, and I'm on my way to try them out. Please excuse me."'

An unexpected conversation with a young man in a waiting-room—and an even more unexpected story. He is a Ukrainian, waiting to speak with someone about a job. He tells how, a year ago, he had a very successful marketing job. But he is now unemployed, penniless, wondering what he is going to do, struggling with a call to become a pastor.

In the job he used to have, his boss would give him a suitcase full of money to wine and dine prospective clients, to take them to the local brothels. His boss's instructions were, 'Give them a good time.' And if he closed a deal, his commission would be about $40,000. This young committed Christian protested, 'I can't do that. I'm a Christian.' And the consequence? He is no longer employed.

In biblical terms, this young man chose to go to the banquet and not to go and take care of his own oxen first. He has been forced to choose: economic security in a fragile economy, or the poverty of faithfulness. He made a courageous choice. Have you ever had to make such choices—when to choose God and his banquet is to say goodbye to assured wealth and security?

Mary and Joseph had a similar choice: would Joseph choose Mary or abandon her in her unusual pregnancy? Would he choose the cultural route or would he listen to the angel messenger? To listen to the angel would complicate their lives considerably, but it would also bring a joy beyond their imagining. And they would be blessed.

God, do the choices have to be so hard? Give us gifts of grace and courage to choose the banquet and leave our oxen behind.

✣

LUKE 9:57–62 (NIV)

Journey with a companion

As they were walking along the road, someone said to him, 'I will follow you wherever you go.' ... Jesus replied, 'No-one who takes hold of the plough and looks back is fit for service in the kingdom of God.'

All I wanted to do was to go home! This wasn't what I had expected following Jesus to be about. I had been invited here to do a particular job and now that job had clearly been taken away. I thought it was time that God started explaining some things to me. I had kept my part of the agreement and had followed him, but now the rug had been pulled out from under my feet. Didn't God have a responsibility in our agreement?

I clearly had a bone to pick with God on this one. I was angry with certain people who, from my perspective, had broken promises. I felt misused. I felt that God had taken a vacation and I was stranded here with a multi-year commitment!

When I stopped ranting, and listened long enough to hear God, I heard his gentle words of love. Underneath my hurt and my anger was fear—fear that I had wrongly heard the call to follow; fear that God had forgotten that I was a stranger here, trying to follow him; fear that somehow I had really messed up and that I deserved being abandoned!

When I listened, I heard him encourage me to keep my hand on the plough—right next to his. He was guiding the plough; his was the power that kept it steady. I just needed to walk alongside him. Even the tears that filled my eyes wouldn't cancel the call if I simply walked alongside him. And although I wanted to turn back and go home, I didn't. I'm still walking alongside him.

Mary and Joseph must have wanted to turn back many times when the journey was hard, when the journey didn't seem to make sense, when they felt alone. But they kept their hands to the plough and followed where Jesus' journey needed to go.

Thank you, Jesus, that your hand is on the plough right next to mine.

⁘

LUKE 2:4–7 (NIV)

Journeys through difficulty

So Joseph also went up from the town of Nazareth in Galilee to Judea, to Bethlehem the town of David... While they were there, the time came for the baby to be born.

Do you notice how often our journeys to follow God happen at the most inopportune time?

We can imagine the excitement of Mary and Joseph after the visit of the angels, and the liveliness of their long conversations, trying to make sense of the strange events in their lives—the way their journey was unfolding. How would a young couple talk about conversations with angels and about the expected birth of God's Son? And then for Mary to find herself in the discomfort of the final days of her pregnancy travelling a long distance only to discover Bethlehem overcrowded and its inns full... well, it sure would make me stop and think about where God was in all this! But Mary seemed to ponder these things in her heart, waiting for God to give her an understanding of all these strange events in her life that were designed by God.

Mary's and Joseph's journeys were custom-designed to achieve God's purposes and plans for them, as are ours. But life's journeys are not without difficulty and challenge. Just think back on your own journeys amid your own difficult times. How seldom we really know ahead of time what God's design looks like, and how much, at times, we long to know what is coming. How surprised we are as we see how our faithful God moulds and shapes us through the difficulties. Yet each difficulty is a potential birth, an opportunity for something new to be born within us—the formation of new attitudes, new understanding, new commitment, the knowledge of God himself.

God, give us faith and hope and understanding when the difficulties in our journey seem to be pointless. Help us to have eyes to see the possibilities of each situation—especially the difficult ones.

✣

LUKE 2:1–7 (NIV)

Journey to register

In those days Caesar Augustus issued a decree that a census should be taken of the entire Roman world... So Joseph also went up from the town of Nazareth in Galilee to Judea, to Bethlehem... He went there to register with Mary.

We were off to the train station to buy train tickets to Simferopol, a city in Crimea—but still in Ukraine. We weren't crossing any borders, so we were a bit surprised when we were asked to show our passports. Later, when we bought plane tickets, we were again asked to show our passports. We weren't used to having to prove who we were for these 'non-passport' activities.

When we asked our friends in Crimea why we needed to do that each time, they pulled their own registration cards out of their pockets and explained that they carry their cards with them all the time. Citizens in the old Soviet empire still do not have complete freedom to move around their own country. They can be stopped at any time and asked by the military to show their registration cards, or risk being taken away for questioning. Their registration cards are proof that they have the right to move and go about their daily business where they are. So now we carry our passports containing our visas with us all the time. It feels strange but they provide the documentation that we have been given permission to be here in this country. They are our identity and our registration here.

Mary and Joseph's journey took them away from Nazareth back to Bethlehem to register—Rome had decreed it. Joseph was required to register in Bethlehem, his ancestral home. Who is Joseph? Oh, he belongs to David's family. Who is Mary? She's pledged to Joseph in marriage. Who are you and who am I? We are registered to God's family, in the kingdom of God. And our passports have a visa stamped with God's seal of ownership upon us: we have his Spirit in our hearts (2 Corinthians 1:21).

Thank you, Father, that we belong in your kingdom.

✣

LUKE 2:34–35 (NIV)

Journey of pain

Then Simeon blessed them and said to Mary, his mother: '... And a sword will pierce your own soul too.'

One minute apart: the contractions were becoming stronger and were coming more rapidly. I was trying to encourage my daughter to keep focused on her breathing exercises and to be strong with the increasing pain. During the pain of the contractions, we both seemed to lose sight of the anticipated joy in the imminent arrival of little Jessica. As the new life of the little baby getting ready to burst into this world got closer, the pain got stronger.

We had been waiting for this moment since three o'clock in the morning—walking around the hospital, sipping juice, talking, clocking contractions—and now, finally, the birth was close. Yet each contraction in itself seemed like an eternity—like it might never end—as we waited and wondered if her husband would actually make it to the hospital before the baby was born, hoping but not sure he would arrive.

Sitting with my daughter through the early hours of the morning gave me an opportunity to think about how pain and anticipated joy inseparably weave themselves together to form a predictable pattern in our journey—and how good it was just to be with my daughter, knowing that giving birth to this little baby was her work, not mine. Mine was simply to walk alongside her, to be there with her until her husband arrived.

It also gave me an opportunity to wonder imaginatively: was Jesus' Father pacing the corridors of heaven watching his son being born in the natural pangs of childbirth? Was he anxious? I wonder if Mary had a sense of her son's heavenly Father being present, encouraging and blessing. And did it reduce the pain? I expect not, because right from the beginning Mary's journey was a mixture of experienced pain—pain far greater than that of childbirth—and anticipated joy. Our journey is the same.

God, give us grace never to lose sight of the wonder and the anticipation of joy as we see you daily brought to birth in new ways; and give us grace to be strong in those times of pain.

✣

LUKE 1:38 (NIV)

Journey with grace

'I am the Lord's servant,' Mary answered. 'May it be to me as you have said.'

It was an old pattern, quickly recognized, but it got me stuck again. I was fighting with the need to be acknowledged and recognized for my contribution—my old Achilles' heel, as my husband said. I was invited to participate, I did my work, and then I was sidelined. I really struggle with situations like this. Something gets triggered deep inside of me. It's as if I am fighting for my very life: it's a suffocating feeling of panic.

At such times, I have heated internal arguments with God, almost demanding that he goes and changes their behaviour instead of asking me to find a holy attitude—like, why isn't it their turn to learn something, instead of mine again! I get quite discouraged because I have so often asked God to give me a gentle, kind forgiveness for these colleagues—to heal my Achilles' heel.

So I am profoundly moved when I read Mary's beautiful and simple response to an angel's visit: 'I am the Lord's servant. May it be to me as you have said.' 'Whatever, God—I trust you with my life,' she's saying. She shows such grace and responsiveness to God's plan for her life.

However, she was greatly troubled by the angel Gabriel's opening comments, 'Greetings, you who are highly favoured! The Lord is with you.' This greeting seemed to unnerve her, perhaps because she had an immediate, intuitive understanding that along with such a greeting there must be mysterious implications that would profoundly impact her own life. She was a wise woman in her youth. But still, she bowed to the circumstances that God's plan would bring into her life.

As my journey continues to unfold, I'd like to be as full of grace in response to the circumstances of my life as Mary was in hers.

Jesus, give me grace to be full of gentle Mary-grace as I journey with you.

⁘

LUKE 2:6–7 (NIV)

Journey into life

While they were there, the time came for the baby to be born, and she gave birth to her firstborn, a son. She wrapped him in cloths and placed him in a manger, because there was no room for them in the inn.

Finally! It was time for little Jessica to be born! My daughter was pushing and Jessica was already emerging. This was the moment we had all been waiting for. It was time. With a final big push, little Jessica was born, kicking and breathing, totally dependent and totally beautiful.

Then it was time to cut the umbilical cord and she was released into this world to begin her journey. The first happening on her journey was to get a big hug and kiss from her mum and hear whispers of, 'You're beautiful. I love you', then more hugs and kisses.

As the more practical things like measuring, weighing and checking Jessica out physically were happening, I was struck with the wonder that I had been watching 'my baby' give birth to 'her baby'. It did make me wonder what it is like for God as he gives new birth and new life to us when we believe in Jesus. Does he feel the same wonder and privilege and joy? I can't help but think that he does. Does he feel birthpangs as we become believers? I don't know, but I do know that I would love to have been present when Mary gave birth to Jesus and to have wondered with her about giving birth to the Son of God. I expect it would have been similar to having shared the experience with my daughter. I expect I would have heard an earthly mother and father, along with a heavenly Father, whispering, 'You're beautiful. I love you.'

And if we stop long enough to listen, I expect we would hear our heavenly Father singing to us in whispers, 'You're beautiful. I love you.'

Jesus, thank you for life and thank you that we have been born again in you.

✣

LUKE 2:15–16 (NIV)

Worship with unlikely people

When the angels had left them and gone into heaven, the shepherds said to one another, 'Let's go to Bethlehem and see this thing that has happened, which the Lord has told us about.' So they hurried off and found Mary and Joseph, and the baby, who was lying in the manger.

Two hours after Jessica had been born, her father came bounding into the room, having just arrived from the airport. He had missed Jessica's birth because she had decided to arrive considerably earlier than expected. Life is like that, isn't it? It just isn't under our control.

It was fun watching him express his joy in his wife and new daughter. In fact, I felt as if I was intruding in a very intimate moment. So before I went off to get a coffee and leave them alone for a moment, I got swept up into the precious gift of love and affection that he was pouring out on his family.

The next visitor who was a delight to watch was Jessica's two-year-old sister, who arrived with her grandad. She walked right up to her mum, patted her tummy, said, 'Baby out', marched over to baby Jessica in her daddy's arms and gave her a big hug and kiss. Grandad, meanwhile, simply beamed from the foot of the bed, enjoying his family and oozing love and joy.

I feel that God the Father must have beamed with similar delight as he began to tell people of his Son's birth. Out in the fields, he told a bunch of shepherds who were quite startled to be informed! What unlikely people to find being invited to the birth of God's Son. But having watched Jessica's dad and her grandad beaming and sharing the news with anyone who would listen, I think Jesus' heavenly Father just couldn't keep it to himself.

As at Jesus' birth, we will find the most unlikely people sharing our journey with us. I'm sure Mary was as surprised as we are to see who God brought into the birthing room. But then, that's just like our heavenly Father, don't you think?

Thank you, Father, for sharing your Son with unlikely people like me.

LUKE 2:10–11 (NIV)

Journey of promise

'I bring you good news of great joy that will be for all the people. Today in the town of David a Saviour has been born to you; he is Christ the Lord.'

Baby Jessica is now a few months old. When she was safely growing in her mother's womb in her initial months of life, she was unseen, a promise of a life to come—a promise that God had plans and purpose for her and that those plans were good. Having now been born, she is known and seen, and greatly loved. All the possibilities and promise of life are being realized in a happy, churgling-gurgling-cooing baby.

For hundreds of years, there were promises of a Messiah, one who would save his people; and now, held in the arms of Mary and Joseph, those promises were becoming a reality. 'Today'—today—'in the town of David a Saviour has been born to you; he is Christ the Lord,' the angels told the shepherds. He has arrived: he has come—no longer just a promise, for the Shepherds saw him and heard him. They had worshipped him! And the skies were filled with angels who also saw and heard the King of kings churgling, gurgling and cooing. They joined the shepherds in praise and worship of this king.

And Mary 'treasured up all these things and pondered them in her heart... And the child grew and became strong; he was filled with wisdom, and the grace of God was upon him' (Luke 2:20, 40)—just as it was promised!

God, the maker and keeper of promises, still meets us today, giving us hope in his promises of life. So we have the possibility of journeying with God who takes the promises out of the future tense of anticipation and puts them into the past tense of our experience. Like Mary, we can ponder these things in our hearts.

Lord Jesus, change your promises for our future into the past tense of our experience. Teach us also to treasure these things and ponder them in our heart.